CW01369629

Live Your Best Life

21 PRINCIPLES FOR PEAK PERFORMANCE, PROSPERITY, AND LIFELONG HAPPINESS

By

Robert N. Jacobs

All rights reserved
Copyright © Robert N. Jacobs, 2025
The right of Robert N. Jacobs to be identified as the author of this
work has been asserted in accordance with Section 78
of the Copyright, Designs and Patents Act 1988
The book cover is copyright to Robert N. Jacobs
This book is published by
Growth Seeker Publishing Ltd.
www.growthseekerpublishing.com

This book is sold subject to the conditions that it shall not, by way of
trade or otherwise, be lent, resold, hired out or otherwise circulated
without the author's or publisher's prior consent in any form of binding
or cover other than that in which it is published and
without a similar condition including this condition being imposed
on the subsequent purchaser.
This book is a work of fiction. Any resemblance to
people or events, past or present, is purely coincidental.
ISBN: 9798282481792

To my daughter, Ava

From the moment you entered my life, you awakened a deeper purpose within me. You've inspired me to grow, to lead by example, and to strive for the kind of life that shows you what's truly possible. Watching your curiosity, courage, and kindness reminds me every day why this work matters. In a world that can sometimes dim bright lights, you shine with a radiance all your own, and I want you to always protect that light. This book is for you, and for every young person growing up in an uncertain world, searching for direction and meaning. If you ever doubt your path, know this: you were born with everything you need. Be bold. Be kind. Be brave. And above all, believe—because your best life isn't ahead of you, it's inside you.

Love always,
Dad

"Your best life isn't found in perfection or waiting for the right moment; it's built, one bold decision at a time, with purpose, courage, and a belief that you are worthy of everything you dream."
Robert N. Jacobs

Introduction

By choosing this book, you have demonstrated courage and clarity of purpose. You've stepped away from passivity and made a firm commitment to actively shape your own destiny. This decision alone sets you apart and places you firmly on a path toward meaningful change.

Within these pages, you'll uncover the extraordinary power you possess to craft a life filled with prosperity and balance. But know this: the abundant life you envision won't happen by accident; it requires conscious effort, purposeful choices, and deliberate actions. Each small step, every challenge you conquer, will build momentum towards your greater potential.

Life moves swiftly, a reminder not to wait or hold back but rather to embrace every moment as an opportunity to redirect your course and elevate your standards. Let each day inspire you to aim higher and push beyond self-imposed limitations. Your past and present circumstances don't define your future; your deliberate and intentional actions do.

As you journey through this book, keep an open mind and an eager heart. You may encounter concepts that challenge your current beliefs or habits. Embrace these moments of discomfort, for they signify growth and a chance to expand your horizons. Remember, genuine transformation often requires stepping into the unknown with trust and bravery.

You are not alone in your quest for improvement. Many have walked this path before you, and their stories of triumph are here to inspire you. Let their experiences motivate you, and remind yourself frequently that the life you want is not only possible, it's waiting for you to claim it.

I sincerely hope this book becomes not just a guide but a trusted companion as you progress. Commit fully to each principle, apply each lesson with determination, and believe deeply that the fulfilling life you desire is achievable and well within your reach.

Today marks the start of your transformative journey. You have everything it takes to live your best life.

Now, it's time to act.

Robert Jacobs
Curious By Design

Table of Contents

Chapter 1

Unleashing the Power of Mindset 1

    1. The Mindset Revolution: Your Path to Lasting Transformation 2

    2. Fixed and Growth Perspectives: Decoding Your Mental Framework 4

    3. Spotting and Reframing Limiting Beliefs 5

    4. Harnessing Challenge: Strengthening 7

    5. Transforming Self-Talk: Affirmations and 9

    6. Elevating Self-Worth: Groundwork for True 11

    7. Mindset in Motion: Real-World Success Stories 13

    8. Building Your Future-Focused Mindset: 14

    9. Shaping Your Environment to Support Your 16

    10. Concluding Your Mindset Evolution: 18

Chapter 2

The Law of Attraction: Your Secret Weapon 21

    1. A Compelling Introduction: Unlocking Your 21

    2. Mastering Your Mindset: From Limitation to 23

    3. The Power of Action and Habit Formation 25

    4. Deepening Your Connections: Building 27

    5. Finding Your Deeper Purpose: The Role of 29

    6. Creating Financial Foundations: Mastering Your Money 31

    7. Leading with Confidence: Career Growth and 32

    8. Health and Vitality: Nurturing Body and Mind 34

    9. Communication as a Cornerstone of 36

    10. Concluding with Momentum: Building a Life 38

Chapter 3

Thoughts: The Architects of Reality 41

    1. The Crucial Influence of Thought 41

    2. Constructing Reality Through Thought 43

    3. Confronting the Power of Negativity 45

    4. Mastering Positive Thinking Techniques 47

    5. Identifying and Overcoming Distorted 49

    6. Harnessing Mindfulness for Mental Control 51

    7. Elevating Emotional Health Through Thought 53

    8. Developing Success-Oriented Thought Patterns 54

    9. Real-World Stories: How Thought Transforms Lives 56

    10. The Future Landscape of Thought 58

Chapter 4

The Art of Habit Formation 61

    1. A Vital Introduction: Why Habit Formation 62

    2. The Brain's Shortcut: How Habits Take Shape 64

    3. Clearing the Path: Breaking 66

    4. The Foundations of New Habits: Setting Strong 67

    5. Building Momentum: The Power of Habit 69

    6. Designing Your Environment for Success 71

    7. Accountability and Support: Strengthening 73

    8. Sustaining Progress: Overcoming Plateaus and 75

    9. The Broader Impact: How Habits Elevate Your 77

    10. Inspiring Habit Transformations: Real Stories 79

Chapter 5

Relationships: The Heart of Human Experience 82

    1. The Hidden Power of Connection: Why 83

    2. Foundations of Harmony: Trust, Sincerity, and 84

    3. Words That Unite: Mastering Your 86

    4. The Boundaries That Liberate: Safeguarding 88

    5. Overcoming Friction: Turning Conflict into 90

    6. The Compassion Factor: Elevating the Human 92

    7. Professional Ties: Building Bridges in the 94

    8. Distance Without Division: Thriving Through 96

    9. Recognising When to Step Back: Freeing 98

    10. A Lifelong Commitment: Strengthening the....................100

Chapter 6

Spirituality: The Path to Inner Peace 103

    1. The Essence of Spiritual Awareness 103

    2. Linking Mind, Body, and Spirit..105

    3. Finding Stillness in a Hyperactive World 107

    4. The Spiritual Foundation of Resilience.............................109

    5. Creating an Everyday Spiritual Routine 111

    6. Spirituality and Its Role in Your Relationships 113

    7. Tapping into a Higher Purpose 115

    8. Confronting Inner Barriers on the Spiritual 117

    9. Nourishing Your Body Through Spiritual 119

    10. Transformational Stories and Ongoing..........................121

Chapter 7

Mastering Personal Finance... 124

    1. Financial Foundations: Laying the 124

    2. Mastering the Art of Budgeting...126

    3. The Saving Mindset: Securing Your 129

    4. Debt Management: Breaking the Chains 131

    5. Investment Fundamentals: Growing Your 133

    6. Retirement Readiness: Planning for the 135

    7. Protecting What You Build: Insurance..............................137

    8. Navigating Taxes: Keeping More of Your 139

9. Real Estate and Other Avenues: 141

10. Sustaining Momentum: Adapting for 143

Chapter 8

Career Planning for Future Leaders 146

1: Why Career Planning Matters for Leadership Potential 147

2: Identifying Your Natural Strengths 148

3: Aligning Passions with Professional Goals 151

4: Short-Term Milestones and Long-Term Vision 153

5: Building Expertise Through Lifelong Learning 155

6: Strategic Networking for Career Growth 157

7: Navigating Transitions and Overcoming 159

8: Developing Leadership Skills for Advancement 161

9: Balancing Professional Ambition and Personal 163

10: Sustaining Career Momentum and Staying Adaptable 165

Chapter 9

Health and Fitness, Your Wealth 168

1. Your Health, Your True Wealth 169

2. The Power of Consistent Movement 170

3. Feeding Your Body with Purpose 172

4. The Unsung Hero Called Sleep 174

5. Mastering Stress for a Stronger Body and 176

6. Crafting a Fitness Routine That Lasts 178

7. How Physical Health Fuels Mental Well-Being 180

8. Overcoming Common Obstacles on Your Health Journey . 181

9. Exploring Outdoors, Embracing Sports 183

10. Transformational Stories: Real People, Real Results 185

Chapter 10

Communication: Your Leadership Tool 188

1. Why Communication Matters for Leaders 188

2. Mastering Verbal Expression 190
3. The Silent Edge of Nonverbal Cues 192
4. How to Listen and Build Trust 194
5. Communication Styles that Drive Results 196
6. Becoming Assertive While Staying Respectful 198
7. Persuasion and Public Speaking 200
8. Writing to Influence and Lead 201
9. Bridging Cultural Gaps 203
10. Resolving Conflict through Clear Dialogue 205

Chapter 11
Flow: The Key to Peak Performance 208
1. The Meaning of Flow and Why It Matters 209
2. The Science Behind Flow and Its Mental Rewards 211
3. Essential Conditions for Tapping into Flow 213
4. The Transformative Benefits of Living in Flow 215
5. Flow and Creative Excellence: Unlocking Innovation 217
6. Entering Flow on the Job: Fostering a Peak-Performance Workplace 219
7. Confronting Barriers: Overcoming the Enemies of Flow 221
8. Flow as a Gateway to Lasting Fulfilment 223
9. Practical Routines and Habits for Flow 224
10. Bringing It All Together: Your Path to Peak Performance .. 226

Chapter 12
The Power of Gratitude 229
1. A Transforming Perspective: Embracing Gratitude 229
2. The Foundation of Gratitude: How it Shapes Your Wellbeing 231
3. Shifting Your Mindset Through Gratitude 233
4. Integrating Gratitude Into Each Day 235
5. Deepening Bonds With Gratitude 237

6. Standing Tall in Hardship: Gratitude as Your Shield 239

7. Elevating Professional Environments With Gratitude 240

8. Gratitude Journals: A Path to Growth 242

9. Unbreakable Ties Between Gratitude and Happiness 244

10. Real-Life Triumphs: Gratitude in Action 246

Chapter 13

Embracing Change 249

1. Why Change Is Inevitable 249

2. The Psychology of Change 251

3. Overcoming Fear of Change 253

4. Strategies for Adapting to Change 255

5. The Role of Change in Personal Growth 257

6. Making Major Life Changes: A Step-by-Step Guide 259

7. Navigating Change in the Workplace 261

8. Change as an Opportunity for Innovation 263

9. Building Resilience for Change 265

10. Inspiring Stories of People Who Embraced Change 267

Chapter 14

The Art of Time Management 269

1. Time: Your Greatest Asset and Why It Matters 269

2. The Power of Prioritisation and Focus 271

3. Planning and Scheduling for Maximum Productivity 273

4. Conquering Procrastination: Strategies for Swift Action 275

5. Sharpening Your Focus in a Distracted World 277

6. Harnessing Time Management Tools and Technology 279

7. Balancing Work and Leisure for a Fulfilled Life 281

8. Navigating Time Management in a Fast-Paced Digital Age. 283

9. The Impact of Time Mastery on Your Success 285

10. Charting Your Path Forward with Intentional Time Management 287

Chapter 15

Lifelong Learning: The Path to Self-Improvement 289

1. A Compelling Start: Why Lifelong Learning Matters 289

2. Building an Unstoppable Curiosity: Cultivating a Passion for Knowledge...291

3. Broadening Your Horizons: Lifelong Learning in Your Career 293

4. Curious Minds Triumph: How Inquisitiveness Drives Your Learning 295

5. Expanding Your World: How Online Learning Transforms Growth 297

6. Confronting Obstacles: Breaking Down Barriers to Lifelong Learning 299

7. Practical Strategies: Elevating Your Learning Habits 301

8. Looking After Your Mind: Mental Health Benefits of Learning 303

9. Embracing the Modern Age: Lifelong Learning in the 21st Century 305

10. True Inspirations: Stories of Lifelong Learners.................307

Chapter 16

Creativity: Unleashing Your Inner Genius 310

1. The Creative Spark: Why Creativity Matters.......................310

2. A Problem-Solving Superpower: Creativity in Everyday Challenges 312

3. Boosting Your Creative Edge: Techniques and Strategies ..314

4. Unlocking Blocks: Overcoming Creative Obstacles...........316

5. Mind-Body Connection: How Creativity Fuels Emotional Well-Being...318

6. Creative Cultures: Fostering Innovation in Workplaces 320

7. The Tech Dimension: Navigating Creativity in a Digital World 322

8. Nurturing Young Minds: Supporting Children's Creativity .. 324

9. The Drive for Innovation: Connecting Creativity and Progress 326

10. Great Creators: Lessons from Inspiring Journeys 329

Chapter 17

Mindfulness: The Power of Now 332

1. Beginning Your Journey: Laying the Groundwork for Mindful Living 332

2. The Inner Mechanics: How Mindfulness Tackles Stress 334

3. Building Emotional Resilience Through Present Awareness 336

4. Meditative Practice: Your Portal to Steady Focus 338

5. Infusing Mindfulness into Everyday Tasks 340

6. Embracing Mindful Eating: Nurturing Body and Mind 342

7. Overcoming Roadblocks: Sustaining Mindfulness in a Demanding World 343

8. Boosting Efficiency: How Mindfulness Fuels Productivity . 345

9. Remarkable Transformations: Lessons from Real-Life Mindful Practice 347

10. Moving Ahead: A Mindful Future of Confidence and Clarity 349

Chapter 18

Resilience: Bouncing Back from Adversity 352

1. The Driving Force Behind Your Power to Adapt 352

2. Mental Foundations: How Your Mind Strengthens Your Resolve 354

3. Practical Steps: Strengthening Your Resilience Day by Day 356

4. Emotional Well-Being: Protecting Your Mind Through Resilience 342

5. Overcoming Life's Highs and Lows: How Resilience Guides You 360

6. Raising Resilient Children: Building a Strong Future 362

7. Thriving Professionally: Resilience on the Job 364

8. Resilience and the Path to Personal Triumph 365

9. Bouncing Back from Defeat: Resilience as Your Safety Net 367

10. Stories of Strength: Learning from Resilient Trailblazers ..369

Chapter 19

Self-Esteem: Embracing Your Worth 372

1. Your Value and the Essence of Self-Esteem 373

2. Invisible Chains of Low Self-Esteem 374

3. Cultivating Unshakable Confidence 376

4. Self-Esteem and Healthy Bonds with Others.....................379

5. Triumphing Over Self-Doubt 380

6. Instilling a Sense of Worth in the Young 382

7. Self-Esteem as Your Edge in the Workplace 384

8. Emotional Well-Being and Self-Worth...............................386

9. Staying Grounded in a Competitive World........................388

10. Stories of Renewed Confidence and Final Inspiration......390

Chapter 20

Emotional Intelligence: Key to Personal and Professional Success 393

1. Emotional Intelligence: Your Foundational Advantage 394

2. Self-Awareness and Emotional Mastery............................396

3. Self-Regulation: Shaping Your Emotional Reactions 398

4. Empathy: Forging Deeper Bonds.......................................400

5. Motivation: Unleashing Drive from Within 402

6. Social Skills: Influencing and Collaborating with Confidence 404

7. Leadership Gains from Emotional Acuity 406

8. Conflict Resolution: Applying Emotional Intelligence 409

9. Overcoming Challenges: Strengthening Emotional Intelligence 411

10. Emotional Intelligence: Your Lasting Pathway to Success 413

Chapter 21

Leaving a Legacy That Resonates 415

1. Legacy: The Ultimate Reflection of Purpose 415

2. The Power of Paying It Forward 417

3. Mentoring the Next Generation 419

4. Financial Pass Down: More Than Money 421

5. Creating Opportunities for the Future 423

6. Designing a Legacy That Outlives You 425

7. Real-World Figures Who Illustrate Lasting Legacy 427

8. Daily Actions and Habits to Strengthen Your Legacy 429

9. Confronting Legacy Challenges and Roadblocks 430

10. Carrying Your Legacy Forward: A Lifelong Journey 432

Final Word

Embrace the Journey to Abundance 435

CHAPTER 1

Unleashing the Power of Mindset

Welcome to the first step on a journey that will fundamentally transform your life. Right now, you're standing at the threshold of something powerful, something capable of shaping every moment of your future: the revolution of your mindset. This isn't a superficial shift or a fleeting trend; it's the key to unlocking the doors of possibility you've always hoped existed. The mindset you adopt from this point forward will define the trajectory of your success, your relationships, your confidence, and your resilience in the face of life's inevitable challenges.

As you embark on this chapter, recognise that your greatest potential isn't dictated by circumstances or past experiences but by the beliefs you hold about yourself and what's achievable. Whether you feel stuck, unsure, or simply hungry for more from life, the strategies in these pages will equip you to replace doubt with determination, hesitation with action, and limitations with powerful possibilities. What you're about to discover isn't abstract theory or motivational fluff; it's practical wisdom rooted in psychological research and proven by individuals who have achieved extraordinary things against all odds.

So, as you turn these pages, do so with the knowledge that your decision to harness the power of mindset is more than a commitment; it's a declaration that you're ready to rise above mediocrity and step into the life you're fully capable of leading. Your mindset revolution begins right here, right now, and the life you've always dreamed of awaits just beyond your next thought.

1. The Mindset Revolution: Your Path to Lasting Transformation

Your mindset is the lens through which you interpret everything in your life. It dictates how you approach challenges, the way you react to both setbacks and triumphs and the level of ambition you bring to each new day. When you harness the power of your mindset, you become capable of achievements that previously felt out of reach. You shift from feeling stuck to realising that growth and progress are entirely within your control. This is not an abstract theory; it is a life-changing shift that starts within.

To begin your revolution, reflect on the daily thoughts that circle through your mind. Do they push you forward, or do they keep you in the same place? Negative patterns often camouflage as realism, convincing you to settle for less or assume that self-improvement is reserved for others. In truth, your thoughts can act like a hidden engine, guiding your behaviour and shaping your future. The moment you begin to choose thoughts that uplift and energise you is the moment you step onto the path of lasting transformation.

A key aspect of this revolution lies in becoming fully aware of the dialogue in your head. If you allow old doubts and insecurities to remain unchallenged, they can grow stronger. Take time each day to identify these limiting notions. Write them down and look at them plainly. Notice how repetitive they might sound: "I'll never be good enough," "I can't keep up," "I've failed too many times." By acknowledging them, you can start to dismantle their influence. Awareness shines a bright light on falsehoods, helping you see that these ideas do not have to be permanent fixtures in your mind.

Adopting a revolutionary mindset also calls for intentional action. Reading about new perspectives, engaging in thoughtful discussions, or learning from those who exemplify positivity can all support your cause. Every small step you take becomes a building block for a life guided by optimism and grounded in the reality that you can improve. Discipline is the driving force behind this evolution, reminding you that your habits shape your outcomes far more than occasional bursts of motivation ever will.

You must also recognise that this transformation is not instantaneous. It takes persistence and a willingness to see failure in a new light. When stumbling blocks arise, view them as lessons rather than confirmations of defeat. Your brain has an incredible capacity to grow through repeated effort, and that growth is linked directly to your ability to keep going in moments of discouragement. Resolve to keep moving forward, and your mindset will begin to match this determination.

Ultimately, the mindset revolution is a commitment to your future self. You are declaring that you refuse to be defined by past limitations and that you choose to steer your thoughts toward solutions and possibilities. From now on, you stand at the helm of your life, not as a passive observer but as the architect of your destiny. This shift in perspective, maintained and protected, will open doors you never realised existed. The revolution starts with a single decision: to set your mind on self-mastery and never look back.

2. Fixed and Growth Perspectives: Decoding Your Mental Framework

Your mindset operates like a personal compass, pointing you either toward growth and progress or keeping you firmly in place. At the heart of your mental framework lies the difference between a fixed perspective and a growth perspective. The fixed perspective insists you were born with certain abilities and that your potential is mostly predetermined. The growth perspective, by contrast, states that you are capable of developing your talents and intelligence through consistent effort and learning. When you see a person who thrives despite challenges, it is usually because they embrace the possibility of growth.

If you have ever told yourself, "I'm not clever enough for that", or "I was never good at these tasks," you have experienced the fixed perspective in action. It leads you to interpret difficulties as proof of your inherent limitations. Even seemingly harmless phrases like "I'm not a numbers person" can create mental barriers. Over time, these statements become internal rules, limiting your readiness to explore fresh challenges or improve yourself. This perspective keeps your talents locked away.

In contrast, the growth perspective centres on seeing yourself as a work in progress. You start to believe you can refine any skill or expand your knowledge with enough discipline and practice. These beliefs prompt you to persevere when facing complex tasks and to see effort as part of the journey rather than a reason to quit. Think of an athlete who doubles her training after a defeat. Instead of viewing a loss as final confirmation of inadequacy, she sees it as a reminder of how much she can still learn.

Shifting from a fixed to a growth perspective begins when you challenge the voice that says you are stuck with what you have. Start by catching yourself whenever you speak in limiting terms, such as "I'm not cut out for this." Reframe that statement to "I'm finding this difficult now, but I can improve if I keep working at it." This seemingly small change reprogrammes your brain to remain open to possibilities. With each repetition, you weaken the hold of fixed, limiting phrases and strengthen your new outlook.

It is also crucial to take practical steps. If your goal is to learn a new language, for instance, do not shy away from intermediate or advanced materials. Stretch yourself. Even if you make errors along the way, view them as stepping stones rather than embarrassments. Every session of practice, every attempt at speaking a challenging phrase, signals to your mind that you are willing to grow. Over time, your confidence in your capacity to learn will rise, matching the effort you invest.

When you adopt a growth perspective, you are no longer a spectator in your own life. Every setback transforms into a clue about where you might focus or how you might adapt. Instead of seeing yourself as lacking, you see undiscovered potential. This mindset shift does not merely boost motivation; it profoundly enhances your performance and resilience, making every step forward feel like a victory in an ongoing journey.

3. Spotting and Reframing Limiting Beliefs

When you pause to evaluate your daily thoughts, you may discover an undercurrent of beliefs that hold you back. These limiting beliefs can stem from past failures, cultural expectations, or remarks from peers that linger long after being heard. They can shape your decisions without your explicit awareness. The ability to spot such beliefs is vital since you cannot overcome what you fail to identify.

One approach to revealing these beliefs is to track your reactions to challenges or opportunities. Each time you sense hesitation or a surge of doubt, ask yourself why. Write down any statements that come to mind, such as "I always mess up under pressure," "I'm too old to learn this," or "I'll never fit in." Look at these statements as though someone else wrote them. Notice how they appear rigid and final, leaving no room for personal development.

With the beliefs visible, your next step is reframing. You must deliberately replace negative narratives with more encouraging alternatives. For instance, if your go-to thought is, "I'm too old to take on this new career path," rewrite it as "I bring unique experience and can excel if I focus on mastering fresh skills." The revised statement acknowledges the gap you need to fill, yet it does not condemn you to failure. Through repetition, your brain starts to accept these reworked beliefs, making them your new reference points.

Reframing is not self-deception. It is an act of clearing away blanket negativity so you can see real possibilities. Notice how people who excel often reframe obstacles into challenges to overcome rather than confirmations of defeat. When an athlete pulls a muscle, they concentrate on healing strategies and physiotherapy instead of lamenting bad luck. When an entrepreneur experiences a product flop, they shift to analysing what went wrong and planning a more refined attempt. By doing so, they preserve their forward momentum.

One critical element of reframing is consistency. You cannot speak one new affirmation in the morning and revert to your old mental habits by noon. It helps to practise daily. Select one or two limiting beliefs that disrupt your focus the most, and commit to challenging them any time they arise. Rehearse your reframed statements out loud, or write them repeatedly until they feel genuine. The key is to treat this practice as a form of mental training rather than a quick fix.

As you integrate reframing into your routine, you will notice subtle changes in how you respond to adversity. Situations that once made you anxious might begin to feel more like solvable puzzles than looming threats. Each success builds your confidence and further dissolves the influence of old, limiting scripts. It is an ongoing process, but each small victory over negative thinking will reaffirm your belief that change is not merely possible; it is already happening. Through reframing, you take ownership of your inner voice and guide it toward empowerment, resilience, and growth.

4. Harnessing Challenge: Strengthening Resilience and Tenacity

Challenges are unavoidable, but your reaction to them is entirely your choice. When you adopt a proactive stance and face difficulties head-on, you sharpen your resilience and develop tenacity. Instead of dwelling on discomfort, you use it as a tool to push beyond your perceived limits. The difference between buckling under stress and thriving under pressure often boils down to your mindset regarding challenge.

Picture an individual who transforms hardship into motivation, a single parent juggling multiple jobs while studying at night. The workload is immense, yet they continue forging ahead, driven by a conviction that they can improve their situation. Although many obstacles block the way, each small triumph fortifies the resolve to keep going. This persistence arises not from unrealistic optimism but from a willingness to embrace challenge as the catalyst for personal and professional evolution.

One highly effective approach is viewing each challenge as an experiment rather than a final test of your worth. This perspective allows you to step back from the pressures of perfection and concentrate on learning. By treating major hurdles as experiments, you can evaluate outcomes without fear of final judgment. If the results fall short of your hopes, you can isolate the variables that went wrong, fine-tune your approach, and try again. This attitude creates a virtuous cycle of iteration and refinement, making each attempt more likely to succeed.

Another valuable tactic is engaging in graduated exposure to challenge. Much like a strength training regime that increases difficulty over time, you can systematically build your capacity to handle stress. Start with smaller tasks that test your persistence, perhaps committing to a daily reading habit or completing a short online course. As you gain confidence in tackling these smaller hurdles, step up to larger ones. The process helps you adapt, forging mental stamina similar to the way exercise builds muscle.

Reflection plays a big role in strengthening resilience. After you overcome an obstacle, take time to analyse how you did it. Did you implement a new study technique or collaborate with someone else for support? Did you alter your daily schedule to accommodate extra practice? By understanding what worked, you can replicate those tactics the next time you face a seemingly insurmountable problem. Likewise, noting what did not work allows you to adjust, avoiding repeated mistakes.

Resilience and tenacity are not superhuman traits reserved for a select few. They are qualities you cultivate through deliberate practice, strategic effort, and a firm belief in your ability to adapt. With each challenge you conquer, you reaffirm that you can prevail. Over time, you will see adversity less as a personal threat and more as a stepping stone to deeper levels of mastery. The satisfaction you gain from overcoming what once felt impossible is enormous. It transforms your outlook, makes daunting tasks feel less threatening, and solidifies your conviction that with the right mindset, you can meet any challenge head-on.

5. Transforming Self-Talk: Affirmations and Daily Mental Conditioning

Your inner voice has immense influence over your behaviour, your goals, and your sense of self-worth. If that voice repeats defeatist statements, your subconscious will be shaped by those expectations, preparing you to fail. On the other hand, a voice that affirms your strengths and potential can propel you forward and sustain you through difficulties. Transforming self-talk is, therefore, a powerful way to condition your mind for success.

One tool to achieve this is through affirmations. These are positive, present-tense statements you speak or write regularly, designed to challenge harmful mental scripts. For example, you might start your day by telling yourself, "I am capable of handling all tasks with confidence," or "I bring unique skills that lead me to new opportunities." Initially, these may feel artificial, especially if you are accustomed to harsh self-criticism. Yet, through repetition and sincerity, affirmations act like seeds planted in your subconscious. Over time, they begin to take root, influencing your beliefs about what you can accomplish.

Timing is an important factor. Reciting affirmations first thing in the morning or before a demanding task sets the stage for better performance. Some individuals prefer recording them on their phone and listening repeatedly, while others opt for writing them in a journal. The method does not matter as much as the consistency of the practice. The more you expose yourself to your chosen statements, the more your mind absorbs them as truth.

Daily mental conditioning extends beyond affirmations. It also involves selecting the ideas that enter your mind. This might mean reading books that uplift you, following motivational accounts on social media, or listening to podcasts that broaden your perspective. Think of it as a mental diet: if you feed your brain with negativity and chaos, that is what will colour your outlook. If you nourish it with hope, resilience, and constructive wisdom, you create a climate more conducive to growth.

It is worth emphasising that affirmations are not replacements for action. They are mental catalysts that boost your commitment to the real steps you must take. Telling yourself you are a proficient public speaker is useful, but backing it up with practice, coaching, and repeated attempts is where genuine development happens. Affirmations and action form a dynamic duo; one fuels your internal drive, while the other builds tangible progress.

Be prepared for resistance, both internal and external. Internally, your mind may cling to old habits of self-doubt. Externally, you might encounter people who dismiss your new outlook as unrealistic. Persist anyway. Your self-talk is fundamentally your choice, and you are free to shift it in a direction that fosters positivity and determination. Over time, a consistent application of affirmations and mental conditioning will elevate your mood, sharpen your focus, and reinforce your readiness to seize fresh opportunities. It is a practice that, once adopted, can become an anchor for building confidence and unlocking your untapped potential.

6. Elevating Self-Worth: Groundwork for True Confidence

Confidence is the visible outgrowth of a more fundamental element known as self-worth. You can attend workshops on public speaking, dress well, and cultivate an air of composure, but if you lack a sense of deep value, your confidence will remain superficial. True self-worth anchors you. It provides the stable foundation upon which you build skills and dare to take bigger leaps.

Cultivating self-worth requires honest introspection. Start by reflecting on any negative patterns you inherited. Were you ever told you would not amount to much? Have you internalised a message that you must please everyone else before deserving anything yourself? These messages, if unaddressed, can erode your belief in your right to learn, grow, and thrive. Acknowledging them is your first step toward dismantling their power.

Next, develop practices that reinforce your inherent value. This might include journaling about your daily wins, however small they may be. List the traits you admire in yourself, such as integrity, perseverance, or empathy, and remind yourself why they matter. Avoid downplaying them or telling yourself that these traits are unimportant. When you emphasise the qualities that make you unique, you gradually reverse any subtle sense of unworthiness.

Establishing strong boundaries is another way to elevate self-worth. If you believe in your value, you do not tolerate consistently disrespectful behaviour or self-sabotaging activities. This could manifest in saying no to requests that overburden you, refraining from toxic relationships, or stepping away from negative environments that drain your energy. Boundaries act as a protective ring around your mental and emotional health, ensuring that your newfound sense of self is not undermined.

An essential aspect of self-worth also lies in embracing your imperfections. If you convince yourself that your worth depends on being flawless, you set an impossible standard. True self-worth grows when you accept that mistakes do not define you; they inform you. Taking ownership of your missteps without catastrophising them paves the way for genuine, enduring confidence. You start to see each challenge as an opportunity to exercise resilience rather than as proof of inadequacy.

Finally, keep in mind that self-worth is not a destination but an ongoing practice. Your sense of value can wax and wane based on stressful circumstances or unexpected setbacks. That is why daily rituals of self-acknowledgement are so helpful. They remind you that your value is neither given nor taken by external events; it is reinforced through mindful care of your own psychological needs. Over time, this consistent dedication to strengthening self-worth will merge with your skill-building efforts and your positive self-talk. The result is confidence that runs far deeper than any surface presentation. When your belief in your own value is solid, you become more willing to take calculated risks, speak your ideas boldly, and recover swiftly from defeats. In essence, robust self-worth is the springboard for living a life aligned with your highest potential.

7. Mindset in Motion: Real-World Success Stories

Nothing illustrates the transformative effect of mindset better than individuals who have applied it to reach remarkable heights. Whether in sport, business, or personal reinvention, their journeys embody the principles of growth, resilience, and the refusal to be limited by circumstance. Reading about these success stories spurs you on, showing that great achievements stem not merely from luck or innate talent but from a powerful commitment to a growth-focused outlook.

One striking example can be found in the life of an aspiring athlete who failed multiple tryouts but kept training rigorously. Undaunted by early dismissals, this athlete doubled the efforts, sought professional feedback, and refined every weak spot in technique. Over time, the tide changed. The training turned those early setbacks into stepping stones, and triumph followed as the athlete secured a place on a national team. This arc from repeated failure to eventual success was powered largely by the belief that abilities can evolve with the right amount of discipline and grit.

In the corporate world, we see innovators who pivoted drastically after being dismissed by investors or losing crucial clients. Instead of interpreting a lost contract as a dire ending, these forward-thinking leaders took it as a nudge to adapt. They revisited their business strategies, listened more closely to market feedback, and motivated their teams to believe in the company's capacity to reimagine itself. The outcome was not always instant, but by embracing a learning mindset, these businesses often rebounded stronger than ever, sometimes creating entirely new product lines or services that redefined their brand.

Stories of personal reinvention are equally telling. Think of someone who battled health challenges or financial adversity yet refused to see those hardships as insurmountable. Through consistent learning, targeted action, and an unshakeable mindset, they found ways to rebuild, occasionally emerging with a sense of purpose deeper than before. Their transformation involved tackling practical problems, like enrolling in skill-based courses or connecting with mentors and sustaining the mental resilience to keep going when progress felt slow.

These narratives share a common thread: an unwavering focus on the possibility of growth rather than the fear of failure. Each person faced doubts and external criticisms, yet responded by working strategically on their shortcomings. That willingness to adapt turned them from would-be failures into success stories. As you study such accounts, bear in mind that their triumph did not hinge on any mystical formula. Instead, it hinged on harnessing a growth mindset to convert stumbling blocks into platforms for learning. Whether you aim to excel in sports, entrepreneurship, or personal development, these examples prove that consistent and intentional mental training can accelerate you toward the outcomes you want. They serve as powerful reminders that the only true limits are those you set for yourself.

8. Building Your Future-Focused Mindset: Strategies for Growth

Building a mindset that propels you forward involves combining vision with concrete action. You need to know where you are heading and believe you can get there through consistent, sometimes challenging, steps. This future-focused approach detaches you from the constraints of your past while providing direction for your present efforts. By establishing a precise aim and backing it up with deliberate strategies, you transform lofty dreams into tangible goals.

Begin by defining your vision. Visualise the person you want to be and the achievements you hope to earn in specific, realistic terms. Perhaps you see yourself leading a successful team, publishing significant research, or mastering a new craft. The key is to be crystal clear, avoiding vague wishes. Commit these details to the paper, describing the end result and how it resonates with your values. A well-defined vision serves as your compass, helping you remain centred when distractions tempt you to wander off course.

Once your vision is set, create a plan of incremental milestones. Break major objectives down into tasks you can handle within days or weeks rather than months. This tactic makes the journey less intimidating and provides continual markers of progress. For instance, if your long-term aspiration is to become a respected public speaker, start by volunteering for small speaking slots. Refine your craft with each engagement, welcoming feedback along the way. Over time, your improvements accumulate, building the competence and composure you need to stand confidently in front of larger audiences.

Discipline is your ally here. Even the strongest vision falters without persistent effort to support it. Schedule times in your day or week to advance your plan, and resist the urge to make excuses when life becomes hectic. Your unwavering dedication becomes the backbone of your future-focused mindset. Routines like reading development-focused material each morning or dedicating a set window for practice sessions can fortify your resolve, making it easier to continue even when motivation wanes.

Adaptability also plays a big role. As you progress, you may encounter changes, new insights, or external shifts that prompt you to adjust your path. Remain open to refining your goals if needed. This is not a sign of weakness; it is a practical alignment with reality. Someone who rigidly clings to a plan despite changing circumstances risks burning out. On the other hand, a flexible approach preserves your momentum, ensuring you keep moving even if you must alter your route.

Throughout this process, keep the bigger picture in mind. There will be times when immediate results feel slow or even non-existent. Yet every productive hour, each newly acquired skill, each supportive connection made, and every lesson gleaned from mistakes draws you closer to your vision. Make time to celebrate small wins to stay enthusiastic about the process. Over time, your consistent actions, disciplined follow-through, and openness to adjustment merge into a formidable force, propelling you toward the future you have imagined. A future-focused mindset is no mere daydream; it is a blueprint for growth built on clear vision and unyielding commitment.

9. Shaping Your Environment to Support Your New Mindset

Your surrounding environment has a profound impact on your mindset and daily discipline. Even with the strongest internal motivation, an unsupportive or chaotic setting can disrupt your progress. Shaping your environment is not about perfection; it is about placing reminders and resources in your immediate reach that steer you toward growth. By doing so, you reduce the reliance on willpower alone, making it simpler to stick to your goals.

Start by examining your physical space. Is it cluttered with distractions or items that encourage procrastination? If you are trying to master a new language, for example, keep textbooks or flashcards within sight instead of stashing them in a corner. If you aim to improve your fitness, place your workout attire in an easily accessible spot so you can change swiftly and begin exercising without fuss. These simple cues signal to your brain that your priorities are important and merit immediate attention.

The digital realm warrants equal scrutiny. Mute or remove apps that derail your focus, such as endless social media feeds or constant notification pings. Curate your online resources so that you frequently see content aligned with your evolving mindset, motivational channels, educational materials, and opportunities for skill development. Setting up your phone or computer for minimal distraction ensures that when you do engage digitally, it supports, rather than hinders, your progress.

People in your orbit also form part of your environment. Seek out those who share a commitment to growth, whether through local clubs, online communities, or professional associations. A positive circle not only offers encouragement but also holds you accountable. Conversely, if certain connections consistently undercut your ambitions or belittle your goals, limit your exposure to them. You are not obligated to remove them from your life entirely, but you should be mindful of how their energy and attitudes might affect your mindset.

Routine is another environment-shaping tool. Structures such as morning rituals, scheduled study blocks, or dedicated practice times help reinforce your new mental framework. By ritualising key actions, you minimise the daily debate over whether or not to work on your goals. You simply follow the structure that you have pre-set. This structure becomes a form of self-support, keeping you on track when motivation ebbs.

Moreover, celebrate small tweaks that remind you of your vision. A post-it on your bathroom mirror with an uplifting message, a progress chart taped to your fridge, or even a motivational quote on your phone's lock screen can all serve as subtle yet powerful nudges. Over time, these environmental cues build momentum, reducing the effort needed to align your daily activities with your ambitions.

Remember that shaping your surroundings is an ongoing practice. As you reach new phases in your personal or professional journey, reassess what needs to stay, go, or shift. The more you adapt your environment to your goals, the more naturally you will inhabit the mindset that drives growth. While you alone are responsible for your progress, a supportive setting can be the hidden ally that helps you keep moving forward without hesitation.

10. Concluding Your Mindset Evolution: Sustaining Momentum and Purpose

You have travelled through the layers of mental transformation, from recognising limiting thoughts to building resilience, using affirmations, and reshaping your environment. By now, you should sense a shift in how you perceive obstacles, as well as in the conviction you hold about your capacity to learn and excel. The real question is, how do you maintain this mindset evolution and integrate it into your everyday living?

First, cement your progress with reflection. Frequent introspection serves as a reality check, ensuring that your actions still match your goals. At the end of each week, dedicate time to assess what went well, where you might have fallen into old habits, and how you can refine your approach. This habit encourages a cycle of improvement, preventing you from drifting back into complacency. Remember that a mindset set to grow thrives on continuous calibration.

Second, remain open to fresh challenges. Stagnation is the enemy of a dynamic mindset. Seek out tasks and experiences that demand you to stretch yourself. Whether it is signing up for advanced courses, tackling new responsibilities at work, or engaging in passion projects, your willingness to try unfamiliar territory keeps the growth-oriented mentality at the forefront of your life. Every achievement, no matter how modest, strengthens your belief in the power of adaptation.

Another key element lies in your relationships. Continue aligning yourself with people who embody the qualities you wish to uphold. Regularly engage in discussions about projects, ambitions, and lessons learned. If your circle lacks this kind of exchange, explore groups or communities where such dialogue is the norm. The collective energy of those pursuing excellence will feed your enthusiasm and nudge you to aim higher than you might alone.

You must also stay vigilant about negative influences. Even if you have significantly reduced destructive thought patterns, random challenges can trigger old insecurities. That is why a routine check on your mindset is essential. Notice if cynicism or resignation starts creeping in. When that happens, revert to your foundational tools, affirmations, reframing beliefs, or the strategies you used to conquer previous hurdles. These techniques are timeless; you can always rely on them to restore your forward focus.

Lastly, root your mindset in a broader purpose. While personal development is admirable, it gains even more meaning when connected to something larger. This might be supporting your family, serving your community, or contributing to a cause you believe in. When you see your own advancement as a stepping stone to improving the world around you, your determination to sustain your new mindset multiplies. Every discipline-based choice and every challenge you conquer becomes part of a far-reaching mission.

Your journey does not end; it evolves. Mindset work is a living process, one you nourish through steady practice, accountability, and exploration. By committing to ongoing introspection, daring to chase bigger goals, fostering enriching relationships, and anchoring it all in a purpose beyond yourself, you cement your mindset evolution for the long haul. This is how you sustain momentum and retain the fire that propels you toward an ever-growing, deeply fulfilling life. When you look back, you will find that the biggest transformation was not solely what you accomplished but who you became in the process.

Chapter 2

The Law of Attraction: Your Secret Weapon

Have you ever wondered why some people seem to effortlessly attract success, wealth, and happiness while others struggle despite their best efforts? The answer lies within the powerful yet often misunderstood Law of Attraction. It's not about wishful thinking or blind optimism but a practical, achievable way to align your mindset, actions, and emotions to shape your reality. By deliberately directing your focus and energy towards what you truly want, you can tap into this force to create the life you deserve.

The Law of Attraction is a principle that works quietly behind the scenes, shaping your experiences in line with your dominant thoughts. When you master this law, you hold the key to a life filled with opportunities, abundance, and joy. Imagine if, instead of fighting your way through obstacles, you could magnetically draw in what you truly desire. This chapter will guide you through the science and practical techniques that can make the Law of Attraction your most powerful ally, empowering you to unlock doors you never thought possible.

1. A Compelling Introduction: Unlocking Your Inner Power

You are the architect of your life, and the power to shape it rests firmly in your hands. This simple truth might sound obvious, yet many people spend their days feeling trapped, doubtful, or underutilised. You might wake up in the morning with a flicker of motivation, only to see it fade as mundane obligations and external pressures take over. But there is another way to live, one that involves tapping into the quiet, potent force within you. By actively recognising your strengths, clarifying your vision, and embracing purposeful action, you can embark on a path that leads to fulfilment in every facet of your life.

Imagine standing at a crossroads where each path represents a different future, one marked by missed opportunities, another by unrealised ambitions, and a third by a dynamic sense of growth. The choice between stagnation and achievement hinges on your willingness to acknowledge your inner power. When you decide to move forward with that power, you begin a journey of transformation that enriches both your inner world and your relationships.

This journey begins with self-awareness. By understanding your values and natural abilities, you learn where your true potential lies. It's not about chasing fleeting pursuits; it's about aligning with a deeper calling that stirs your heart. As you grow more aware of what you genuinely want, you begin to see that obstacles are not insurmountable barriers but stepping stones toward who you can become. Challenges turn into opportunities, and setbacks morph into lessons that refine your resolve.

Next comes the critical step of taking consistent action. Daydreaming can spark enthusiasm, but genuine progress requires deliberate decisions, daily tasks, and the courage to adapt when faced with unexpected twists. The more action you take, the more proficient you become at navigating change with agility rather than fear. This consistency fosters discipline, an essential trait for anyone seeking to reach new heights. Discipline is not a punishment or a drudgery; it's the anchor that holds you steady when doubts arise.

Throughout this process, you must give yourself permission to aim high. Too often, we shrink our dreams out of fear or rely on external validation. Real empowerment emerges when you embrace bold goals and show up for them fully. Even if a goal feels ambitious, your inner power gives you the spark to persist. As you harness that power, life's challenges may still appear, but you will face them with greater resilience, clarity, and determination.

In the following pages, you will uncover key principles that help you harness this power in practical ways, focusing on personal growth, forming supportive habits, deepening relationships, nurturing faith or spirituality, and achieving success with integrity. You will learn to direct your mental energy, expand your skills, and navigate challenges with unwavering resolve. By the end, you will see that your inner power, once unlocked, can set you on a trajectory of lifelong achievement. Embrace it, and step into a future where every choice, every morning, and every action pulses with purpose and self-belief.

2. Mastering Your Mindset: From Limitation to Possibility

Your mind is the control centre of your experiences, decisions, and the reality you create. If you have ever felt stuck or convinced you lack the intelligence, talent, or drive to reach your ambitions, you have witnessed the power of mindset. When that mindset is rigid, it chains you to a predefined level of accomplishment, preventing you from taking the bold steps that spark real change. However, when your mind is set on growth, you begin to see challenges as tools for development. Every trial, critique, or setback transforms into a new layer of strength.

Fostering a growth mindset starts with recognising that you are not trapped by your current abilities or any label that has been imposed on you. You are free to learn, adapt, and excel in ways you never thought possible. This sense of freedom arises when you see obstacles as useful friction, providing opportunities to refine your strategies and hone your dedication. Many high achievers have spoken about the importance of having a mindset that welcomes hurdles instead of fleeing from them. They don't crave comfort as much as they crave progress.

One of the most effective ways to reshape your mindset is by examining your internal narrative. Reflect on the words you tell yourself daily, do they lift you up or hold you back? If a discouraging phrase echoes in your mind, replace it with a constructive statement. Instead of saying, "I'm not good at this," you might say, "I will get better with practice." Such linguistic shifts may appear small, but they undermine the momentum of negativity and spark belief in your potential.

Discipline also plays a key role in building a growth-oriented mindset. By sticking to a routine or consistently tackling difficult tasks, you teach your mind to persist under pressure. Self-discipline signals that you value long-term gains more than short-term comfort. Each time you choose a walk in the morning over sleeping in or practise a skill instead of watching mindless entertainment, you reinforce the belief that your actions matter. This steady determination builds mental muscle, making you more resourceful.

You also strengthen your mindset by surrounding yourself with mentors and peers who embody the growth philosophy. Seek environments that promote learning and honest feedback. A conversation with someone who has turned their limitations into stepping stones can inspire you to do the same. Observing their methods, hearing their struggles, and witnessing their resilience teaches you that success is not reserved for a select few; it is available to all who are willing to refine their mindset and make purposeful choices.

Once you embrace a growth mindset, you'll notice a fundamental shift in how you view yourself and the world. Barriers will look smaller, opportunities will seem closer, and your ability to persevere will intensify. By moving from a restrictive mentality to one that sees possibility everywhere, you make a decisive move toward a life marked by genuine transformation.

3. The Power of Action and Habit Formation

Ambitions remain idle fantasies until they are paired with consistent action. You may have profound aspirations, a dream career, solid relationships, or a strong physique, but without action, those ideas stall. Developing effective habits is the key to bridging the gap between what you intend to do and what you actually achieve. Habits transform repeated efforts into second nature, relieving you from daily battles of willpower and freeing up mental energy for creativity and learning.

At the heart of habit formation lies simplicity. When you identify a single habit that aligns with your goals, such as a ten-minute morning exercise session, your success rate significantly improves. Trying to overhaul every aspect of life in one swoop can overload your discipline, leading to burnout. Instead, take an incremental approach. By introducing small, manageable actions, you lay a sustainable foundation for future expansion. Over time, these small, consistent efforts accumulate to produce remarkable progress.

Structure also matters. Think of each habit as having a trigger and a reward. If your habit is to read 20 pages of a book each night, set a cue, perhaps placing the book on your pillow during the day. Then, select a reward that signals completion, whether it's a relaxing stretch or a calming piece of music. By attaching a pleasant outcome to the routine, you encourage your mind to repeat it. Through repetition, the action shifts from something that demands mental effort to a process that unfolds automatically.

Habits don't merely improve productivity; they deepen your sense of commitment. By faithfully executing tasks, you provide evidence to yourself that you are someone who follows through. This self-trust boosts confidence and carries over into other areas of your life. If you consistently show up for a daily writing session, you build the conviction that you can apply the same discipline to eating well, exercising, or nurturing essential relationships.

Still, you must keep your habits flexible. Life is unpredictable, and sticking rigidly to an exact schedule under all circumstances can cause unnecessary frustration. When unexpected obligations arise, adapt the routine to fit the day's challenges. Even doing a shorter workout or reading fewer pages can keep you on track psychologically and maintain the sense of continuity that habits foster.

It's also vital to check your environment. If you wish to reduce screen time, store your devices in another room or disable notifications that disrupt your focus. If you want to eat better, fill your fridge with nutritious options and limit junk food at home. Such seemingly simple environmental tweaks make it easier to sustain new habits because the path of least resistance now points in a direction that aligns with your goals.

By shifting your lifestyle one routine at a time, you evolve from hoping to doing. The fortitude born from consistent habits propels you beyond fleeting motivation toward a steady momentum. Each action you repeat weaves a secure layer of discipline around you, safeguarding your dreams until they flourish into concrete achievements.

4. Deepening Your Connections: Building Healthier Relationships

Your life gains much of its colour and vitality from the relationships you nurture. Whether shared with family, friends, colleagues, or romantic partners, meaningful connections enrich you emotionally, offer companionship, and act as a buffer in times of stress. Strong relationships are based on mutual respect, genuine communication, and empathy. Cultivating them requires thoughtful action and a readiness to learn from missteps.

The cornerstone of every thriving relationship is trust. You build trust by doing what you promise, respecting boundaries, and being transparent. Trust is not formed in a day; it's established over time through consistent behaviour. If a friend confides in you, your willingness to guard their confidences and provide non-judgemental support speaks volumes about your dependability. Similarly, if someone sets a personal boundary, honouring it communicates respect and deepens the sense of safety in the relationship.

Open communication is equally significant. Authentic dialogue goes beyond discussing everyday niceties; it involves sharing fears, hopes, and even vulnerabilities. Speaking honestly about what troubles you or what excites you might feel unsettling at first, especially if you fear judgment or rejection. However, real bonding often develops when you show up as you are. This transparency invites the other person to reciprocate, gradually creating a nurturing environment where both parties feel understood.

Learning to listen actively is another way to enhance closeness. Too many conversations die because each party waits for the other to stop talking so they can speak. When you pause to truly absorb someone else's perspective, asking clarifying questions, mirroring back their feelings, and refraining from unsolicited advice, you transform casual exchanges into moments of genuine connection. This approach nourishes empathy, encouraging you to see life through another's eyes.

Boundaries play a pivotal role, too. A boundary is not an act of aggression but an expression of respect for yourself and others. If certain topics, behaviours, or demands feel uncomfortable, articulating your boundary prevents lingering resentment. Healthy relationships thrive when both sides are free to express needs without fear. When boundaries are routinely crossed, relationships can become toxic, draining your emotional energy.

When conflicts arise, as they inevitably will, turn to constructive resolution. Resist the pull to score points or prove that you are right. Instead, concentrate on identifying root causes and discovering solutions. The aim is to resolve disagreements with mutual respect intact so that your bond emerges stronger, not weaker. Viewing conflict as a chance to learn more about yourself and the other person shifts the conversation from hostility to collaboration.

Strengthening relationships is an ongoing journey, not a one-time fix. Maintain them through supportive actions, consistent presence, and honest communication. The reward is a robust network of people who brighten your accomplishments, soften your hardships, and stand by you through every twist life brings.

5. Finding Your Deeper Purpose: The Role of Spirituality and Belief

Whether you identify as religious, spiritual, or guided by a personal moral philosophy, an inner sense of purpose often shapes how you handle life's challenges. Connecting with something greater than your daily routine can inspire gratitude, resilience, and a more expansive perspective. You find yourself tapping into resources of strength and calm that help you stay balanced when life feels uncertain.

Finding this deeper purpose does not require elaborate rituals or rigid doctrines. It can emerge when you reflect on your place in the world, the legacy you aspire to leave behind, or the higher principles that resonate with you. Sitting quietly each day to gather your thoughts, praying, meditating, or even contemplating the natural world can spark spiritual insight. These moments nurture humility, reminding you that your personal journey intertwines with something larger than your immediate concerns.

Many people who have cultivated a strong sense of spirituality note a decrease in fear of failure because their sense of self extends beyond external outcomes. If you root your worth in something more profound than a job title or social standing, you are less likely to crumble under stress. This spiritual grounding serves as a reservoir of hope. Even in the face of obstacles, you remain steadier, recognising that the hardships are not the entire story.

Acts of kindness and service also reinforce this sense of connection. When you devote time, effort, or resources to benefit others, you reinforce the bonds that tie us all together. Compassion, empathy, and charity become tangible reflections of a higher calling. Rather than feeling drained, you often experience a surge of fulfilment, knowing that your existence brightened another person's day.

If you find it difficult to integrate spirituality or a guiding belief system into your life, start by reflecting on what lifts your spirit. Perhaps it's daily gratitude journaling, breathwork, or spending time outdoors. Build simple practices around these uplifting activities. By focusing on regular, small rituals, you slowly weave a sense of meaning into each day. Over time, these routines anchor you, giving you internal stability in a fast-paced world.

Still, it's worth noting that belief systems vary widely. Healthy spirituality never aims to condemn or demean others. If you share your beliefs, do so with a willingness to understand different viewpoints. A fruitful exchange of ideas can enlarge your perspective, teaching you that universal lessons, like love, compassion, and perseverance, unite humanity across various faiths and philosophies.

As you deepen your spiritual or moral grounding, you carry that calm into your relationships, ambitions, and daily choices. Life's achievements and setbacks begin to feel less random; each event becomes part of a broader tapestry that shapes your growth. This sense of purpose makes each day feel significant, transforming what might seem like mundane tasks into steps that serve a calling beyond yourself.

6. Creating Financial Foundations: Mastering Your Money

Financial stability can provide a springboard for many of your life's goals, whether you seek independence, security, or the resources to fund your dreams. When managed wisely, money becomes a tool that broadens your options. Conversely, neglecting finances can lead to stress, limiting your freedom to seize promising opportunities or cope with life's inevitable surprises.

A strong starting point is awareness: regularly track your income and expenditure. This might sound obvious, but many people only glance at their account balances when bills are due, never forming a clear overview of where their money goes. By diligently tracking every purchase, housing, food, transport, and leisure, you develop a sharp sense of your financial inflows and outflows. From there, you can make a structured budget that categorises expenses, sets saving targets, and pinpoints areas to cut back if needed.

Building up savings is another cornerstone. An emergency fund, typically three to six months' worth of living expenses, shields you from unplanned costs, car repairs, medical bills, or job loss. This cash cushion reduces the likelihood of relying on high-interest loans or credit cards in a crisis, keeping financial stress at bay. Once your emergency fund is solid, you can set your sights on bigger goals, such as purchasing a home, funding education, or investing in business ventures.

Investing is equally critical for long-term prosperity. Simply stashing cash in a savings account often won't keep pace with inflation, meaning your buying power diminishes over time. By exploring investments in equities, bonds, or property, you put your money to work for you. Begin modestly, research thoroughly, and, if necessary, consult a trustworthy professional. Compound growth over years or decades can significantly grow your capital, granting you a comfortable retirement or the funds to chase passion projects.

Debt management should also be prioritised. Distinguish between debt that fuels worthwhile opportunities, like a reasonable mortgage or tuition, and high-interest consumer debt that drains your resources. If you carry credit card balances, focus on settling these swiftly. High-interest liabilities can act like anchors on your progress, absorbing funds that could be devoted to saving or investing. Promptly paying down such debts frees you to dedicate future income to pursuits that align with your long-term goals.

Frugality and intentional spending round out the financial foundation. Avoid comparing yourself to others, whether that's buying designer items or chasing the latest gadget. Instead, place your financial energy into pursuits that match your values. If travel enriches your perspective, budget for it. If professional development is vital, invest in courses or certifications. By choosing a path of thoughtful, value-driven spending, you minimise waste and preserve resources for what truly matters to you.

Financial wellness is not about chasing empty material milestones; it's about securing a base that supports your aspirations. With a stable foundation under you, your stress decreases, and your mental space expands. You gain the freedom to shape your life's direction, unfettered by mounting debt or limited cash flow, focusing instead on a broader, more purposeful horizon.

7. Leading with Confidence: Career Growth and Professional Impact

In a world brimming with opportunity, your career can become a platform for personal expression, leadership, and lasting impact. When you anchor your professional journey to clear goals and a sense of direction, your work shifts from a routine obligation into a source of pride and accomplishment. To lead in any domain, be it business, education, or the arts, you need clarity of purpose, honed skills, and the audacity to speak your mind with conviction.

One of the first steps to career progression is identifying your genuine interests. When you operate in a field that sparks your curiosity, the line between work and passion blurs. You become eager to refine your craft, staying alert to emerging trends and new technologies that shape your sector. This thirst for knowledge sets you apart, making you nimble and valuable to any team or organisation.

Networking is also pivotal. True networking is not about collecting superficial contacts; it's about cultivating relationships that are mutually beneficial. You share insights, learn from peers, and exchange constructive feedback. Over time, a robust network offers you insights into industry shifts and opens the door to opportunities you may not have discovered independently. Building these relationships also teaches you about different leadership styles, showing you how to handle diverse personalities and workplace challenges.

Developing communication skills moves you from being a background player to a figure who can influence decisions. Effective leaders speak openly while being attentive listeners. Whether presenting to a group, explaining complex data, or leading meetings, your capacity to articulate ideas and empathise with your audience often determines your level of impact. This process also involves refining nonverbal cues, such as maintaining confident posture and attentive eye contact, helping you come across as trustworthy and composed.

Emotional intelligence underpins much of your leadership potential. When you identify your own emotions and sense how others feel, you create an atmosphere that values candour and mutual respect. Empathy is more than a buzzword; it's a core tool for any leader striving to unify a team behind a shared mission. When employees or colleagues feel understood, they offer their talents and time with greater enthusiasm and loyalty.

Yet, leadership is not a linear path; setbacks and uncertainties will appear. Embracing a mindset that sees these as natural learning phases can help you persist. If a project fails or you encounter workplace tension, use it to refine your strategies and deepen your resilience. Great leaders rarely coast through easy triumphs; they grow stronger by conquering trials.

As your career evolves, remain anchored in humility. You can hold expertise without ceasing to learn. The market, your profession, and even your personal interests can shift. This flexibility, coupled with integrity, keeps you relevant, valued, and prepared to guide others responsibly. Through continuous development and daring leadership, you elevate not only your professional standing but also the community and organisations you touch.

8. Health and Vitality: Nurturing Body and Mind

Health stands at the heart of your overall ability to achieve, excel, and savour life's joys. A balanced approach that includes regular exercise, nourishing foods, adequate sleep, and emotional care paves the way for you to operate at your best. Disregarding your body's needs can undermine your ambitions, while prioritising your vitality adds fuel to everything else you do.

Movement is one of the most straightforward and impactful parts of health. Activities like brisk walking, cycling, or resistance training not only keep your muscles and bones in strong condition but also alleviate stress. Physical exertion triggers the release of endorphins, mood-lifting chemicals that provide a natural burst of positivity. Even brief exercise sessions can sharpen your concentration and boost energy, qualities that prove invaluable in a busy schedule.

Nutrition is equally fundamental. When you fill your plate with whole foods, fresh vegetables, fruits, lean proteins, and healthy fats, you are providing your body with crucial building blocks for recovery, growth, and mental acuity. On the other hand, a diet high in refined sugars or overly processed meals often leaves you feeling lethargic. By making thoughtful food choices, you support consistent energy levels and strengthen your defences against common ailments.

Quality sleep often slips through the cracks, but it is vital for cognitive performance, emotional stability, and physical rejuvenation. Aiming for seven to nine hours of uninterrupted sleep allows your body to repair muscles, consolidate memories, and regulate hormones. If you find yourself struggling to rest, set an evening routine that dials down stimulation, dim the lights, silence notifications, and engage in a calming activity such as reading or gentle stretching. By valuing rest as much as your daytime pursuits, you replenish your mental reserves and wake up primed for the day ahead.

Emotional well-being weaves into overall health more strongly than many realise. Persistent worries, guilt, or sadness can sap motivation. When negative emotions mount, employing strategies like journalling, counselling, or mindfulness can help you confront them before they spiral. Sharing your feelings with a trusted friend or professional often relieves emotional strain and offers a fresh perspective on persistent challenges.

Finding equilibrium among these pillars- exercise, nutrition, rest, and emotional care- requires intention. Each facet works synergistically, so neglect in one area can weaken gains in another. Yet, the reward for consistency is profound. Life's daily obstacles become more manageable when you are physically energised, mentally sharp, and emotionally stable. Your self-confidence grows as you observe progress, such as lifting a heavier weight, enjoying clearer skin, or feeling more optimistic.

Caring for your health is neither indulgent nor optional. It is a crucial part of your self-leadership, informing how effectively you interact with family, engage in your job, and handle unpredictable events. By nurturing your body and mind, you create the conditions for sustained growth, creativity, and satisfaction, ensuring that the life you build can be fully enjoyed.

9. Communication as a Cornerstone of Leadership

Any vision, however promising, remains powerless if it cannot be conveyed effectively to others. Communication is the heartbeat of leadership, determining how well you inspire, encourage, or unite those around you. Whether you lead a company, coach a sports team, or run a household, how you speak, listen, and empathise influences whether people trust your guidance and follow your direction.

First, clarity is essential. You could have a brilliant plan, yet if your message is mired in rambling or technical jargon, the spark will be lost. To hone clarity, organise your thoughts before you share them. Outline the key points you want to emphasise and use straightforward language that resonates with your audience. Clarity fosters confidence; when listeners grasp your direction without confusion, they are more inclined to participate wholeheartedly.

Listening holds equal weight. Many individuals only pretend to listen, formulating their responses while someone else speaks. In contrast, active listening requires full presence, making eye contact, nodding, and asking open-ended questions. This genuine engagement not only offers deeper insights into problems and solutions but also validates the other person's perspective. When people sense that they are heard, they respond with greater respect and cooperation.

Nonverbal cues amplify or undermine your spoken words. Purposeful gestures, upright posture, and steady eye contact can convey commitment and calm. Meanwhile, slouching or avoiding eye contact may hint at uncertainty or disinterest, eroding your credibility. A confident stance is not about dominating a room; it is about aligning your physical demeanour with your spoken convictions.

Another pillar of communication is empathy. Tailor your approach to the emotional states and cultural backgrounds of those you address. When you attune yourself to how people feel, you choose words or examples that strike a chord. You reduce defensiveness and foster unity instead. This empathetic style is effective whether you are launching a project at work or resolving tensions among family members.

It is equally important to note that communication does not end when the talking stops. Follow-up turns words into outcomes. If you announce a new plan, check in on its execution. If you promise resources to colleagues, provide them. If you ask for feedback, show gratitude for the input and act on it when viable. This follow-up cements the link between the spoken message and tangible results.

Ultimately, communication is about partnership. You present ideas, listen to alternative views, refine plans, and inspire collective action. Maintaining an environment where others feel comfortable sharing thoughts without judgment can keep innovations flowing. People gravitate toward leaders who not only talk but also create a safe space for dialogue.

Communication is not an empty exercise; it is the vehicle through which you mobilise hearts and minds. By striving for clarity, truly listening, leveraging nonverbal cues, and speaking with empathy, you set the stage for effective teamwork. When words and actions align, you become a leader who consistently earns trust, guiding your circle toward collective success.

10. Concluding with Momentum: Building a Life of Growth and Purpose

You have the power to design a life that brims with progress, unity, and fulfilment. Each chapter of your journey, whether focused on mindset, habits, relationships, belief systems, financial stability, or physical health, feeds into the mosaic of who you are becoming. It is not a single grand gesture but a tapestry of actions, decisions, and reflections that add richness to every day. This closing segment draws together the insights explored so far, urging you to transform knowledge into consistent action.

As you move forward, remember that growth is not a destination but a steady upward climb. Expect detours and plateaus. When disappointment or weariness creeps in, refocus on why you started. That deeper purpose, be it forging a legacy, uplifting your family, or realising a personal dream, fuels perseverance. By keeping your sights on that anchor, you weather challenges with confidence and bounce back stronger.

Meanwhile, remain aware of the extraordinary potential within you. Embrace discomfort as a chance to expand your abilities. Reject voices, whether internal or external, that belittle your ambitions. Instead, channel your energy into self-improvement. Whether it is mastering a new skill at work, strengthening relationships, or building a healthier body, your ongoing efforts build long-lasting pride. Each achievement then serves as evidence that you possess both the capacity and the resilience to excel.

Life often changes course, so flexibility is key. Clinging rigidly to outdated plans can breed frustration. Allow your vision to adapt as you gain experience and broaden your interests. Stay informed about the world around you, incorporating new insights or pivots into your plans. At the same time, stay true to your core values. These unchanging guidelines act as a compass, ensuring that even if your path shifts, you remain faithful to what matters most to you.

It's also wise to keep kindness at the forefront. True success extends beyond self-interest, spilling over into how you treat loved ones, co-workers, and the broader community. A simple expression of gratitude or a timely act of support can encourage others who are on their own journeys. By contributing positively to those around you, you strengthen bonds that sustain you in times of need. When you invest in the success of others, your own life flourishes in unexpected ways.

The Law of Attraction: Your Secret Weapon

Finally, do not underestimate the power of reflection. Set aside brief moments to track what went well, where you stumbled, and how you might improve. Regular introspection refines your approach, helping you avoid repeating mistakes. Through reflection, you deepen your awareness of who you are, ensuring that your evolution remains intentional.

At this stage, you stand equipped with tools and insights to shape a remarkable life, yet it is consistent, purposeful steps that bring your aspirations to fruition. Keep your motivation alive by remembering that each day offers a blank canvas. You hold the brush. By painting your ambitions, values, and dreams with deliberate strokes, you create not only a personal achievement but a lasting impact on everyone blessed to witness your unfolding journey.

Chapter 3

Thoughts: The Architects of Reality

You've probably heard the saying, "You are what you think," but have you ever truly considered just how powerful your thoughts can be? Every goal you've achieved, every challenge you've overcome, and every moment of growth started as a simple thought, a seed planted in your mind. Your thoughts are the invisible architects of your reality, quietly shaping your beliefs, actions, and, ultimately, the life you lead.

Think about a time when a negative thought held you back, causing self-doubt or hesitation. Now, contrast that with a moment when positive thinking opened doors you never imagined possible. Whether you realise it or not, your thoughts influence your emotions, your choices, and even your interactions with the world around you. By understanding and harnessing this power, you can transform not only your outlook but your entire life.

In this chapter, we'll explore how thoughts shape your reality, delve into techniques for overcoming negativity, and discover practical strategies to nurture a mindset that aligns with your aspirations. Prepare to unlock the profound potential that lies within your own mind and begin constructing the reality you've always envisioned.

1. The Crucial Influence of Thought

Thoughts: The Architects of Reality

You hold a vast amount of power inside your mind, and your thoughts are the gatekeepers of that power. From the moment you wake up in the morning to the instant you drift off to sleep, the quality of your thoughts affects how you feel, the choices you make, and the direction your life takes. Your internal dialogue shapes your overall perspective, guiding how you interpret success, failure, and the many experiences in between. Although you might think your circumstances dictate how you feel, it is often your thoughts that set the emotional tone of your day. If you harness this power wisely, you can positively transform your outlook and steer your actions toward greater achievement, growth, and fulfilment.

There is a story of a once struggling author who believed passionately in her work and refused to surrender to years of rejection. Though poverty and repeated setbacks weighed heavily on her, her unwavering conviction in her storytelling kept her writing late into the night, convinced that her words would one day connect with readers around the world. Eventually, those stories found an audience, leading to one of the most beloved literary franchises in modern history. Her example shows that thought precedes victory, planting seeds of possibility even when the external world seems bleak. Had she allowed discouragement to rule her mind, the world might have missed out on an entire magical universe.

Thoughts do more than colour your emotional state. They also influence your decisions, which accumulate into outcomes over time. A thought can turn into the motivation to attempt something daring, such as starting a new business, seeking a better job, or writing that novel you have always dreamed of creating. Equally, a thought can undermine you, instilling doubts that keep you fixed to the same routines, never venturing forward or exploring your fullest potential.

Crucially, you are not a bystander to these mental processes. You can take command by deciding which thoughts to accept and which ones to challenge. This level of responsibility may feel daunting, but it is also freeing. Instead of viewing your thoughts as uncontrollable events, you can see them as mental habits that can be redirected toward new opportunities and higher accomplishments. Every time you make a choice about where your focus goes, you are shaping your inner narrative. Over time, these narratives become the foundation of how you perceive the world and your place within it.

In short, your thoughts function like a master architect. They create the framework for how you behave, what you believe, and the goals you pursue. Even if your circumstances are not ideal, nurturing an optimistic and tenacious mindset can shift how you approach each obstacle, ultimately reshaping your future. If you choose to see thoughts as valuable building blocks rather than random impressions, you will discover that life opens up in profound ways. The next stage in your journey is to delve deeper into the mechanisms behind this phenomenon, learning how these inner ideas build the reality you inhabit.

2. Constructing Reality Through Thought

You have an exceptional ability to influence the world around you by choosing how you think about it. This concept extends beyond a motivational slogan; science and psychology echo the same perspective. Your internal narrative frames your expectations, emotional responses, and interpretations of events. When you frequently concentrate on possibilities instead of limitations, you prime your mind to spot opportunities where others see barriers. Conversely, if you fixate on past failures or presumed shortcomings, you may miss out on the very openings that could alter your path.

Research in neuroscience shows that persistent thought patterns can reshape your brain's neural pathways. Neural plasticity means that your brain is not a rigid structure, it is dynamic, continually rewiring in response to what you dwell on. Reflect on an inventor who envisions solutions before they even exist. By maintaining a mental image of what is possible, they pave the way for their breakthroughs. This inventor's mind is not clouded by assumptions that something is out of reach. Instead, they develop a flexible brain primed to spot every hint of a workable idea.

Take, for example, a tech entrepreneur who, at one point, saw rockets explode and finances plummet yet continued to hold a vision of human advancement and interplanetary travel. Many people dismissed these endeavours as too risky or impractical, but the entrepreneur's resolute belief in success guided decisions and sparked relentless effort. Over time, these once outlandish ideas evolved into world-altering industries that pushed technology to new heights. By choosing to view obstacles as part of a grand experiment rather than dead ends, this individual reshaped modern engineering.

This idea of self-fulfilling prophecies further underscores how thoughts shape reality. If you consistently regard yourself as incompetent or bound to fail, you may shy away from golden opportunities. You might not put in the required effort or might sabotage your own progress out of worry. Over time, these actions confirm the very negative belief you harbour. In contrast, when you regard yourself as resourceful, able, and prepared to improve, you tend to invest more energy, spot solutions more quickly, and display resilience in the face of setbacks.

Crucially, this is not about ignoring genuine hurdles. Reality can present enormous challenges, and unwavering optimism alone cannot fix everything. Instead, it is about recognising that negative or limiting thoughts often undermine the talents you already possess. When you train your mind to look for openings, even small ones, you teach yourself to respond rather than withdraw. If you make it a habit to ask, "What can I do about this?" you start shaping a reality brimming with creative solutions.

Therefore, constructing your external world often begins with nurturing an inner environment directed at possibility, resilience, and purposeful action. Rather than being at the mercy of circumstances, you are refining the lens through which you see them. The next step is to examine how destructive thinking patterns can hold you back from accomplishing your ambitions, prompting you to find methods to break the cycle.

3. Confronting the Power of Negativity

Negative thinking can stand like a fortress, blocking you from advancements in your professional, personal, or emotional life. Though occasional self-doubt or critical thoughts may be expected, persistent negativity can create a harmful cycle that is difficult to escape. Once you start believing that you are undeserving of achievement or incapable of surmounting hurdles, you reinforce these ideas each time they crop up. In the end, negativity can stifle your natural gifts and undermine your motivation to aim for something more rewarding.

Thoughts: The Architects of Reality

Imagine you have an inner critic, a persistent voice pointing out every flaw, doubting each intention, and predicting failure before you even begin. When this critic takes control, you become trapped in self-fulfilling outcomes. You forgo applying for a position because you feel unqualified, or you avoid forging new connections because you assume you will be rejected. These actions confirm the critic's gloomy forecast, and the cycle persists unchallenged. It becomes a self-built barrier erected by thoughts rather than undeniable facts.

Various high-achieving individuals had pivotal moments where negative thoughts could have overwhelmed them. A famous business leader once slept in his office, faced multiple rejections, and had every reason to abandon his ambitions. However, by challenging bleak expectations, he channelled negative energy into a relentless push for success. Without that mental shift, no amount of financial backing or outside advice could have propelled him past self-imposed mental constraints. It was the internal decision to confront negativity that guided every subsequent step.

Chronic negativity takes a toll on your physical health, too. Studies in psychology and medicine show that you release stress hormones like cortisol each time you dwell on worst-case scenarios or imagined failures. Over time, prolonged exposure to these hormones raises blood pressure, disrupts sleep, and weakens the immune system. If you have found yourself more tired, anxious, or susceptible to illnesses, your constant negative mindset may be a hidden culprit.

Yet there is hope. The first step is recognising that negative thoughts are habitual patterns, not indisputable truths. They might feel genuine, but in reality, they are stories you repeatedly tell yourself. Once you see them for what they are, mental narratives shaped by fear or past disappointments, you reclaim the power to question them. This realisation can be liberating, revealing that you can rewrite old mental scripts. You are not destined to remain stuck in a spiral of self-defeating beliefs.

Confronting negativity does not mean pretending life is perfect. Instead, it involves validating your fears while refusing to allow them to govern your outlook. By doing this, you open space for constructive thinking, rational problem-solving, and openness to fresh possibilities. The challenge is to replace negativity with a more balanced mental environment. This sets the stage for using tried-and-tested methods that shift your focus toward productivity and confidence rather than endless self-criticism or gloom.

4. Mastering Positive Thinking Techniques

Cultivating a mindset oriented toward optimism is a learned skill rather than an inborn trait. Positive thinking does not involve pretending that difficulties vanish or that life is devoid of complexity. Instead, it centres on developing a constructive viewpoint that fuels resilience, creativity, and an unshakable belief in your ability to overcome challenges. This approach protects you from becoming mired in despair and helps you remain flexible when facing obstacles.

One popular way to foster positive thinking is through the power of visualisation. By mentally rehearsing favourable outcomes, you prime your brain to spot and seize opportunities. Successful athletes, for example, often mentally run through their entire performance, timing each movement, feeling every muscle contraction, before ever stepping onto the court, track, or field. This mental exercise boosts their confidence and conditions their minds to anticipate triumph. When executed consistently, visualisation can reshape how you approach major tasks, personal goals, or significant life changes.

Another crucial method is the practice of gratitude. Spending a few moments each day reflecting on what you appreciate instils a habit of focusing on gains instead of losses. Scientific studies have linked regular gratitude practices to greater well-being, lower stress, and a heightened sense of connectedness. You may find that gratitude paves the way for a steadier mental outlook, providing an anchor during tense or overwhelming situations.

Affirmations also help by counteracting the damaging impact of self-critical thoughts. When you repeat empowering statements, statements about your competence or resilience, for instance, you gradually retrain your internal dialogue. Think of it as updating your internal software. Affirmations are not magic words that erase problems overnight, but they help override harmful mental habits. You develop an internal environment that favours problem-solving and motivation rather than self-sabotage.

Yet applying these techniques requires consistency. It is not enough to visualise once or note down gratitudes sporadically. You must make them part of your daily routine, integrating them into your lifestyle. A short period of visualisation each morning, a few minutes to list what you appreciate in the evening, or the repetition of encouraging statements, whenever doubt arises, can cumulatively shift your mental perspective. Over time, these small, regular habits transform your outlook and influence how you tackle trials in every sphere of your life.

Crucially, positive thinking is not a replacement for strategic planning or skill development; you still need to pair optimistic thought with practical action. However, these methods can dramatically affect how you perceive difficulties, handle setbacks, and maintain momentum. They give you an internal framework that supports, rather than hampers, your aspirations. With this foundation in place, you are well-prepared to identify and resist the mental pitfalls known as cognitive distortions, which often sneak in and twist your perception of reality.

5. Identifying and Overcoming Distorted Thinking

Cognitive distortions are misrepresentations that your mind can generate, warping how you interpret events and relationships. These distortions may emerge as sweeping assumptions about yourself, such as believing a single setback defines all future attempts. They can also present as magnifications of problems or minimisations of achievements. In essence, these distorted views undermine your clarity and lead to skewed conclusions.

A well-known example of such patterns includes all-or-nothing thinking, where you perceive only extremes in any outcome. For instance, you might believe you are either a complete success or a total failure, neglecting the shades of grey that reflect real life. Another common trap is catastrophising, where minor issues quickly balloon into imminent disasters in your mind. This false narrative fuels anxiety and hinders your capacity to address the situation calmly. Over time, repeated distortions lead to a self-confirming cycle: you expect misfortune, you notice signs that affirm that expectation and the cycle entrenches itself further.

Thoughts: The Architects of Reality

Overcoming distorted thinking starts with awareness. You need to trace moments when your thoughts feel exaggerated or unfairly dismissive. Ask yourself if there is any evidence supporting the dire conclusion you have drawn or if you are overlooking data that contradicts it. Writing down these thoughts can be beneficial. Seeing them on paper often reveals how disproportionate or flawed they are, helping you gain a more accurate perspective.

Several leaders and visionaries have discussed the importance of breaking through these mental illusions. An influential figure in the retail sector once remarked that early failures did not label him incompetent; they merely pointed out areas needing adjustment. By reframing setbacks as feedback rather than condemnation, he avoided all-or-nothing thinking. This shift prevented him from becoming stuck in discouragement and encouraged him to refine his approach instead. Without that reframing, he would have been trapped by destructive thought patterns.

Confronting distortions also includes developing alternative interpretations. When a thought like "I messed up this presentation, so I will never excel professionally" crosses your mind, you could counter with, "One underwhelming presentation indicates a need for improvement, not a permanent inability. I can study the mistakes, refine my skills, and deliver better results next time." This does not mean sugar-coating reality. Instead, it is about aligning your thinking with logic and actual evidence rather than letting fear or perfectionism dictate the narrative.

Be patient during this process. Cognitive distortions can be deeply engrained, becoming default mental routes that the brain follows automatically. Through consistent effort, you can forge fresh neural connections that challenge these inaccuracies. Over time, you will retrain your mind to interpret difficulties in a rational, balanced way, enhancing both your decision-making and emotional well-being. The next step is to harness mindfulness as an effective method to stabilise and focus your thoughts, preventing them from veering into distortion.

6. Harnessing Mindfulness for Mental Control

Mindfulness is more than a trendy buzzword. It is an enduring practice of being alert to the present moment, your thoughts, feelings, and environment, without judging them as good or bad. This heightened awareness creates a buffer between your emotions and your reactions, allowing you to respond wisely instead of being driven by impulsive, knee-jerk reflexes. Through mindfulness, you can systematically tame the chaos of the mind, gradually minimising the influence of unhelpful distractions or anxieties.

Visualise yourself in a challenging situation at work. A deadline draws near, your inbox is overflowing, and tension is mounting. In these moments, your mind may race with worries about failure or embarrassment. Mindfulness training teaches you to recognise these anxious thoughts instantly. Rather than engaging with them or letting them spiral, you simply note their presence and observe how they come and go. This pause disrupts the automatic fear response. You discover that many of your stress-inducing thoughts are fleeting unless you keep feeding them with attention.

Well-known individuals in high-pressure fields often credit mindfulness with giving them the mental composure to excel. A prominent hedge fund founder, for example, has cited daily meditation sessions as instrumental to his clarity under fast-paced market pressures. By practising mindfulness, he remains more balanced, responding thoughtfully to unexpected changes rather than panicking. This strategic calm grants him a decisive edge, especially in a domain where impulsive moves can wreak havoc on results.

Consistent mindfulness also physically restructures the brain. Research shows it can lessen activity in the regions linked to stress and heighten activity in areas that regulate self-control and emotional stability. Over time, you cultivate a mental environment less susceptible to negativity or irrational fears. This transformation in brain function, achieved through regular mindfulness, paves the way for clearer judgement and enhanced problem-solving.

In practice, mindfulness can be woven into everyday routines. You might set aside a few minutes each morning to sit quietly, focusing on your breath. Whenever you notice your mind drifting, perhaps to an unresolved task or a fleeting emotion, acknowledge that shift, then gently guide your attention back to the present moment. No condemnation, no frustration, simply a return to now. This exercise, repeated regularly, teaches your mind to remain centred amid life's bustle. Alternatively, you could bring mindfulness to daily activities, paying close attention to how you move, eat, or even wash dishes, turning what was once a mindless routine into a grounding exercise.

By using mindfulness to anchor yourself, you disrupt the repetitive loops of self-doubt or rumination. The result is a more solid and balanced mental landscape, one that fosters productive habits and keeps you from tumbling into emotional extremes. Next, you will see how this steady mental foundation can enhance emotional health, revealing how thoughts directly shape whether you remain balanced, anxious, or content as life unfolds.

7. Elevating Emotional Health Through Thought

Your emotions do not simply arise out of nowhere; they often emerge from the thoughts percolating beneath your awareness. Each time you interpret an event, be it a trivial mishap or a major life change, your mind issues a judgement that elicits a corresponding emotion. Understanding this relationship between thoughts and feelings is vital if you aim to improve your emotional well-being.

Various psychologists have noted that your emotions frequently stem from your interpretations, not merely the external events themselves. If a colleague forgets to invite you to a meeting, you might immediately assume they dislike you or doubt your competence. This thought triggers feelings of hurt or anger. Another person in the same scenario might interpret it as a simple oversight and experience no such distress. The event is the same, but the emotional outcomes differ due to contrasting thought processes.

High-profile personalities have highlighted how a healthy mindset supports emotional stability. A media innovator who reimagined an entire industry once dealt with multiple rejections and near-bankruptcy. She disclosed that whenever self-pity or worry crept in, she deliberately pivoted her thinking toward problem-solving and opportunity discovery. This stance preserved her enthusiasm and helped her navigate major career setbacks with less emotional turmoil.

Studies also indicate that long-term negative thinking can lead to chronic anxiety or depression. When you repetitively think in catastrophic or defeatist ways, you set off a sequence of stress responses in your body, essentially teaching it to remain in a state of perpetual alert. Over extended periods, this undermines mental health, leaving you more vulnerable to further negativity and emotional swings. Breaking free means unlearning reflexive negative interpretations.

Conversely, nurturing thoughts that champion resilience and hope sets off emotional states that promote healing and balance. Reminding yourself that you can adapt to challenges and learn from mistakes helps you remain steady in turbulent times. These balanced emotions make you more open to problem-solving, supportive relationships, and constructive action. The result is a cycle where positive thoughts enhance emotional health, which in turn supports better thinking.

Ultimately, you are not entirely at the mercy of your moods. By developing an awareness of how your thoughts affect your emotions, you gain control over your psychological well-being. This control does not mean forcing yourself to be cheerful at all times; it means seeing how your interpretations drive how you feel. Recognising this interplay allows you to stay mindful, challenging unhelpful narratives and replacing them with balanced views that better reflect reality. As you solidify this emotional resilience, you also strengthen the mental bedrock for building enduring, success-oriented habits, a crucial ingredient for long-term achievement.

8. Developing Success-Oriented Thought Patterns

Success emerges not solely from ambition or raw talent but also from the mental habits you maintain day in and day out. The most accomplished figures in business, sports, or the arts often share a common trait: a disciplined inner world that pushes them forward, even when the path is unclear. Adopting success-oriented thought patterns is akin to building an inner engine that continually drives you beyond perceived limits.

One core mental habit is resilience. Rather than interpreting setbacks as personal failings, you learn to see them as catalysts for improvement. When you train your mind to interpret each obstacle as a temporary challenge, your determination multiplies. This resilience thinking is essential for progress, whether you are an entrepreneur launching a new product or someone seeking a promotion in a competitive field.

Another important habit is keeping an eye on future possibilities rather than remaining stuck in present constraints. A visionary business leader once made what seemed like absurd decisions based on a belief in future technology that few others recognised. That conviction shaped the direction of entire industries. Instead of dwelling on every short-term hindrance, a forward-thinking orientation allows you to lay the groundwork for breakthroughs that alter your trajectory. This applies not just to technology but to all facets of life, from planning a meaningful career shift to working toward personal development milestones.

Beyond resilience and a future orientation, successful individuals also adopt what can be termed abundant thinking. Instead of ruminating on what they lack or what might go wrong, they fixate on avenues for progress and the resources at their disposal. This mental framework fuels creative solutions because the mind stops obsessing over barriers and starts hunting for fresh angles. Over time, abundant thinking evolves into an ingrained habit of asking,

"How can this be done?" rather than "Why can't this be done?"

These thought patterns do not materialise overnight. They require repeated practice, shifting from a mindset of "I am stuck" to "I am learning." By acknowledging that your mental habits are malleable, you empower yourself to make changes. Small daily acts, such as noting lessons learned from mistakes or envisioning your five-year goals, gradually forge these success-oriented pathways in your brain.

As you refine these patterns, you will see that success is less about a single breakthrough moment and more about sustained psychological discipline. Even if external circumstances get messy, a well-tuned mental approach keeps you centred. This steadiness paves the way for consistent progress and achievements you once doubted were possible. Now, let us investigate people who have truly walked this path, using the power of their thoughts to elevate themselves to remarkable heights. Their stories highlight how tangible it becomes when determined thinking transforms into concrete, world-changing outcomes.

9. Real-World Stories: How Thought Transforms Lives

Nothing illustrates the force of thought better than real individuals who propelled themselves from difficult circumstances to unimaginable success by changing their mental approach. These stories remind you that your mindset can redefine what is achievable, no matter how formidable the barriers may appear.

One actor lived in a small apartment, struggling to cover daily expenses, yet clung to an unwavering belief in his capacity to succeed. He envisioned a future where he would be compensated lavishly for a film role, penning himself a cheque as a tangible reminder. Despite abundant rejections and disappointments, he held onto this symbol of eventual triumph. Years later, he was paid the exact sum for a major movie, a moment that felt fated given his persistent mental rehearsal. His story underscores how resilience, joined with a firm vision, can defeat uncertainty.

A world-renowned fashion entrepreneur launched her career well into adulthood, shattering the misconception that it is ever too late to excel. Despite the scepticism of those around her, she chose to reinterpret each setback as a learning experience, attributing her later success to a refusal to nurture negative thoughts about her perceived age disadvantage. By steadfastly picturing her designs captivating the global market, she persisted through the initial difficulties. Today, her label stands as proof that mental fortitude can overrule what others deem an impassable boundary.

Another luminary overcame repeated failures when shaping an entertainment empire. He faced mockery and financial disasters yet continually leaned on the idea that imagination could captivate hearts worldwide. His mental blueprint guided him through every phase, ultimately giving rise to creations that resonate with millions. He regularly spoke about dreams and curiosity as essential ingredients, revealing that the narratives you tell yourself can pioneer entire worlds if you stay committed to them.

These individuals, spanning diverse industries and backgrounds, share a unifying theme: the mind set the stage for their ultimate achievements. They encountered doubt encountered rejection, and stared down hopelessness. The difference lay in their refusal to let those defeats cement themselves into their identity. Each negative episode was interpreted as a stepping stone, fuelling ambition rather than erasing it. This alignment of thought, aspiration, and unyielding action is what carved their paths from obscurity to significance.

Recognising the patterns in these transformations can spark your own re-examination of personal obstacles. You might not be planning to be a Hollywood star, a global designer, or an entertainment pioneer, yet the underlying principle is the same: when you transform your mindset from despair to possibility, your options multiply. Doors, once invisible, can swing open. Challenges you once thought unconquerable can serve as catalysts for growth. By absorbing these lessons, you prepare to look ahead at emerging ideas in thought research, where evolving science illuminates ever more intriguing ways your mental processes can shape not only your reality but possibly the broader environment around you.

10. The Future Landscape of Thought

As research on brain plasticity, quantum theories, and advanced mental technologies pushes forward, the future of thought holds exciting potential. Scientists are peeling back additional layers of how your consciousness interacts with reality, suggesting that your mental landscape may be even more influential than previously believed. These insights point to new frontiers where the power of directed thought could affect learning capacities, emotional states, and even the realm of creative imagination.

One area of intense exploration is the possibility that your conscious focus might shape interactions at micro levels, perhaps even at subatomic scales. While still under rigorous investigation, these ideas hint that the observer may play a role in determining outcomes in ways we do not fully comprehend. If proven, it would highlight an even deeper link between your thinking and the fabric of the reality you experience. Rather than viewing thoughts as intangible or ephemeral, you would see them as active contributors to the ongoing evolution of your environment.

Rapid advancements in brain-computer interfaces also show how thought may move from the intangible realm of ideas to more tangible forms of expression. Already, experimental interfaces allow individuals to control devices solely with their minds. If this trend continues, your thoughts could one day directly shape the world through technology, bridging the gap between intent and action in unprecedented ways. Such innovations hold immense promise for those with physical limitations, granting them broader agency in daily life. Yet this technology also raises ethical queries about privacy, free will, and the essence of identity itself.

In the midst of these discoveries and innovations, one unchanging truth stands: how you think remains pivotal to your personal evolution. Regardless of how sophisticated technology becomes or how the outer world shifts, the fundamental choice about which thoughts to cultivate still rests in your hands. By deliberately guiding your mind toward productive ideas, supportive narratives, and curiosity about what is possible, you enrich your capacity for transformation. Challenges and setbacks become part of a bigger story of growth instead of final verdicts on your potential.

Embracing this perspective does not require you to abandon rational thinking or ignore obstacles. It means acknowledging that the mind is a vibrant and creative force, at times able to locate hidden paths through seemingly impossible terrain. The future, shaped by science and your own willingness to believe in the power of thought, appears filled with potential. You now have a comprehensive understanding of why your thinking patterns deserve attention, how they reshape your life circumstances, and what you can do to channel them for extraordinary results.

As you step beyond these pages, you hold the choice to see yourself not as a bystander but as an active architect of your experiences. By applying the strategies for mindful awareness, balanced self-talk, and openness to greater possibilities, you encourage a reality where your inner victories become outward transformations. It begins with one single idea: that each thought holds the possibility of renewal, leading you closer to the life you envision and the person you aspire to be.

Chapter 4

The Art of Habit Formation

Picture waking up each morning feeling energised, knowing precisely how your day will unfold, not because you're trapped in routine, but because you've intentionally shaped habits that guide you towards success. Your life is a reflection of daily actions, and when these become second nature, you're not just coasting through life; you're steering it confidently in the direction you choose. Habit formation puts you firmly in control, turning mundane activities into powerful drivers of your ambitions.

Now, imagine those small actions you repeat each day. From your morning coffee ritual to how you unwind at night, each choice impacts your path. These automatic actions, when aligned with your goals, effortlessly propel you forward, freeing your mind for greater creativity and problem-solving. But when they're misaligned, they silently erode your potential. Recognising this empowers you to swap out those harmful habits for ones that genuinely support your dreams.

This chapter dives into the fascinating mechanics behind habit formation, exploring how your brain thrives on repetition, making even complex tasks feel effortless. You'll uncover how to intentionally craft habits that not only stick but profoundly enhance your life. With real-world insights and practical strategies, you'll learn how to build a foundation of habits that sustain motivation, foster resilience, and deliver remarkable, lasting change. The art of habit formation isn't about rigidly controlling your life; it's about wisely choosing behaviours that support your vision for success.

1. A Vital Introduction: Why Habit Formation Matters

You deserve to step into each day feeling in control of your actions, and habit formation is the key to achieving that. Your daily choices shape the overall path of your life, guiding everything from physical health to professional accomplishments. When you master habit formation, you place yourself in the driver's seat, deciding which patterns will help you thrive and which ones need to be left behind. This introductory section lays the groundwork for understanding why habits matter so profoundly, showing you how they can become your most valuable assets in the pursuit of success, fulfilment, and balance.

Picture your morning routine: perhaps you wake up, reach for your phone, browse the news, and sip a hot drink. You might then get dressed, head to work, and settle into a string of behaviours repeated so often that you scarcely notice them. These automatic actions save mental energy, freeing you to focus on bigger tasks. However, what if some of these automatic routines fail to serve you? Worse yet, what if they hold you back? By exploring the art of habit formation, you become alert to any self-sabotaging patterns, allowing you to replace them with ones that contribute to your goals.

A crucial reason habit formation matters is the way your brain works. Repetition builds neural pathways, transforming conscious choices into instinctive actions. This reduces mental strain; your brain loves shortcuts because they lighten the cognitive load. Although this system is beneficial, especially when used to form positive habits such as consistent exercise or strategic planning, it can also cement negative habits. By learning to build awareness and intention into your routine, you replace counterproductive cycles with healthier ones that elevate your life rather than limit it.

Habit formation also offers a sense of stability. In a fast-paced world full of unexpected events, routines bring structure to your day, ensuring that important tasks never slip through the cracks. You create a mental anchor by cementing essential habits, like preparing nutritious meals, committing to regular workouts, or dedicating time to meaningful relationships. This anchor keeps you steady in the face of life's changing circumstances. Rather than feeling adrift when challenges appear, you lean on carefully chosen behaviours to provide continuity and a sense of control.

In this chapter, you will uncover the science behind habit formation, from the subtle cues that trigger your routines to the powerful rewards that keep them going. You will learn how to set up effective new habits while also breaking free from unhelpful cycles. Drawing upon principles of psychology and real-life examples from high achievers, you will be shown practical techniques, enabling you to transform daily actions into stepping stones toward your grandest vision of success. By mastering habit formation, you direct your own path, shaping each day with renewed clarity, determination, and purpose.

You are now invited to explore how these principles apply to your life. Recognise the power you hold to build the habits that reflect your aspirations. With time and the right methods, you will cultivate routines that support your best possible future, forging a daily rhythm that propels you to success on your own terms.

2. The Brain's Shortcut: How Habits Take Shape

Picture your brain as a master strategist, constantly seeking ways to conserve energy and work more efficiently. Habits are the strategies it deploys. Each time you repeat a behaviour, your brain builds a more solid neural pathway, eventually making the action nearly automatic. This phenomenon explains why you can perform tasks like driving to a familiar location without consciously thinking about every movement of the steering wheel. In this section, you will see exactly how habits become ingrained in your mind, revealing the profound effect of consistency on your everyday life.

From a scientific perspective, habits form through what psychologists call the cue-routine-reward loop. First, you encounter a cue, perhaps you feel stressed; then you respond with a routine, such as opening social media, and finally, you experience a reward, which might be the brief relief of distraction. Over time, your brain links the cue to the routine, looking forward to the reward. With repetition, this loop becomes so entrenched that the behaviour unfolds automatically whenever the cue appears. Although this mechanism can serve you well by creating beneficial patterns, it can also lead you down roads you would rather avoid, such as late-night snacking or procrastination.

The basal ganglia, a region deep inside your brain, is fundamental in storing and reinforcing these habits. While the frontal cortex handles conscious decisions, the basal ganglia excels at patterns built through repetition. When a behaviour first begins, you must actively concentrate. However, as your neural pathways strengthen, the basal ganglia takes over, freeing your conscious mind to focus on more complex tasks. This switch explains why initially challenging actions, think of learning a new instrument or adopting a daily exercise routine, can become easier with dedication. Your brain transforms novel tasks into a seamless routine, saving you willpower in the process.

Yet, your brain's habit-forming efficiency can be a double-edged sword. If a behaviour brings a short-term reward, your mind can lock onto it before you realise the long-term consequences. These harmful loops often include mindless scrolling on devices, binge-eating sugary snacks, or relying on unproductive coping mechanisms whenever you encounter stress. Overcoming those ingrained patterns may appear daunting, but by unravelling the brain's process, you will gain the insight needed to change them.

To start reshaping your habits, focus on the cue-routine-reward loop. Identify the trigger for any behaviour, pinpoint the actions that follow, and evaluate the resulting outcome. Is it helping you, or is it undermining your goals? Replacing the negative routine with a more positive one while still obtaining a satisfying reward is a proven way to steer your brain toward healthier loops. You are not battling laziness or lack of willpower; you are working with a brain that prioritises efficiency and immediate gratification. By re-routing that efficiency, you can develop habits that push you forward instead of holding you back.

Ultimately, this exploration of how habits take shape in the brain is designed to empower you. Once you understand your mind's built-in preference for routine, you can harness it to strengthen any area of your life, health, relationships, productivity, or personal growth. That knowledge lays the groundwork for transforming your daily actions into powerful building blocks of lasting success.

3. Clearing the Path: Breaking Counterproductive Cycles

Before you can build the kind of life you desire, you must dismantle the routines that threaten your progress. You know those moments when you catch yourself repeating a behaviour you promised to eliminate, whether it is an unhealthy snack before bed or mindlessly checking messages when you should be focusing on a task. Breaking counterproductive cycles is not about brute force; it requires strategy, patience, and an understanding of how habits become so resilient in your mind.

To dismantle an unwanted habit, you must first highlight the cue triggering it. Ask yourself: is there a certain time, emotional state, or environment setting it off? Imagine, for instance, you have a habit of reaching for your phone whenever boredom creeps in. The cue is the sensation of boredom, the routine is scrolling through apps, and the reward is a brief moment of stimulation. Once you see that pattern clearly, you can swap out the routine for something healthier, like reading a few pages of a book or stepping outside for fresh air. Although your phone habit felt unstoppable at one time, identifying the cue empowers you to respond differently.

One stumbling block is the immediate gratification that keeps unwelcome routines alive. If you indulge in junk food when you feel stressed, you get a swift burst of pleasure, even though you pay for it later with low energy or regret. In these moments, short-term rewards overshadow long-term goals; your brain interprets them as urgent forms of relief. To confront this, you should introduce alternative rewards that provide satisfaction without undermining your bigger aspirations. Maybe you replace the sugary snack with a comforting cup of herbal tea, or you go for a quick walk to shift your mood. By doing so, you still soothe that craving for comfort, but in a way that aligns with who you want to become.

It is also crucial to lessen your exposure to triggers whenever possible. If your evenings revolve around mindless television marathons, remove the temptation by having your workout gear visible or by planning a social activity that pulls you away from screens. If you overspend while browsing online shops late at night, hide those shopping apps or set digital spending limits. By reducing the friction around good alternatives and increasing the friction around harmful routines, you adjust your environment to support your choices.

Another aspect of breaking counterproductive cycles is embracing self-compassion. You might think berating yourself for slipping up will keep you on track, but shame often pushes you into the very spiral you hope to escape. Instead, accept occasional setbacks as part of the process. Acknowledge that you are learning to redirect deeply ingrained patterns and that small missteps are natural. This approach keeps you from spiralling into hopelessness and enables you to bounce back quickly.

By systematically revealing triggers, replacing routines, managing reward structures, and practising self-compassion, you weaken any habit that does not serve you. This clearing of the path sets the stage for intentionally constructing new cycles that reflect the person you are becoming. With each unwanted routine dismantled, you create space for healthier, more fulfilling behaviours to take root.

4. The Foundations of New Habits: Setting Strong Cornerstones

The Art of Habit Formation

Now that you have cleared away or at least weakened the unwanted habits, it is time to lay the foundations for new, beneficial ones. Much like constructing a house, you want your habits to have strong, steady cornerstones that withstand the pressures of everyday life. These cornerstones are built through small, strategic steps that gradually foster resilience, dependability, and genuine progress.

To start, remind yourself that every major transformation begins with one modest, meaningful action. Rather than setting an enormous goal right away, choose a miniature version of it. If you desire a daily exercise routine, begin with a simple five-minute session. If you want to meditate consistently, start with two minutes each evening. This technique, sometimes called "micro-habits," addresses the psychological hurdle of taking the first step. Once you have satisfied your smaller target, you can feel victorious, which motivates you to scale up gradually. The sense of accomplishment triggers a rush of positive emotion in your brain, reinforcing the new pattern.

Clarity stands out as one of your strongest allies when creating new habits. Spell out precisely what the habit entails. If your aim is to read more, identify the book, the specific time, and the location you will do it. You might say, "Each evening, after I finish washing up, I will read two pages of a self-improvement book while seated on the living-room sofa." By removing ambiguity, you signal your brain that there is no guesswork involved; the plan is set in stone. This clarity also shortens the window where you can talk yourself out of taking action.

Rewards, even small ones, are invaluable for habit formation. As you build a routine, make sure you celebrate your successes. This could mean treating yourself to a pleasant break, sharing your achievement with a friend, or simply allowing a moment of satisfaction and self-praise. That reward cements the neural link, signalling to your brain that the new habit is worth repeating. Over time, the behaviour itself might become its own reward, but in the early stages, an external incentive can make all the difference.

Be aware of potential hurdles to your new habit. If you tend to run late in the morning, scheduling a new habit for that time might invite frustration. If your weekends are constantly chaotic, planting a new routine there could lead to missed attempts. Think through where your habit will fit most naturally. You want to stack it onto an existing, stable routine, perhaps straight after lunch or right before bedtime. This technique, often called "habit stacking," glues your new behaviour to something already ingrained in your schedule, making it much harder to skip.

By using micro-habits, clarity, thoughtful rewards, and smart scheduling, you develop a robust framework for lasting change. Each of these elements unites to form the strong cornerstones of your new habit. Over time, the consistent application of this foundation ensures the routine does not collapse under the demands of everyday life, growing steadily into an unshakeable part of who you are becoming.

5. Building Momentum: The Power of Habit Stacking and Repetition

Once you have selected a habit and laid its foundations, momentum becomes your greatest ally. Momentum transforms a fragile seedling of a routine into a flourishing, self-sustaining pattern. Think of habit stacking and repetition as the twin engines that propel you forward, keeping you on track during those inevitable moments when motivation wanes, or life gets complicated.

Habit stacking is a method that ties your new behaviour to an action you already perform without fail. It leverages the well-practised routines anchored deeply in your brain's basal ganglia. Suppose you habitually enjoy a hot drink each morning. You can attach a new action, like writing in a journal or stretching for two minutes, right after making your morning beverage. This linkage means you rarely forget your new habit because it is tied to something you do naturally. The more you stack, the more your day becomes a guided set of positive steps, making each habit feel far more automatic.

Repetition, meanwhile, provides the cement that anchors habits in place. Every time you complete a new action, you reinforce the neural connections that drive it. This repeated practice ultimately shifts the behaviour from conscious effort to subconscious automation, freeing your mental energy for other tasks. Athletes, musicians, and high performers of all kinds rely on repetition to hone their skills; the same principle applies to daily tasks like reading, cooking healthier meals, or tidying up. You want to ensure that each day includes consistent practice, however small. Those daily touches, accumulated over time, create the unshakeable sense that your habit is a regular part of your identity.

Timing is crucial. If you wait for the urge to strike, you might find yourself at the mercy of changing moods. Instead, set a specific time or a clear trigger for each repetition. "After I brush my teeth, I will do ten push-ups," or "During my lunch break, I will walk around the block for five minutes." By scheduling the habit rather than leaving it to chance, you remove the ambiguity that can derail even the best intentions. This predictable scheduling also helps you measure consistency, which is vital for tracking progress and maintaining accountability.

People often talk about a magical threshold, some say it takes three weeks to form a habit, others claim more. The truth is that habit formation time varies widely based on complexity, personal circumstances, and level of motivation. Rather than fixate on a set number of days, focus on maintaining momentum day after day. Embrace the mindset that each repetition fortifies the foundation. If you skip a day, return the next without punishing yourself. Consistency, not perfection, is the ultimate goal; you want to embed the habit so deeply that it feels wrong not to carry it out.

In the end, habit stacking and repetition merge into a powerful formula for success. By aligning your new action with an existing routine and committing to regular practice, you create an unstoppable force. Momentum becomes second nature, making it far easier to sustain beneficial habits and drive them into your life's core.

6. Designing Your Environment for Success

Your environment is far more than a background setting; it holds the potential to shape your behaviours more powerfully than sheer willpower ever can. When you adjust your surroundings to make good habits easier and bad habits harder, you take advantage of a subtle yet formidable force. This principle emphasises that your success often relies on how well your environment nudges you toward or away from certain actions.

Begin by examining what your environment currently encourages you to do. If you find snacks scattered around the kitchen, they will entice you each time you walk through.

The Art of Habit Formation

If your phone sits prominently on your desk, any passing boredom might push you to scroll through it. You can make simple changes right now: storing snacks in an out-of-reach cupboard, placing your phone in another room during work hours, or having your workout clothes neatly folded and waiting by your bed for a morning routine. These small but strategic adjustments reduce the mental friction of choosing a healthy behaviour.

On a broader level, consider the people you surround yourself with. If your closest contacts engage in habits contrary to what you want to develop, you may face continual temptation or discouragement. Although you might not change your entire social circle overnight, be mindful of spending more time with those who support or share your goals. Joining a sports club, a reading group, or any community that champions a habit you want to build can drastically increase your motivation to continue. Humans are social beings, and your determination thrives when those around you value the same direction.

Digital environments also play a pivotal role. The notifications on your devices can fragment your attention, pulling you away from important tasks. A cluttered email inbox can create anxiety, making it hard to focus on the habit you are attempting to cultivate. By adjusting app settings, unsubscribing from unnecessary mailing lists, or scheduling tech-free periods, you create an online world that supports your intentions rather than undermining them. This digital discipline allows you to craft a mental space conducive to growth.

Be prepared to re-evaluate and adapt your environment periodically. As you evolve, so do your needs. Perhaps your initial approach to working out at home was effective, but after a month or two, your living room arrangement no longer feels motivating. It might be time to shift your exercise area or move sessions outside. Similarly, if your personal or professional life changes, like starting a new job or moving houses, you might need to adjust your environment to safeguard your habits.

Ultimately, environment design is not about eliminating personal responsibility; it is about making wise choices that nudge you in the right direction. Rather than relying on willpower to overcome every temptation, you make success more natural by structuring your surroundings effectively. This method spares you from constant internal battles, leaving you free to devote energy to creative work and meaningful relationships. By managing your environment, you lay a supportive foundation that helps your habits flourish no matter what challenges arise.

7. Accountability and Support: Strengthening Your Habit Journey

Though personal resolve is invaluable, accountability and support from others can dramatically strengthen your habit-building journey. When you openly commit to a habit goal, you step beyond the realm of private ambition and invite a network of allies. This encouragement can come from a friend, family member, colleague, or online community. Having someone check your progress can make the difference between slipping back into old routines or pushing forward with renewed determination.

Accountability takes many shapes. You could partner with someone who shares the same habit target, whether it is a daily run, writing project, or improved diet. Working with a buddy fosters a sense of camaraderie as both of you celebrate each other's wins and recover from setbacks together. Alternatively, you might announce your plans to a few trusted allies, letting them know you will keep them updated. Their positive influence forms a soft but constant pressure to remain true to your word. It is not about shaming you if you fall short; rather, it is about gently reminding you that your goal matters.

Support can also be formal and structured. Coaches, mentors, or experts in your particular habit domain can accelerate your progress by offering tailored advice, spotting pitfalls early, and recommending adjustments to your plan. Seeking professional guidance might involve sessions with a fitness trainer, a nutritionist, or a financial advisor, depending on what habit you are trying to solidify. This investment pays off by reducing guesswork and boosting your confidence as you progress. Knowing an expert is in your corner can disarm any insecurities you have about making mistakes.

In your quest for accountability, do not overlook the power of community-based solutions. Online forums, social media groups, or local clubs dedicated to similar goals bring together people of diverse backgrounds who share a passion for improvement. Whether you connect in a virtual running group or a personal development forum, the shared enthusiasm and occasional healthy rivalry fuels your motivation. You realise you are not alone in tackling difficulties or celebrating milestones, which creates a sense of belonging and drives you to stay consistent.

Alongside seeking external support, it is crucial to keep a personal record of your efforts. Track your progress in a journal or a digital app. Document not only your successes but also the obstacles you encounter. By periodically reviewing entries, you spot emerging patterns: moments in the day when your motivation is strongest or common triggers that threaten to sabotage your momentum. This self-awareness allows you to refine your approach. The simple act of noting, "Today I felt less driven to work out because I skipped lunch," can remind you to handle basic needs so your energy remains stable.

With accountability and support, you add layers of security to your habit-building process. Gone is the notion that you must accomplish everything alone. By enlisting caring partners, mentors, or communities, you surround yourself with encouragement. The result is an environment that keeps you on course, helps you rebound from lapses, and enriches your journey with shared inspiration.

8. Sustaining Progress: Overcoming Plateaus and Staying Motivated

Forming a habit is a major victory, but sustaining it presents a separate test of commitment. You have advanced through the initial excitement, established a routine, and maybe seen noteworthy gains. Then, without warning, you may reach a plateau where your once-flourishing momentum stalls. This phenomenon is surprisingly common. Plateaus occur when your body or mind adjusts to the new normal, leaving you with the sensation that you are stuck on a flat road, lacking the steep climb or downward rush that keeps you sharp.

One effective tactic for smashing through plateaus is to adjust the parameters of your habit. If your routine involves exercising for 20 minutes daily, increase the intensity slightly or vary the activities. Trying new forms of movement, such as swimming or yoga, challenges your body in fresh ways, rekindling your enthusiasm. If your habit involves reading personal development books for 15 minutes each morning, change the genre occasionally or add a step like writing a brief reflection afterwards. These tweaks restore a sense of novelty and ensure that you continue to stretch your capabilities.

Monitoring your progress can also restore motivation when you feel stuck. If you are on a fitness journey, keep track of metrics like the number of push-ups, the weight you can lift, or your running times. For a writing habit, note your daily word count or how many pages you finish each week. When you glance back at where you began, you may realise how far you have come, igniting pride and determination. Tracking progress does not have to be complicated; a simple spreadsheet, journal, or app can remind you that each small victory adds up to a bigger transformation.

Motivation can fluctuate, which is entirely natural. It is wise to have alternative motivators lined up for low-energy periods. Perhaps you are initially driven by the pure excitement of self-improvement, but that feeling dims over time. In that case, anchor your habit to a deeper objective. If you are cultivating a writing routine, connect it to a vision of publishing a book or sharing meaningful stories with others. If your habit is meditating daily, remind yourself that stress reduction helps you be more patient and compassionate around your loved ones. Linking your actions to an outcome that resonates with your heart keeps you engaged even when fleeting enthusiasm dips.

Another tool for sustaining progress is reflection. Give yourself moments to evaluate how the habit aligns with your evolving goals. Life changes, jobs shift, relationships grow, interests expand. If you started a morning workout routine but now work earlier hours, you may need to switch to afternoons. Staying flexible helps your habit live on rather than wither. By continually adapting, you stay faithful to the core value of self-improvement, even as the details of your situation change.

Overcoming plateaus and maintaining long-term motivation hinge on variety, consistent tracking, deeper purpose, and adaptive thinking. You do not have to accept stagnation as inevitable. Instead, you can refine your approach and deepen your commitment so that your habits deliver lasting benefits, ensuring your journey remains both engaging and rewarding.

9. The Broader Impact: How Habits Elevate Your Entire Life

The power of habits radiates beyond the single act you repeat each day. Whether it is doing push-ups, reading before sleep, or making a nutrient-rich breakfast, your habits produce ripple effects that transform many aspects of your life. Through seemingly small choices, you cultivate discipline, sharpen your decision-making, and strengthen your sense of self-efficacy. These positive qualities then spill over into your relationships, career, and overall well-being.

One of the most profound effects of strong habits is the enhanced self-trust they bring. When you repeatedly honour a promise to yourself, like going for an evening walk even when you feel tired, you reinforce the belief that you can rely on your own word. This sense of integrity boosts your confidence, making you more decisive in other areas. You may become bolder at work, presenting new ideas without the old hesitation or setting clearer boundaries with friends.

In essence, your consistent self-care fosters resilience and an inner voice that says, "I follow through."

Better habits often go hand in hand with improved mental health. Regular exercise, a structured sleep pattern, and mindful breaks fight stress, anxiety, and low mood more effectively than many short-lived fixes. Your brain benefits from the hormonal balance created by physical activity, while steady rest keeps your emotional state balanced. This stable foundation allows you to cope with day-to-day demands without feeling perpetually overwhelmed. Bit by bit, your resilience grows. Instead of reacting impulsively when facing a setback, you can approach difficulties with calm analysis, secure in the knowledge that you have cultivated a robust internal framework.

Additionally, your enhanced discipline can prompt you to prioritise what truly matters. Instead of battling with procrastination or spending energy on trivial tasks, you organise your day around the key actions that align with your ambitions. Even simpler routines, such as daily planning, transform your approach to productivity. You become strategic, dedicating your peak energy hours to critical work or personal projects. This calculated approach spreads into everything else: your finances, your social life, and your creativity, because you learn to structure and direct your efforts more wisely.

Your relationships also stand to benefit. A well-chosen habit often elevates not only your mood but also your empathy and patience. If you meditate daily, you may find that minor irritations roll off you more easily, and you respond with kindness in tense moments. If you carve out consistent reading time, you might expand your knowledge, giving you richer perspectives to share in conversation. Over time, those closest to you may notice a steadier, more focused demeanour, and your improved presence can encourage them to follow similar paths.

Through the lens of habit formation, you come to see that each small action is a seed with the power to grow into a significant force in your life. You start with one behaviour, and the transformation unfolds like concentric circles, spreading outward. In capturing that momentum, you can shift multiple areas of your world, confirming that sustainable habits are truly the stepping stones to a more purposeful and fulfilled existence.

10. Inspiring Habit Transformations: Real Stories to Ignite Your Journey

To bring it all to life, think about individuals who have harnessed habit formation to unlock new heights of achievement. Perhaps you have heard of someone who started running for just a few minutes a day and ended up completing marathons. Or someone who committed to writing a page daily, which eventually led to publishing a book. These stories matter because they remind you of the boundless possibilities that emerge when habits align with ambition.

Take, for instance, the story of an office employee who determined to boost personal fitness and began walking around the block during each lunch break. Initially, the walks were brief, providing only a modest gain in step count. Yet, the momentum built quickly. After a few months, those walks turned into short jogs, then weekend runs, until the employee felt confident enough to train for a half marathon. Over a year later, that once-sedentary individual crossed the finish line. The transformation did not appear overnight, but each step formed part of a chain reaction that strengthened both body and mind.

Another powerful narrative comes from a young professional overwhelmed by the chaos of multiple deadlines and personal obligations. Eager to curb stress and enhance focus, this professional chose a simple habit: writing a five-minute journal entry each evening. The goal was small, perhaps only a few sentences about the day. Still, the consistency soon expanded to include reflection on triumphs and challenges, leading to better emotional regulation. Over time, decision-making improved, tasks were prioritised with ease, and daily anxieties receded. That unassuming writing habit was the catalyst for deeper self-awareness and improved performance across all areas of life.

You might also recall someone who found themselves in a toxic cycle, spending nights scrolling on devices, neglecting relationships, or feeling disconnected. By committing to healthy habits such as digital-free evenings and daily mindfulness activities, they gradually reclaimed mental clarity and social connections. While these transformations are deeply personal, the universal lesson is that a single, well-chosen routine can spark a cascade of positive changes. The reward of seeing tangible results, like improved physical health, a calmer mind, or renewed confidence, reinforces the habit further, creating a self-sustaining loop.

Perhaps you have a friend or family member whose morning rituals energise them for the rest of the day. They might wake early, read or pray for five minutes, complete a brief workout, then sit down for a wholesome breakfast. After adopting these practices, they notice improved focus and a steadier mood. Their example lights a spark in you, illustrating that sometimes the best motivation comes from seeing real, relatable journeys.

You hold that same capacity for transformation. Your habits are the daily building blocks of your life's trajectory. Whether you dream of running marathons, launching a creative venture, or simply finding more peace each day, the process starts with the smallest, most deliberate actions. These stories of everyday people achieving remarkable results demonstrate that the path is open to you. Begin with one habit, nurture it with consistency and patience, and watch as the gradual, cumulative impact reshapes your life in ways you scarcely imagined.

Chapter 5

Relationships: The Heart of Human Experience

As you step into this new chapter, you're entering the very core of what it means to be human: relationships. Think about it; every meaningful moment in your life, every significant joy or challenge, is shaped by the connections you have with others. Your relationships aren't just a part of your life; they are the heartbeat that fuels your happiness, your growth, and your sense of belonging.

Throughout this chapter, you'll discover the profound impact relationships have on your emotional health, your aspirations, and even your physical well-being. You'll explore why trust, sincerity, and empathy form the foundation of true harmony and how mastering communication skills can transform everyday interactions into deeper, more rewarding connections. We'll also uncover how to set boundaries that strengthen rather than strain your bonds and how compassion can elevate even the simplest exchanges into profound acts of human kindness.

Relationships aren't always easy, but when you approach them with intentionality and openness, they become your greatest source of strength and fulfilment. Get ready to enrich your connections and experience firsthand how relationships truly are the heart of your human experience.

1. The Hidden Power of Connection: Why Relationships Are Your Core

You stand on the threshold of a powerful truth: your relationships shape the fabric of your everyday life. You might think your achievements or personal ambitions define you, but genuine fulfilment thrives on how well you connect with others. Picture yourself in a room full of individuals you trust and value. The warmth of shared memories, mutual respect, and loyalty envelops you. In that moment, you sense a level of purpose and security words alone cannot fully express. This illustrates that relationships are not peripheral elements in your life; they lie at your core, influencing your emotional well-being, your aspirations, and even your health.

A relationship is more than a casual connection; it is an exchange of insights, mutual support, and encouragement. When you form meaningful bonds, you forge alliances that sustain you during difficult times and inspire you to aim higher when new challenges appear. Yet, relationships require your input. They demand your time, energy, and willingness to be vulnerable, even when vulnerability feels uncomfortable. Whether you are interacting with a long-time friend who understands your history or meeting a new colleague who sparks fresh possibilities, every relationship calls for genuine engagement.

Healthy relationships can transform isolation into belonging and motivate you to carry on when you feel inadequate or uncertain. For instance, think of a moment when you faced a considerable obstacle, such as a career setback or a personal disappointment. Chances are a trusted friend or loved one was there, offering practical help, encouragement, or a simple reminder that you were not on your own. That sense of companionship eased your worries and reinforced your resilience. While your own resolve played a part, the emotional undercurrent of a supportive relationship often forms the lasting influence that helps you move forward stronger than before.

Yet, relationships are not solely about receiving. When you uplift someone else, share in their successes, and remain present when they stumble, you create an environment of trust and goodwill that benefits everyone involved. By showing kindness, listening attentively, and being dependable, you strengthen not only the bond but also your personal sense of purpose.

When you step back and assess how crucial your relationships are to your overall happiness, you gain clarity about where to focus your time and energy. These connections reflect who you are, what you hold dear, and how you want to be remembered. Aligning your decisions with the relationships that energise and elevate you is vital for building a rewarding life.

In the chapters that follow, you will learn techniques to refine communication, set healthy boundaries, and nurture relationships even when obstacles arise. By remaining aware of the power that relationships hold over your emotional and physical well-being, you will see that forming and tending to positive connections is a choice worth making. Embrace the idea that your core identity flourishes through strong, uplifting bonds, and allow this principle to guide your journey as you move closer to a life marked by joy and purpose.

2. Foundations of Harmony: Trust, Sincerity, and Empathy

You may believe that relationships flourish by chance, but genuine, long-lasting bonds require deliberate effort. In every strong connection, three foundations consistently rise to prominence: trust, sincerity, and empathy. When these elements align, you create an environment where mutual respect and growth are not only possible but natural.

Trust might appear elusive, yet it is surprisingly straightforward to nurture when you invest in daily gestures of honesty and consistency. It does not matter if you are engaging with a beloved family member or collaborating with a new colleague; people need to know that they can rely on you to keep your promises and honour your commitments. If you become known as the person who does what you say, trust will grow organically. Trust also calls for vulnerability: if you are genuine about your own experiences and acknowledge your flaws, you demonstrate that authenticity is more important to you than trying to appear perfect.

Sincerity moves beyond surface politeness or compliments. It is about your willingness to speak the truth, even when the truth might challenge someone's assumptions. You aim to communicate in a way that lifts others and respects their dignity. Speak with clarity and kindness, and people will feel your openness. By speaking from the heart, you reinforce a sense of safety in your relationships because the other person senses there is no hidden motive at play. Your sincerity tells them: "We can share thoughts without fear of manipulation."

Empathy, meanwhile, completes the triad by allowing you to see the world through another person's eyes. You no longer listen solely to respond; you listen to genuinely understand. When someone trusts you enough to confide, and you respond with sincere interest, empathy blossoms. It becomes the connective tissue that holds relationships together, particularly during times of conflict. Without empathy, you risk misreading signals, taking offence unnecessarily, or disregarding legitimate concerns. That leads to division rather than collaboration.

Of course, none of these qualities exists in isolation. When you show empathy in your interactions, you also illustrate sincerity by respecting another person's experience. When you display trustworthiness through action, you demonstrate sincerity and empathy for their sense of security. Together, these elements form a strong alliance that fortifies every bond you create or maintain.

You do not need to be flawless to practise trust, sincerity, and empathy. Mistakes happen, misunderstandings occur, and sometimes, you might catch yourself sliding into indifference or impatience. Yet by consciously returning to these three principles, you realign yourself with the spirit of connection. Each time you choose to trust, speak truthfully, or empathise with someone's viewpoint, you feed an environment of collective growth.

Your relationships mirror the effort you devote to them. Allow trust, sincerity, and empathy to guide your words and actions. In doing so, you will create interactions that leave you energised rather than drained. This dedication to the underlying pillars of harmony not only elevates your personal life but resonates throughout your community, offering stability, warmth, and the joy of genuine human connection.

3. Words That Unite: Mastering Your Communication Skills

Language is a force that can uplift or deflate, include or isolate. When you harness the power of communication with deliberation and thoughtfulness, you ignite positive change. People tend to listen more closely when they sense you genuinely value their perspectives, and they respond with openness when you choose phrases that respect their intelligence and emotions. In that way, your words become a bridge that spans differences, fosters understanding, and knits relationships closer together.

To start, clarity is your most trusted ally. Speaking in circles or overwhelming others with unnecessary detail leaves people confused. Pinpoint your central message before you speak. Are you aiming to persuade, to inform, or to invite collaboration? With that end in mind, shape your communication in a way that directly addresses your goal. If you notice your listener's attention drifting, refocus and keep your conversation concise. Brevity, when used wisely, makes your point more memorable.

Tone is another factor that holds remarkable influence. If you speak in a rushed or harsh manner, others might feel hurried or discouraged from contributing their ideas. In contrast, a calm and encouraging tone suggests you truly want to build mutual understanding. Your choice of words is important, but your vocal inflection can elevate or erode your message faster than you might expect. By controlling your tone, you guide the emotional undercurrent of the discussion.

Active listening goes hand in hand with effective speaking. Rather than waiting for your turn to talk, direct your attention to the speaker's words and the feelings behind them. Affirm what you hear by rephrasing key points in your own words, then follow up with questions. Doing so confirms that you care about their viewpoint, setting a strong foundation for collaboration. When someone senses you are listening rather than merely tolerating their speech, they feel respected, which boosts the likelihood of a harmonious exchange.

Timing and context are crucial as well. Delivering delicate criticism or sensitive news while someone is in the midst of stress rarely produces a calm response. Choose moments when the person is most likely able to engage thoughtfully. If a conversation begins to heat up, stepping aside momentarily can cool tensions. Also, remain mindful of cultural nuances in your language. Certain expressions might come across as harmless to you but could carry negative connotations for someone from a different background.

You can further strengthen relationships by learning how to ask questions that spur genuine dialogue. Shift from closed-ended queries that yield yes-or-no answers to open-ended ones that invite depth. For instance, rather than asking, "Are you okay with this plan?" you might ask, "What do you think of this direction, and where might we improve?" Such an approach fosters an inclusive atmosphere, letting others know their insights are integral, not peripheral.

Ultimately, mastering communication is not about perfect oratory skills or a scripted approach. It is about seeing each person you talk to as an equal stakeholder in the conversation. When you speak to connect, clarify, and respect, your words serve as a uniting force, drawing people into a shared space of deeper understanding.

4. The Boundaries That Liberate: Safeguarding Emotional Space

It might seem counterintuitive, but establishing healthy boundaries in relationships is a profound way to create more closeness and understanding. Far from shutting people out, boundaries work to protect and uplift everyone involved. When you give yourself permission to define what is acceptable and what intrudes on your emotional well-being, you empower both parties to interact more freely and respectfully. This results in an environment where each person's time, needs, and personal limits are acknowledged.

Setting boundaries begins with self-awareness. Ask yourself how certain interactions, schedules, or responsibilities make you feel. If a routine chat with a friend leaves you regularly drained, perhaps it has become a one-way conversation. Let them know, gently yet firmly, that while you treasure their thoughts, you also need space to recharge or speak your mind. Alternatively, if an ongoing pattern at work causes constant anxiety, ask how you can reframe the situation or limit after-hours demands. These steps are not selfish; they protect your mental resilience and help you engage more positively when you do spend time with others.

You will find that boundaries are never one-size-fits-all. Every relationship and situation carries its own distinct context. The boundary you set with a colleague about weekend communications might be different from the boundary you set with a close friend regarding daily phone calls. Being specific is beneficial. Instead of vague guidelines such as "I do not like too many messages," try something like "Please email me for major updates, but if it is not urgent, I prefer we catch up during work hours." By articulating precisely what you can manage, you reduce misunderstandings and potential conflicts.

Another factor is consistency. Standing by your boundaries means recognising that once you set them, you must also honour them yourself. For example, if you inform a family member that you will not answer calls after 8 pm unless it is an emergency, but then you break your own rule repeatedly, your boundary loses its impact. Consistency demonstrates seriousness and invites others to respond with respect.

Though initially challenging, boundary-setting often strengthens trust. Instead of letting tension build silently, you address issues head-on in a respectful way. People who respect and value you will likely appreciate the clarity. Those who find your boundaries off-putting might reveal a relationship dynamic that needs re-evaluation. That clarity, in itself, can be helpful, allowing you to adapt accordingly.

Boundaries also promote a healthier mindset toward conflict. If someone crosses a line you have clearly drawn, you have a logical framework for discussion. You can approach them calmly: "We agreed on this arrangement, but the situation has changed. Let us see how to move forward." In doing so, the focus remains on facts and solutions rather than shifting into blame or emotional outbursts.

By safeguarding your emotional space, you show that you value yourself and the relationships you nurture. It might involve difficult conversations and a period of adjustment, but the end result is a life where you engage with others on terms that preserve your energy and foster mutual respect. Healthy boundaries free you to be open-hearted without feeling overwhelmed or compromised in the process.

5. Overcoming Friction: Turning Conflict into Growth

Conflict can feel like a block in your path, an unwelcome hurdle that jeopardises the harmony of a bond you have worked hard to build. Yet conflict, when approached with the right mindset, can also become a catalyst for growth and deeper understanding. If you shift your perspective, you might discover that disagreement does not have to tear people apart; it can help them strengthen their connection when addressed thoughtfully and calmly.

The first step to transforming conflict is recognising that it often stems from differing expectations or perceptions. Imagine you and a friend have drifted into an argument about how much time you spend together. Beneath the disagreements, perhaps you had conflicting assumptions about each other's availability or level of interest. When you strip away heated emotions and examine the root, you start to see the bigger picture: two individuals who each have their own needs. If you acknowledge that both viewpoints carry validity, you create common ground for resolution.

Open dialogue serves as the second step. In a moment of tension, the urge to speak over the other person can be strong, but you can only find solutions if you step back and listen first. Let them outline their viewpoint. Resist the impulse to form a rebuttal in your head while they speak. True resolution emerges when you both recognise that your aim is to coexist positively, not to triumph at the other's expense.

A powerful technique for negotiation is focusing on needs rather than positions. Positions might be inflexible statements such as, "I need you to be free every weekend." In contrast, needs revolve around deeper motivations: "I want to feel supported and valued, and weekends are when I need some companionship." When you phrase your concerns in terms of needs, the conversation moves away from demands and toward an exploration of possible compromises. You can then brainstorm solutions that work for both parties.

Humour and levity can also help. If an argument is spiralling, a lighthearted comment can remind you that you share a bond beyond this disagreement. Of course, timing is important. A sarcastic remark in the midst of anger may pour fuel on the fire, but a gentle moment of warmth or a shared memory can dissolve tension and shift the mood.

Finally, do not skip the follow-up. A successful conversation that ends on a positive note should not mark the end of your efforts. Relationships evolve, and so should your understanding of each other's needs. Checking in a few days or weeks later helps keep any new agreements alive and fosters an environment where both parties feel heard and respected. This also encourages you both to refine your conflict-resolution skills for the future, reinforcing a cycle of open, growth-oriented dialogue.

Remember, your aim in any conflict is not to point out faults or emerge victorious. Rather, you want to deepen the relationship by addressing differences in a constructive way. If handled with patience, empathy, and the willingness to find common ground, friction can act as sandpaper, smoothing rough edges until a more polished bond emerges.

6. The Compassion Factor: Elevating the Human Touch

Compassion is frequently overlooked in a culture that celebrates fast success, individual achievement, and constant competition. Yet, it remains one of the most influential forces that can elevate any relationship from a polite acquaintance to an unshakeable bond. When you offer genuine compassion, you provide safety, reduce the weight of someone's troubles, and help them feel valued. This element of human kindness has the power to turn a transactional interaction into a caring alliance.

Imagine you are speaking with a friend who is going through a setback at work. You could rush through the conversation, offering generic clichés like "Better luck next time." Alternatively, you could ask them questions about how they truly feel, reflect on their concerns, and respond in a way that shows you recognise the scale of their disappointment. That depth of understanding, knowing they are not judged or trivialised, can restore their self-esteem and remind them that someone genuinely cares about their emotional state.

When you extend compassion, you also help yourself. Research in emotional wellness suggests that acting kindly toward others encourages the release of beneficial hormones in your own body, improving mood and even reducing stress. Compassion, therefore, serves as a two-way street: while it benefits the person receiving empathy, it also enriches your emotional experience, making you more aware and resilient. This does not mean you become a selfless doormat; rather, it highlights that you can combine strength with warmth.

Some confusion arises when people equate compassion with unconditional agreement. You do not have to accept every viewpoint as correct or sugar-coat serious issues. Compassion is about recognising that every individual has struggles and emotions and that they long to be validated in those feelings. If you disagree with someone, you can still respond with kindness: "I see where you are coming from, and I recognise the frustration that led you to that perspective, though I have a different view." This gentle approach avoids placing the person on the defensive and keeps the doorway open for deeper dialogue.

To cultivate compassion, begin by acknowledging your shared humanity. Recognise that everyone navigates challenges, insecurities, and hopes. From an acquaintance on a public bus to a close friend you see weekly, each person you encounter yearns for acceptance. Make a habit of engaging in small acts of compassion daily: offer a helping hand without being asked, listen attentively rather than hastily, or send an encouraging message to someone who appears overwhelmed. These seemingly small gestures accumulate into a tangible atmosphere of support.

As your compassionate mindset grows, you will likely discover that people warm to your presence. Those you meet sense that you are not merely ticking a box but genuinely caring about them as individuals. This, in turn, creates a cycle of reciprocated goodwill, transforming how you form new relationships and reinforcing those you already hold dear. At its core, compassion is not a show of weakness; it is a reflection of your humanity, paving the way for more meaningful, uplifting connections that enrich your life and others.

7. Professional Ties: Building Bridges in the Workplace

When you walk through the doors of your workplace or switch on your computer in the morning, your success relies on more than the knowledge you bring or the tasks you accomplish. Your relationships with managers, colleagues, and clients can propel you to new heights or hold you back if neglected. Professional ties may begin as formal interactions, but they have the potential to flourish into supportive, mutually beneficial networks that shape your career path and overall satisfaction.

Start by recognising that strong professional relationships often stem from simple, everyday acts of cooperation. Perhaps you share resources with a colleague who is behind on a deadline or offer thoughtful insight during a team discussion without seeking any immediate return. These moments of kindness and collaboration not only ease the flow of work but foster a culture where everyone feels inclined to reciprocate. You might find that these small gestures lead to unexpected invitations, recommendations, or mentorship.

One vital element is authenticity. While professional environments sometimes encourage formality, do not underestimate the power of genuine human warmth. If you regularly hide your true thoughts, you deprive your workplace of the unique insight you alone can offer. When you speak sincerely, whether presenting an innovative idea or addressing a concern, you encourage others to do the same, building an atmosphere of trust. If your manager sees you as dependable, open, and respectful, you increase your visibility as a candidate for new responsibilities or promotions.

Conflict resolution also shapes the tenor of professional relationships. Disagreements about budgets, timelines, or role responsibilities are bound to occur. How you manage them marks you as either a conflict escalator or a peacemaker. If you tackle tension calmly, aiming for problem-solving over blame, people notice. Over time, you build a reputation for fairness, reason, and collaboration.

Another important aspect is learning how to navigate different personalities and communication styles. Some colleagues might prefer direct, concise messages; others appreciate warm, friendly small talk before delving into work matters. Adapting your approach based on these nuances shows respect and consideration, essential for cultivating goodwill. Keep in mind that everyone has off days; extending patience or empathy when a co-worker seems distant or stressed can pay off in a more harmonious work environment.

Networking beyond your immediate circle can also be invaluable. Attending industry events, participating in cross-departmental projects, or engaging in online forums allows you to meet professionals from diverse backgrounds. These external connections might offer unique solutions to workplace challenges or open doors to future collaborations. Remember that networking is not solely about self-interest; it is about establishing a reciprocal rapport. When you share resources, knowledge, or helpful contacts, you demonstrate your willingness to be of service, a trait that others often remember.

Ultimately, professional relationships are not static. They shift as teams reorganise, careers progress, and your own skill sets develop. By investing in open communication, thoughtful collaboration, and authentic engagement, you construct bridges that can weather time and change. In a workplace where bonds are fortified by trust and mutual support, you set a stage for steady growth, success, and a sense of genuine accomplishment in every project you undertake.

8. Distance Without Division: Thriving Through Separation

Physical distance in relationships can arise for many reasons: a job transfer, educational pursuits, or even personal preference. Although miles may lie between you and the people who matter, a gap in location does not have to equal disconnection. When managed with purpose, long-distance relationships, romantic, familial, or friendships, can remain fulfilling. They may even encourage you to strengthen your communication and reinforce the core of your bond.

The first principle is deliberate effort. Without daily face-to-face interactions, your natural cues to keep in touch are fewer. You might lose track of how long it has been since you last spoke. This is where a structured plan helps: schedule weekly video calls or set days to exchange messages. A consistent routine creates a sense of stability, ensuring that distance does not turn into neglect. In addition, sending spontaneous updates or small gestures, like a postcard or a funny anecdote, keeps the other person at the forefront of your thoughts.

Transparency about expectations is equally important. You might imagine daily chats while the other person is comfortable communicating once a week. Discuss your preferences openly: "How often would you like to talk, and through which method?" By making these points explicit, you avoid misinterpretations. If you cannot meet a planned call because of a schedule clash, let them know promptly. Such courtesy prevents misunderstandings and reassures the other person that you still value their time and emotional investment.

Trust becomes the linchpin of maintaining intimacy across physical divides. Genuine trust arises when both parties are certain that their relationship remains a priority despite the distance. Though you may not share all your daily experiences together, the foundation of trust means you can still confide in one another, celebrate each other's milestones, and rally in difficult moments. Virtual communication platforms, whether video chats, shared online spaces, or simple voice notes, become your lifelines to keep trust alive.

Distance can paradoxically offer a benefit: it forces you to articulate your feelings and thoughts more precisely. Because you cannot rely on an occasional hug or a shared meal to smooth over tensions, you become more aware of the significance of words and nonverbal signals that translate through video or voice. You might discover deeper emotional insight into the other person's life because you spend a concentrated amount of time listening when you do connect.

When opportunities arise to meet in person, make those moments count. Plan activities that nurture your relationship's unique dynamic, whether it is revisiting old haunts or exploring a new place together. Save some key updates or celebrations for when you can share them face-to-face, preserving the sense of excitement and closeness. A reunion after time apart often reveals how communication, trust, and small acts of connection have kept your bond strong.

Ultimately, distance need not sever strong ties. Through honesty about expectations, proactive connection, and a commitment to seeing every conversation as a chance to deepen understanding, you can thrive through separation. In that sense, physical gaps become an invitation to test the resilience of your mutual devotion and to innovate your approach, proving that meaningful bonds can outlast any geographical barrier.

9. Recognising When to Step Back: Freeing Yourself from Toxic Ties

You may come across a relationship that brings more grief than growth, where negativity overshadows positivity. These are toxic ties: connections that undermine your self-worth and leave you feeling drained. Perhaps it is a colleague who relentlessly belittles your ideas or a close contact who manipulates your generosity for their benefit. You might persist for fear of losing the familiar or from a misplaced sense of loyalty, but clinging to such relationships can cause deeper harm in the long run.

The first step to breaking free is learning to spot the red flags. If every interaction concludes with you feeling anxious, guilty, or resentful, that is a strong signal something is wrong. You might also notice the relationship revolves around the other person's demands, with no reciprocal regard for your needs. You try to communicate your viewpoint, yet they twist your words or ignore them entirely. Over time, the constant friction erodes your confidence, leaving you doubting your instincts.

Open dialogue, when possible, should be your next step. Sometimes, a relationship seems toxic due to misunderstandings or unexpressed frustrations. A frank conversation can clarify the issues. You can explain the patterns that harm you and suggest healthier ways to engage. However, do remain prepared for resistance. If the other person refuses to acknowledge the impact of their behaviour, you cannot progress together toward a solution. In that scenario, preserving your own well-being should be the priority.

Establishing and maintaining boundaries becomes crucial here. Firmly communicate what you will not tolerate, such as relentless criticism or manipulative tactics, and follow through if those boundaries are crossed. A boundary is meaningless if you do not back it up with action. This might mean reducing contact to a minimum or, in severe cases, cutting ties altogether. These decisions are rarely easy, but you are not obligated to sustain a bond that inflicts emotional harm.

It is also wise to seek support from those you trust: a mentor, a family member, or a friend who can offer perspective. Sometimes, you can get lost in a cycle of hoping the situation will improve. A fresh opinion can help you see that you are investing emotional energy into a relationship that consistently returns negativity. That external validation can strengthen your resolve to break free if necessary.

Deciding to leave a toxic relationship can trigger guilt or fear of hurting the other person. However, preserving your mental and emotional health is not an act of cruelty. You will be in a stronger position to show empathy and kindness to others when your own boundaries are safeguarded. It might be painful in the short term, but liberating yourself from toxic ties ultimately paves the way for healthier connections that affirm your worth, encourage growth, and restore your peace of mind. In these new, brighter spaces, you regain the emotional capacity to forge deeper bonds with those who genuinely respect and value you.

10. A Lifelong Commitment: Strengthening the Bonds

Consider for a moment what genuine commitment to your relationships looks like day to day. You are not ticking boxes or following a routine. Instead, you are choosing to be present and attentive in a way that cultivates depth and trust over the long term. This commitment shapes how you show up in every interaction, ensuring each relationship receives consistent, wholehearted effort.

A practical starting point is making time for regular, meaningful contact. Rather than waiting for major life events, birthdays, holidays, or a big promotion, look for smaller opportunities to share everyday moments. A quick call, a meal out, or even a supportive text at the right time can stop your bond from slipping into complacency. Embracing these chances to engage reinforces the idea that the relationship extends beyond formal occasions and is nurtured through simple acts of connection.

Continual learning forms another part of this lifelong commitment. You do not arrive at a point where you have mastered all the nuances of family dynamics, friendships, or partnerships. People evolve, and so should your understanding of their personalities, preferences, and potential stressors. Being curious about someone's changing interests or new experiences keeps your conversations lively and prevents you from slipping into stale assumptions.

A relationship can lose vitality when neither party invests effort into fresh experiences or knowledge. Even simple changes, trying a new hobby together or delving into topics you have never explored, can revitalise your shared perspective. Breaking out of predictable patterns encourages laughter, reinvigorates curiosity, and reminds both of you why you connected in the first place.

It is equally crucial to handle setbacks responsibly. Every relationship faces strain at various points, whether triggered by external pressures or internal misunderstandings. The question is how you respond when troubles arise. Do you shut down in frustration or approach the issue with honesty and a desire to move forward together? In a long-term bond, the ability to address challenges without harming the trust you have cultivated is what sets you apart. Committing to proactive solutions, rather than finger-pointing, makes it easier to navigate difficulties and emerge with renewed stability.

Finally, remember to recognise and celebrate progress and growth. When you look back on how far your bond has come, it encourages you to keep building. Maybe you have improved your communication style or learned how to respect each other's boundaries more effectively. These gains deserve acknowledgement. Sharing gratitude fosters an appreciation for what you have overcome and instils hope for what lies ahead.

By consistently choosing to invest in your relationships, you establish a culture of respect, acceptance, and optimism. You transform a simple acquaintanceship or an ordinary friendship into something more layered and impactful. This has a ripple effect: the more you strengthen each bond, the more your sense of belonging and emotional security rises, influencing all aspects of your life. When you direct effort toward your connections every day, you live out the reality that the greatest wealth truly lies in the warmth, comfort, and encouragement a well-tended relationship can provide.

Chapter 6

Spirituality: The Path to Inner Peace

Have you ever felt as though your life is racing past you, leaving you feeling disconnected, drained, or longing for something deeper? You're not alone in sensing there's more to life than simply going through the motions. Perhaps you've had moments when the noise of the world faded away, and you felt a profound sense of calm and connection. Those moments aren't accidental; they're a gentle nudge inviting you to explore the realm of spirituality. Spirituality isn't about adhering strictly to religious rules or rituals. Instead, it's a deeply personal journey that guides you to find meaning, peace, and fulfilment right where you are.

In the pages ahead, you'll uncover how spiritual awareness can transform ordinary experiences into moments of profound joy and insight. Whether you're drawn to quiet meditation, inspired by nature, or seeking the warmth of community and shared values, spirituality offers a way to navigate life's challenges with a steady heart and clear mind. This chapter is your invitation to slow down, reflect, and connect to something greater, laying a solid foundation for lasting inner peace.

1. The Essence of Spiritual Awareness

You have likely wondered about the deeper dimensions of life, those moments when the daily grind feels hollow, and

Spirituality: The Path to Inner Peace

you sense there must be something richer waiting to be discovered. This longing is not unusual; it is a clue that you are ready to explore spiritual awareness. Spirituality goes beyond any single practice or faith. It touches on the universal search for a deeper meaning behind your actions, thoughts, and connections with the world around you. When you look beyond the material, you see that spirituality can illuminate every aspect of your life, bringing comfort and direction that transcend ordinary routines.

Spiritual awareness rests on the notion that there is more to existence than achieving goals or collecting possessions. It highlights the importance of aligning with values that enrich your inner life, whether you are drawn to quiet reflection, inspired reading, or a sense of community with others who share your yearning for a higher understanding. Some individuals find this through prayer or attending a place of worship, while others sense it in serene moments of solitude by the sea, in the forest, or anywhere that brings stillness and presence. The goal is not a rigid set of rules; it is discovering what brings you a feeling of inner calm and reverence for life.

One of the best-known figures who exemplified spiritual awareness was Mahatma Gandhi, who drew upon universal values like peace and truth. Although rooted in his own faith tradition, his mainstay was that the inner journey unifies people of all beliefs. His actions showed that spiritual awareness nurtures courage, calmness, and forgiveness, qualities that allowed him to champion non-violent change. You can apply this lesson to your own path by remembering that genuine spirituality fosters compassion, steadiness under pressure, and the capacity to see the good in others.

Spiritual awareness brings you closer to an inner peace that does not buckle under setbacks. While worldly pursuits may bring fleeting highs or lows, a spiritually attuned mindset reminds you that your worth extends beyond job titles or social status. When you live in alignment with spiritual principles, you acknowledge your inherent value and that of those around you. This sense of unity calms the restless part of you that constantly seeks external validation. Over time, you build a strong internal compass that helps you navigate life's storms with grace.

This first step toward spiritual awareness sets the tone for a profound transformation. It begins with a willingness to slow down, reflect, and ask what makes you feel truly alive. In daily life, it might look like pausing before reacting in anger or extending kindness to someone in need. These small acts, guided by deeper awareness, accumulate into a life of meaning and emotional stability. In the sections that follow, you will learn how to harness this awareness, explore different pathways to spiritual growth, and discover the peace that waits when you connect to something greater. Every step you take toward deepening your spiritual awareness lays the foundation for the abiding calm that marks a spiritually fulfilled life.

2. Linking Mind, Body, and Spirit

When you aim to enrich your inner life, it is useful to explore how your thoughts, physical wellness, and spiritual understanding intertwine. This trio forms the basis of a holistic approach to living. Picture a three-legged stool, where each leg, mind, body, and spirit must be balanced to keep you steady. If your mind is churning with worries, your body becomes tense, making spiritual calm far more difficult to maintain. Equally, if you disregard your physical needs, no amount of mental positivity will produce a deep sense of harmony.

Spirituality: The Path to Inner Peace

Many ancient traditions highlight that caring for the body is not an indulgence but a necessary component of spiritual growth. If you read about early monastic lifestyles or the practices of indigenous communities, you will notice they often paired contemplative exercises with disciplined care for the body. The reason is simple: your body houses your spirit, so it deserves respect and attention. Nourishing meals, enough rest, and regular physical activity all serve to keep you grounded. When your physical state is strong, you experience a calmer, more focused mind, setting the stage for deeper spiritual reflection.

Consider the life of Tina Turner as an example. She dealt with extreme hardships, from personal turmoil to health scares, yet found renewed vitality by integrating her spiritual beliefs with healthy daily routines. Alongside her practice of Buddhist chanting, she placed value on maintaining physical strength and stamina through consistent exercise and mindful eating. As a result, she tapped into reserves of resilience that allowed her to reinvent her career and find peace on her own terms. You, too, can draw from this holistic viewpoint, ensuring your daily actions encourage both bodily health and spiritual insight.

Your mind can be both an ally and an adversary. When it is overwhelmed by stress or negativity, it drags you away from spiritual calm. However, when guided by spiritual ideals, your mind can become a source of encouragement and clarity. Mindfulness and meditative practices help you remain in the present, reducing the endless chatter of internal doubts. By grounding your mind in spiritual values such as humility, empathy, or selfless service, you elevate your daily thoughts from trivial concerns to matters of enduring significance.

Fostering a balanced interplay between mind, body, and spirit requires a plan. Make time for physical self-care; choose an activity that renews your energy. Protect moments of mental stillness in your schedule, whether for breathing exercises, prayer, or silent observation of nature. Each measure reinforces the other: a relaxed body supports clearer thinking, a focused mind raises spiritual awareness, and spiritual convictions guide healthier choices. It is a cycle of mutual support, reflecting a life lived in complete alignment.

As you move forward, remember that the goal is not perfection. Perfection is elusive. Rather, aim for consistent small steps, each reinforcing your intention to unify mind, body, and spirit. In doing so, you lay firm groundwork for experiencing inner calm, clarity of purpose, and a solid emotional core that can thrive even in challenging conditions. By acknowledging the interdependence of mental health, physical wellbeing, and spiritual depth, you prepare to embrace each day with confidence and inner poise.

3. Finding Stillness in a Hyperactive World

Your life may feel like an endless carousel of obligations, digital notifications, and rushing from one task to the next. In such a frantic setting, you might wonder how to find the calm you crave. Spirituality reminds you that stillness is not some luxury reserved for monks on mountaintops. It is an accessible retreat within you, even in the midst of modern chaos. Seeking out a space of stillness offers a gateway to discovering your deeper essence and reconnecting with priorities that have been overshadowed by daily stress.

Spirituality: The Path to Inner Peace

To begin, identify pockets of quiet within your usual routine. It might be the first few minutes after you rise in the morning, a break during your lunch hour, or the moments before bedtime. Embrace the simple act of sitting quietly. Let the swirl of thoughts come and go without forcing them away. Over time, this practice helps you observe the mind's habits without becoming enslaved by them. You do not need an elaborate ritual; you only need the willingness to stay with yourself in a calm, focused state, if only for a short period each day.

Many notable figures who lived productive and public lives nonetheless carved out moments of stillness. Winston Churchill often withdrew for short intervals during high-pressure times, choosing a silent space for reflection and mental restoration. You can adopt a similar method by giving yourself permission to pause. This small discipline, repeated consistently, sharpens your awareness of mental over-activity and opens the door to spiritual insight. The breath itself becomes an anchor: when you follow each inhalation and exhalation, you tether your mind to the present rather than letting it wander into stressful thoughts.

Stillness fosters spiritual insight by placing you face-to-face with your inner world. Rather than running from feelings of unease, you can notice them with a compassionate eye, gaining a deeper understanding of what drives your anxieties. This shift from avoidance to gentle acceptance can bring surprising relief. You might discover new perspectives on a recurring problem or find the courage to address hidden emotional burdens. Stillness becomes not a place of idleness but a wellspring of clarity and potential resolutions.

In addition, true stillness does not merely reduce stress; it also fine-tunes your capacity for empathy and calm responses. When your inner state is less chaotic, you approach interactions with more patience and kindness. Those around you sense this shift, often responding with equal respect or openness. In this sense, your personal stillness radiates outward, subtly improving the tone of your environment. When faced with confrontations, this inner calm acts as a steady anchor, preventing you from getting swept away by anger or fear.

Stillness represents one of the most essential spiritual practices, offering both an antidote to modern pressures and a channel for deep self-discovery. As you incorporate brief intervals of quiet into each day, you strengthen the root of your spiritual growth. By simply pausing on purpose, you create a zone where genuine insight, emotional healing, and renewed vitality can emerge. In the next sections, you will see how this foundation of stillness can carry you through personal challenges and lead to true resilience and peace.

4. The Spiritual Foundation of Resilience

Hardships are unavoidable. Whether triggered by personal loss, professional setbacks, or internal struggles, challenges test your inner resources. Spirituality can be a strong ally in these situations, serving as a bedrock of resilience when life feels like it is crumbling around you. Far from being a mere distraction, spirituality empowers you to navigate storms with composure and dignity, reminding you that your value does not hinge on external achievements. Your spiritual bedrock grounds you, allowing you to stand firm even when everything else feels uncertain.

Spirituality: The Path to Inner Peace

Resilience hinges on your ability to reframe difficulties. Instead of seeing them as disasters, you see them as opportunities to draw upon deeper strengths. A spiritual outlook teaches you to accept that life will not always adhere to your preferences, but it also reminds you that your essence remains intact regardless of events. This openness to life's unpredictability allows you to adapt with far less anxiety or bitterness. Over time, resilience bolsters an assurance that you have the mental and spiritual fortitude to handle disappointments and keep progressing.

Another advantage of spiritual resilience is its capacity to foster a sense of community or unity with others. You may find hope in reading about individuals who overcame immense struggles by holding tight to a higher principle or belief in something beyond their hardships. Sharing stories or fellowship with like-minded friends can strengthen your resolve. You no longer feel isolated in your troubles because you recognise that countless people have turned adversity into growth when buoyed by spiritual convictions. This sense of belonging and moral support can be the difference between succumbing to despair and soldiering on with faith and purpose.

Spiritual resilience also helps you cope with grief and loss in a healthier way. You learn that while sadness is real, it does not define the entirety of your existence. You can honour your grief while also remembering that life carries on, offering new chances for connection and personal development. Some spiritual traditions hold that the soul endures beyond physical existence, providing comfort that the bonds you share are not lost even when a person departs. Although beliefs may differ, the solace drawn from spiritual resilience offers common ground: you have a safe inner sanctuary to which you can retreat when sorrow feels overwhelming.

When challenges inevitably arise, lean on practices that deepen spiritual composure. For some, this might be reflective reading or journaling to process complex emotions. For others, silent meditation or prayer reaffirms a sense of calm amid turmoil. Each of these methods ensures that resilience is not a hollow optimism but an active, constructive approach to life's tests. By melding acceptance of hardship with faith in your innate capacity to endure, you wield a powerful toolkit against despair.

As you remain rooted in these principles, you will begin to trust your ability to handle whatever emerges. This trust is not naive; it is grounded in repeated experiences of facing down challenges without losing sight of the bigger picture. In the sections ahead, you will discover the daily practices that transform spiritual resilience from an abstract idea into a living, breathing shield against life's storms, enhancing your capacity to remain unshaken even in the direst of circumstances.

5. Creating an Everyday Spiritual Routine

Spiritual development often flourishes through simple, repeated actions embedded in your daily life. When you create an everyday spiritual routine, you are effectively weaving spiritual reflection into your morning, midday, and evening patterns. This grounded approach ensures that spirituality is not a distant concept you recall only during crises or occasional retreats. It becomes a living force that shapes how you respond to tasks, relationships, and even minor setbacks throughout the day.

Spirituality: The Path to Inner Peace

An initial step might be designating small segments of time for a calm, inward focus. Perhaps you begin at dawn, taking five or ten minutes to acknowledge your hopes for the day ahead and centre yourself. During lunch, you could pause to review your morning's encounters, reflecting on moments of kindness or frustration and finding lessons within them. Finally, before sleep, you may take a few more minutes to release any tension, expressing gratitude for what went well. These micro-habits bring consistency and help the spiritual dimension of your life remain vivid, guiding how you behave and feel.

Daily routines can also integrate mindful eating or mindful movement. If you approach each bite of breakfast with a calm awareness, you reduce mindless snacking or agitation. By paying full attention to the flavours, aromas, and textures of your food, you transform a routine meal into a practice of gratitude and focus. Similarly, any chosen exercise, a short walk or structured workout, can become a chance to align with deeper awareness. You feel your breath, sense your body's movements, and appreciate the life force sustaining you. Although these may be small, they collectively shift your entire day's tone, reminding you that spirituality is not an isolated domain but a lens through which every moment can be appreciated.

Some people find an everyday spiritual routine through reading, studying quotes, or journaling. These reflective pauses expand your understanding of spiritual themes, whether drawn from scriptures, philosophical works, or modern teachings that resonate with you. Writing your thoughts can provide a tangible record of evolving insights, allowing you to notice patterns and track your growth over time. By integrating reflective or meditative writing into your daily routine, you crystallise fleeting insights into actionable wisdom.

Your environment plays a role as well. Placing a serene object in your home or workplace, such as a calming picture or a small statue, can provide a gentle reminder of your spiritual intentions. A simple glance can be enough to recapture a sense of presence and peace. Keep in mind that routines need to be flexible rather than rigid, adjusting to life's variations but consistent enough to anchor you when circumstances grow turbulent. Ultimately, it is your commitment to regular practice that deepens your sense of inner calm and heightens the awareness that spiritual wisdom is a resource available at any time.

As you continue evolving, you will discover which daily practices resonate best. Some may prefer silent prayer, others recitation of meaningful lines, and still others mindful breathing or journaling. There is no single formula because spirituality is personal. What matters is your dedication to sustaining this ongoing dialogue between the mundane and the sacred. In the following sections, you will learn how strengthening this daily routine extends into your connections with other people and the broader world, further grounding your spiritual perspective in every layer of your existence.

6. Spirituality and Its Role in Your Relationships

Your spiritual path does not exist in isolation. It permeates every conversation, each gesture, and the tone you set in your relationships. Whether you are interacting with family, friends, or colleagues, your spiritual insights shape how you see others and respond to their needs. Far from pulling you away from daily responsibilities, spirituality can enhance the depth and warmth of your connections, promoting a compassionate stance that inspires trust and harmony.

To begin, awareness of the sacredness in yourself often translates into recognising dignity in others. If you hold yourself in respectful regard, you are more likely to treat people around you with fairness and empathy. When tensions flare up, as they inevitably do in close relationships, a spiritual mindset urges you to pause and revisit your core values instead of reacting impulsively. You may recall how each person, despite differing opinions or behaviours, has a spirit worthy of respect. Such reminders can defuse hostility and keep interactions grounded in respectful dialogue.

Imagine a tense work meeting where frustrations threaten to boil over. A spiritually guided approach helps you observe your thoughts and physical reactions calmly. Rather than snapping or retreating in silence, you address the issue while honouring the other person's perspective. This kind of response fosters understanding, preserving team morale. In personal relationships, the same principle applies: by staying present and seeing conflicts as a chance to practise patience and kindness, you build stronger, more genuine bonds. You become the calming presence in a room, encouraging others to behave more responsibly as well.

Spiritual beliefs often stress the importance of compassion, forgiveness, and humility. These qualities serve as potent tools for healing wounds in relationships. Perhaps you have experienced betrayal or disappointment. While it does not mean you ignore harmful actions, spirituality encourages you to approach resolution from a place of sincerity. This might require honest communication or setting healthy boundaries, ensuring that you do not enable repeated harm.

Even so, you carry forward the belief that reconciliation or understanding is possible, or at least that you can release bitterness for your own peace of mind.

Examples of renowned leaders show how spirituality can bridge gaps between individuals and communities. Many historical peacemakers, grounded in their spiritual convictions, managed to mediate intense hostilities. They approached adversaries with empathy, aiming to unveil the humanity that often gets obscured in conflict. You can replicate that spirit in smaller daily conflicts, reminding everyone involved that beyond disagreements lies a shared desire for respect and well-being.

Though spirituality can foster deeper relationships, it can also raise challenges. Friends may not share your perspective. Family members might question your choices if they sense unfamiliar changes in your attitude or practices. In these cases, be patient and remain open. Show them through consistent actions that your spiritual focus enhances your ability to love and support them. Over time, the benefits of a more centred, understanding version of you may win them over. Ultimately, the beauty of spirituality in relationships is its capacity to illuminate the inherent worth of each person you encounter, bringing harmony where conflict or indifference previously held sway. In the next section, you will see how this same spiritual foundation can guide you to discover a higher purpose in your everyday existence.

7. Tapping into a Higher Purpose

Human beings often search for meaning, wanting to align their deeds with something beyond mundane routines. Spirituality can guide you in pinpointing a higher purpose, a calling that resonates with your sense of identity and values. Pursuing such a purpose transcends typical definitions of success, measuring achievement by the fulfilment you feel rather than accolades or wealth. Finding and embracing this higher purpose lends vitality to all you do, transforming tasks into meaningful contributions.

You do not need to stand on a global stage or lead major movements to act on your higher purpose. It might be as personal as offering compassionate care to a family member, volunteering in your community, or finding creative ways to brighten someone's day. What matters is how aligned your intentions are with the convictions you hold sacred. If you value compassion, your higher purpose might revolve around helping those who are vulnerable. If truth matters to you, your purpose might involve honest communication or research that promotes informed decisions. Aligning actions with personal ideals forms the crux of living an extraordinary life.

Some individuals describe this higher purpose as a "calling," an inner prompt that continues to nudge them toward certain paths or activities. They feel incomplete or restless until they respond to it. Malala Yousafzai personifies this sense of mission; driven by a belief in each child's right to education, she risked her own safety to champion that cause. Although her journey is extraordinary, the underlying principle applies broadly: a purpose anchored in spiritual convictions can kindle unwavering dedication, even in grim circumstances. Likewise, you can draw strength from your own sense of calling. Whether large-scale or humble, your mission can keep you focused when obstacles appear.

When seeking your higher purpose, avoid fixating on a single definition of "purpose." It can evolve. Spiritual awareness keeps you open to fresh insights, enabling you to adjust your path if necessary. One chapter of your life might revolve around personal healing, another might emphasise community service, and later phases might focus on guiding younger generations. Regardless of form, the underlying essence remains a spiritual impulse that draws you out of self-absorption into a world that hungers for empathy and goodwill.

A higher purpose also shields you from burnout. The typical approach to work or responsibilities might drain you, especially if your efforts feel aimless. But when your actions are animated by spiritual motivation, you tap into an inner reservoir of energy and endurance. Challenges no longer signify dead ends; they become stepping stones that test and refine your commitment. With each hurdle overcome, you strengthen your sense that your life's work matters. You return to your tasks reinvigorated, aware that your efforts hold meaning that stretches far beyond momentary setbacks or external validations.

By identifying and living your higher purpose, you breathe life into each day, forging a unique legacy that uplifts you and those around you. Rather than drifting through work or family duties, you infuse them with depth and gratitude. In the sections that follow, we will explore how you can tackle those internal obstacles that sometimes sabotage this quest for purpose, opening the way for genuine growth and lasting serenity.

8. Confronting Inner Barriers on the Spiritual Path

While the advantages of spirituality are many, the path is not a seamless stroll. Inner barriers, doubt, fear, or deep-seated habits can hinder your progress. Imagine starting a new spiritual practice brimming with enthusiasm, only to be derailed by persistent negative self-talk or the worry that you might be doing it "wrong." Recognising and confronting these internal obstacles becomes essential if you want to continue moving forward on your journey.

Self-doubt frequently arises as soon as you attempt something unfamiliar. Old conditioning might whisper that you are incapable of changing or that you lack the discipline to sustain a practice. The key is to acknowledge these doubts without letting them become self-fulfilling prophecies. You can learn from individuals like Elizabeth Gilbert, who overcame creative fear through ongoing reflection and a willingness to be imperfect. Her example reveals that doubt is not a signal to stop; it is a chance to refine your approach and understand that progress, not flawlessness, is the real objective.

Fear of judgment, whether from friends, family, or society, can also be an obstacle. You might hesitate to share your evolving beliefs or new routines, worried about ridicule or rejection. Although it is wise to maintain privacy around certain sacred aspects of your life, do not let the fear of others' opinions extinguish your spiritual curiosity. If you sense a genuine calling toward deeper spiritual exploration, your life will ultimately benefit from being genuine. Pretending otherwise only postpones your growth, leaving you unsettled and missing opportunities to cultivate an inner peace that also benefits those around you.

Another subtle barrier is complacency. Once you find a small measure of calm in your practices, it is easy to become satisfied and avoid further effort. You stop challenging yourself, and eventually, you may slip into old patterns. To move past this plateau, recall the larger potential that awaits. Like an athlete who keeps training even after winning initial matches, you can keep pushing the boundaries of your spiritual depth. By consistently setting fresh intentions, perhaps learning about different meditative techniques or exploring advanced teachings, you sustain the momentum and remain humble, understanding there is always more to learn.

Overcoming inner barriers does not demand radical measures; you can start by engaging in self-reflection. Keep a personal journal where you document recurring negative thoughts or anxieties, along with any victories, no matter how small. Each entry is a step toward identifying patterns that try to sabotage your progress. Meditative introspection can also help you spot these barriers in the moment, giving you a chance to address them calmly instead of reacting impulsively.

A vital takeaway is that these internal challenges are a natural part of spiritual growth; they are not signs that you have veered off course. In surmounting doubt, fear, or apathy, you make space for a more resilient, evolved version of yourself. The very barriers that once stood in your way become catalysts for heightened self-awareness and compassion, enriching both your inner life and your relationships. Next, you will see how harnessing spirituality not only tackles internal blocks but also benefits physical health, providing even more reasons to keep going.

9. Nourishing Your Body Through Spiritual Perspectives

It might surprise you to learn how profoundly your spiritual framework can influence your physical health. While your mind and spirit rise through silent prayer or meditation, your body does not stand on the sidelines. Instead, it responds to the emotional and mental states that arise from spiritual practices. When you nurture a sense of inner calm and purposeful living, your body often reflects that harmony in the form of reduced stress, better immunity, and improved energy.

Many faith traditions and philosophies point out that your body is not merely a vessel but a partner in your earthly journey. If you see yourself as connected to a higher order, it follows that this earthly form deserves respect and careful maintenance. You might approach food choices, for instance, with newfound mindfulness. Rather than stuffing yourself mindlessly or relying on quick, unhealthy meals, you slow down and choose nourishing options. This does not require an extreme diet; it is about honouring your body's needs and savouring mealtimes as an opportunity for gratitude rather than a rushed pitstop.

Physical activity also enters a different light when seen through a spiritual lens. Exercise ceases to be a chore you undertake out of guilt; it transforms into a celebration of your life force, a tangible way to connect with the gift of movement. Some people find that gentle yoga, walking in natural settings, or even mindful stretching can spark spiritual awareness. Through intentional, unhurried exercise, you strengthen muscles, improve cardiovascular health, and invite moments of reflection where your mind grows still, merging with your spiritual longings.

Another key area is the relationship between stress and physical ailments. Stress, if left unchecked, can take a toll on your body through hypertension, weakened immunity, and various chronic conditions. A robust spiritual practice helps to counteract these effects. When your convictions reinforce hope and resilience, your body's stress responses are less likely to spin out of control. Regular contemplative moments, such as breathing exercises or guided meditations, equip you with tools to dial back tension, offering your body a break from the relentless fight-or-flight state that can lead to illness.

Historical figures like Florence Nightingale understood the link between spiritual insight and caring for the sick. Her nursing approach addressed not only cleanliness and medical care but also the morale and emotional support of patients. In your life, a spiritually driven outlook encourages you to see health as a holistic project, one that involves mind, emotions, spirit, and body working in harmony. By aligning your lifestyle habits with your spiritual attitudes, you produce a positive ripple effect that supports a more balanced existence.

Adopting this perspective does not mean you will never face health challenges, of course. The body remains vulnerable. Nevertheless, your spiritual grounding can shift your mindset from one of helpless victimhood to one of mindful stewardship. You better equip yourself to pursue medical advice proactively, follow through with treatments, and remain patient during the healing process. Seeing your body as a valuable ally makes each health choice resonate with deeper significance. Up next, we will explore how real-world stories of transformation highlight the power of spirituality to spark remarkable shifts in people's lives, reinforcing the lessons shared so far.

10. Transformational Stories and Ongoing Growth

Spirituality: The Path to Inner Peace

Throughout history, countless individuals have encountered life-altering shifts upon embracing a spiritual perspective. These stories, while specific to each person, share a universal pattern: a change in thinking and behaviour that leads to renewed purpose, inner peace, and resilience. You can draw encouragement from these transformations, recognising that your own journey may hold similar moments of breakthrough when you remain open to spiritual direction.

One prominent story is that of Eckhart Tolle, who battled severe anxiety and despair until a single night brought a deep inner realisation. He awoke with a quieter mind, leading him to explore consciousness more deeply. Tolle then shared his experiences worldwide, guiding others to silence mental turmoil and discover deeper awareness in each moment. His journey teaches that even in the shadow of emotional darkness, a turning point can usher in profound spiritual awakening, reshaping everything from priorities to how everyday life is experienced.

A different sort of tale comes from individuals who adopt small spiritual practices yet experience sweeping changes over time. They may start by dedicating minutes daily to silent reflection, only to realise months later that they have gained better emotional control, more empathy, and a stronger sense of connection to others. By anchoring themselves in daily spiritual routines, they create fertile ground for major shifts in mindset and relationships.

These accounts, whether dramatic or gradual, are not restricted to celebrities or renowned authors; they include neighbours, colleagues, or relatives who quietly demonstrate how spirituality can guide someone through heartbreak, addiction, professional burnout, or simple apathy. Their transformations reveal that spiritual growth does not come from escaping real-world challenges but from engaging them with faith, persistence, and moral clarity. Even those who begin spiritual exercises sceptically may find themselves surprised by the emotional relief and purpose that unfolds.

Yet, it is crucial to remember that transformation is not a final destination but an ongoing journey. Once you have a breakthrough, whether small or large, you continue to nurture the insights gained. Regular introspection ensures you do not slip back into harmful habits. Setting incremental spiritual goals pushes you to keep learning. This steady progress is how you maintain a flourishing spiritual life well beyond any initial surge of inspiration.

Your own life can stand as a testament to spiritual development. You need not wait for dramatic upheavals to justify a spiritual shift. Even if you start by taking one mindful breath in moments of stress or by showing extra patience toward a loved one, you are treading the path of growth. Over time, those single acts accumulate, steering you toward a more serene, compassionate, and purposeful way of being.

Closing this chapter, you have seen that spirituality is not limited to remote retreats or doctrinal adherence. It weaves itself into every domain of your existence, guiding how you balance body and mind, handle emotional pain, give meaning to work, and foster relationships. These stories of transformation affirm that the path is ever-unfolding. With each fresh day and each renewed intention, you can delve deeper into a wellspring of peace that no external trouble can completely disturb. This unshakeable spiritual grounding helps you stand tall, even amid life's fiercest storms, carrying forward a radiance that touches both you and the wider world.

Chapter 7

Mastering Personal Finance

You might not always think about money in an emotional sense, but personal finance touches nearly every part of your life. It's more than just keeping track of numbers or paying bills on time; it's about feeling secure, having the freedom to choose, and building a future you're excited about. Mastering your finances gives you power over your circumstances, allowing you to pursue your dreams without the constant worry of financial stress hanging over your head.

Everyone starts somewhere, and the beginning can feel daunting, but getting your financial house in order doesn't have to be complicated. By understanding where your money comes from, being clear about where it goes, and having a straightforward plan to manage debt, budgeting, savings, and investing, you build strength and confidence. This chapter is your guide to gaining control, eliminating anxiety around money, and creating a financial life you're proud of.

1. Financial Foundations: Laying the Groundwork

You stand at the threshold of a journey that can reshape the way you approach life's many demands. Personal finance is not a sterile set of numbers; it is the heartbeat of your security and freedom. By taking charge of your finances, you arm yourself with discipline, peace of mind, and the flexibility to pursue goals without the suffocating weight of looming debts or scattered funds.

This is where you begin, and it is crucial to start strong. At its core, personal finance is about understanding where your money comes from and how it leaves your hands. You might have already experienced the anxiety that accompanies mid-month uncertainty, unsure if you can manage the week's remaining expenses. You do not need to live in that state. When you decide to take the reins, you move closer to a life where you know your income, your outgoings, and the precise steps needed to fortify your future.

A powerful first move is to review your monthly finances line by line. Imagine your cash flow as a river with various branches. Your salary or main source of income flows in, and each branch represents an expense, rent, groceries, phone bills, transport, and so on. If one of those branches grows too large, you will notice your main current weakening. By mapping these expenses clearly, you give yourself the power to spot imbalances and correct them before they wreak havoc.

Debt also factors heavily into your financial foundation. Student loans, credit card balances, or personal loans can accumulate, leaving you unsure of what to pay off first. A straightforward approach is to list every debt, right down to the penny, and rank them by either interest rate or balance. A higher interest rate often means a greater financial burden in the long run, so tackling it first can save you more money over time. However, you might also feel motivated by paying down the smallest balance first, boosting your morale as one debt disappears from the list. No single route works for everyone, so choose what keeps you focused.

Think of the initial stage of your financial journey as an architectural blueprint. You would not build a house without a plan, and your finances deserve the same respect. Even if you feel far from comfortable discussing terms like assets or portfolios, you can begin with something as simple as a spreadsheet or an app. Creating a snapshot of your income against your expenses is akin to sketching a house plan. This picture offers clarity, and clarity sets the stage for transformation.

There is a powerful sense of agency when you lay down these foundations. You start thinking beyond the present day, looking at the next year, five years, or decade. This shift in perspective helps you see that every penny you allocate responsibly can strengthen your future. Far from being restrictive, this approach empowers you. You begin to see that small steps, like directing savings to a secure account or chipping away at a credit card balance, add up to something greater than the sum of its parts.

Ultimately, the groundwork you establish now will guide all your financial decisions. It shapes how you address debt, how confidently you invest, and how resiliently you handle unexpected emergencies. It is not about self-denial; it is about knowing your numbers, mapping out goals, and making daily choices that keep you aligned with a better future. By focusing on these fundamentals, you elevate your sense of control, stability, and confidence, setting the tone for everything that follows in your quest to master personal finance.

2. Mastering the Art of Budgeting

Once you have a solid grasp on your current financial landscape, you move to a practice that underpins every other step: budgeting. A properly managed budget stands between you and financial chaos. Rather than robbing you of spontaneity, it offers liberation from those midnight worries about unpaid bills or impulsive splurges that leave you panicked by month's end.

Budgeting begins with awareness. You have already compiled an overview of income and expenses; this is your runway. Now, you allocate funds in a way that reflects your priorities. That might mean devoting a fraction of your monthly earnings to essentials like housing, utilities, groceries, and transport. Then, you decide how much can go toward leisure, future goals, or paying down debt faster.

One popular approach is to divide your take-home pay into percentages. Perhaps you direct half toward necessities, around a fifth toward savings and debt clearance, and the remainder toward discretionary spending. The proportions may shift depending on your unique circumstances, but the guiding principle remains: each pound, dollar, or euro is a resource you direct with purpose. The brilliance of budgeting lies in how it transforms mere hope ("I hope I have enough at month's end") into strategy ("I know precisely how much goes where").

When you first adopt a budgeting mindset, you might feel it is tedious. You could be tempted to log every coffee purchase or small transaction, which can seem exhausting. Yet, the payoff of consistent tracking is clarity. If tracking each expense down to the smallest detail overwhelms you, you can opt for weekly reviews where you summarise categories instead. This small effort helps you spot areas where costs might be rising too quickly. Perhaps you notice far more money going to takeaways than you realised, prompting a decision to cook more at home.

Another dimension to budgeting involves deciding how you automate payments and savings. Many find it easier to manage finances when a portion of each paycheck is automatically diverted to a savings or investment account. This approach reduces your ability to spend more than intended and ensures you are consistently progressing toward the future you envision. It is one thing to resolve to set aside money each month; it is another to have it transferred before you even see it in your current account.

Over time, budgets must evolve. Maybe you earn more, relocate, or undergo a life transition, and your priorities shift. Periodic reviews, monthly, quarterly, or annually, allow you to adjust. You also want to anticipate future milestones. If you know you will need a new vehicle in a year, build a car fund into your budget. If you plan to move to a new city, factor in possible relocation costs. The earlier you plan, the less likely you will experience a cash flow crisis.

Of course, nobody claims budgets are failproof. Life throws curveballs: a medical bill here or an unexpected household repair there. Budgeting does not shield you from all hardship, but it provides a structure that can absorb shocks more effectively than scattershot spending. By maintaining discipline in better times, you create breathing room for when adversity strikes.

Budgeting, ultimately, is your financial anchor. It helps you decide if you can afford that weekend getaway without derailing your long-term plans or if you can treat yourself to a fancy dinner without resorting to debt. Through budgeting, you adopt a proactive stance, guiding your financial journey instead of being tossed about by impulses. That sense of calm, combined with strategic foresight, underpins everything else in your personal finance world, setting you on a course toward empowerment rather than restriction.

3. The Saving Mindset: Securing Your Tomorrows

Once you have grasped your budget, you take a crucial leap by embedding a strong saving habit into your routine. Saving is about more than safety nets; it is the backbone of long-term prosperity. By establishing a saving mindset, you give yourself the power to face unexpected challenges without living in fear of financial ruin, and you also invest in the freedom to act on future opportunities.

For many, the first goal is an emergency fund. This fund is not meant for everyday expenses; it is a buffer for times when life blindsides you. Imagine the boiler failing in the middle of winter or an urgent medical cost. Without an emergency fund, you may spiral into high-interest debt or juggle other bills precariously. Yet, with a cushion covering three to six months of living costs, you protect your essential commitments, from groceries to housing, even if your income is temporarily compromised.

Beyond emergencies, saving ties directly into your ambitions. You might dream of home ownership, launching a business, or funding your child's education. These goals become attainable when you systematically set aside funds over months or years. This practice shifts your mindset from short-term indulgences toward viewing your paycheque as a tool to create something lasting. If you have never tried saving seriously, you may be surprised by how quickly your funds accumulate once you decide to lock away a certain amount or percentage each month.

One of the most powerful allies to your saving goals is compound growth. When you place money in a savings account or invest in assets, your returns can be reinvested, generating further gains. Over time, this compounding effect can produce surprising wealth. By starting early, you allow compounding to work for you longer, making each pound saved in your twenties or thirties more potent than those set aside later. This is not reserved for financial geniuses or high-earners; it is available to anyone disciplined enough to consistently put money away.

Of course, modern life is awash with distractions and enticing ways to spend. The act of saving demands forethought and discipline. By reminding yourself that each saved pound is a pledge to future growth, you quiet the voice urging you to spend on the latest gadget or holiday you cannot truly afford. You can still enjoy life, but you weigh each purchase against its potential impact on your broader plans. You begin to see that skipping a night out or an impulsive online purchase can funnel more into savings that may later fund an investment, pay down a mortgage, or allow you to retire comfortably.

Automating the saving process remains one of the most effective techniques. If a set portion of your income travels automatically to a savings or investment account, you adapt to living on the remainder. This approach minimises the temptation to dip into funds earmarked for your future. Over time, the money in these accounts grows in the background, guiding you toward bigger milestones.

That said, saving does not need to be joyless. Your monthly budget can include allocations for leisure and personal treats, so long as you uphold commitments to short-term security and long-term ambitions. The aim is balance and enough discipline to fortify your future without destroying your zest for the present. The saving mindset, once internalised, can truly revolutionise your relationship with money, enabling you to absorb life's setbacks and seize new prospects, free from constant financial unease.

4. Debt Management: Breaking the Chains

Debt can be the invisible chain stifling your financial freedom. It starts small, a credit card purchase here, a personal loan there, but can soon feel overwhelming. The essence of debt management lies in taking charge before the chain grows too heavy. While not all debts are destructive, failing to keep them in check can derail even the most carefully laid financial plans.

First, identify your debts in detail. Create a list of every liability, from credit cards and overdrafts to any lingering loans. Note the interest rates and minimum payments for each. You might see that certain balances carry punishingly high rates, effectively siphoning off extra cash monthly. This knowledge is your starting point; you cannot solve what you have not defined.

One strategy involves paying down the highest-interest debt first. This route ensures you eliminate the costliest balances early, potentially saving you more in total interest. Another approach, often called the "small wins" strategy, involves clearing the smallest debts first. Though you may pay a bit more in interest over time, the psychological boost you gain from erasing entire balances quickly can motivate you to keep going. Either way, the objective remains the same: regaining control of your finances by stopping interest charges from ballooning.

The reality of modern life means you may carry a mortgage or a student loan for decades, but these forms of debt can be seen as investments in property or education. The real trouble arises when you rely on credit cards for everyday living or keep multiple high-interest loans on your back. Rather than letting debt define your monthly outlay, you become proactive. Make extra payments whenever possible. Resist the allure of new credit lines until you have stabilised your existing debts. Each pound allocated toward principal beyond the minimum shortens the overall repayment term, easing the grip of your creditors.

You may worry about the idea of losing your leisure spending. True, there could be short-term sacrifices. Perhaps you postpone an expensive holiday or reduce your online shopping. Yet, the sense of relief and future flexibility you gain is a reward in itself. Imagine the liberating moment when your take-home pay belongs to you rather than split among lenders. Your money can then flow toward savings, investments, or experiences that add lasting value to your life.

Consolidation is another avenue to consider. If you juggle multiple high-interest debts, you might find a consolidation loan at a better rate, simplifying your repayments. However, this step requires discipline. The risk is that once your balances consolidate, you may feel tempted to use the newly freed credit lines again, compounding your problem if you lack self-control.

Ultimately, tackling debt is an act of self-empowerment. You are declaring that your earnings will no longer be devoured by interest payments or hidden fees. There is no magic wand to erase debts overnight, so it hinges on strategy, discipline, and the willingness to break the pattern of living beyond your means. While the journey can be challenging, each balance you clear brightens your financial outlook, giving you more ownership of your destiny.

5. Investment Fundamentals: Growing Your Wealth

Once you have contained your debts and built a habit of saving your financial world expands to the realm of investment. Here, you begin to transform idle funds into a force for growth. The basics of investing revolve around one principle: your money works on your behalf rather than gathering dust in a low-interest account. Investments are not wizardry; they are tools you can harness with informed strategies and consistent attention.

The first hurdle often lies in demystifying investment jargon. Shares, bonds, mutual funds, exchange-traded funds, these might sound complicated if you are new to them, but their essence is simpler than it appears. When you buy shares in a company, you own a small piece of that organisation, potentially benefiting from its future earnings or growth in share value. Bonds are essentially loans you issue to governments or corporations, receiving steady interest in return. Mutual funds and exchange-traded funds bundle a variety of assets, offering diversification without requiring you to select individual companies.

A core tenet of investment is diversification. Rather than placing all your funds in one stock or sector, you spread them around. By diversifying, you protect yourself somewhat from catastrophic losses if one company or market segment slumps. Indeed, seasoned investors emphasise that putting your "eggs in different baskets" smooths out the inevitable ebbs and flows of market cycles. This approach helps maintain stability, especially when the broader market experiences turbulence.

Time is your closest ally. The longer you invest, the more chance you give your assets to ride out short-term drops and capitalise on overall upward trends. This is where compound growth truly shines. Reinvested dividends and accumulated interest can create a compounding loop, enhancing your returns over years or even decades. Short-term speculation, chasing quick profits, can be risky, leaving you exposed to unpredictable market swings. A more measured, long-term strategy suits most individuals aiming for consistent wealth building.

Even so, you cannot neglect your tolerance for risk. Some can stomach volatile price swings, while others prefer steadier if slower, growth paths. It is wise to align investment choices with your comfort level and future plans. If you see yourself needing the money in a couple of years, you probably want more conservative vehicles. If you are looking toward retirement decades away, you might embrace more risk for higher potential returns.

Harnessing professional guidance can be valuable. A trusted financial advisor or credible online resources can help you determine the right mix of shares, bonds, and funds. While you pay fees or commissions, you may gain insights that protect you from misguided speculation. Alternatively, low-cost index funds often appeal to those who favour simplicity, as they track entire market indices rather than individual stocks. This route offers diversification in a straightforward package.

Finally, keep a level head. Markets go up, they go down, and fear or greed can tempt you into rash decisions. You might witness a sharp drop in your portfolio value, leading you to panic-sell at the worst moment. Or you could chase trends, investing in overhyped assets. Both tendencies can undermine your long-term strategy. Discipline is paramount, setting clear goals, automating monthly contributions, and reviewing your portfolio periodically ensures you remain on track without succumbing to emotional swings.

By entering the investment arena with a balanced mindset, you position yourself to grow wealth beyond the confines of a traditional savings account. Over time, prudent investments can outpace inflation, preserve the value of your funds, and allow you to fund major life goals. It takes patience, risk management, and a willingness to learn, but that is a small price for the potential to secure your financial future and enrich your life with greater opportunities.

6. Retirement Readiness: Planning for the Long Haul

Retirement might seem distant, especially if you are in your early career, but the sooner you address it, the stronger your eventual position. Retirement is not about idling through later years; it is about ensuring you can maintain the lifestyle you want when you no longer rely on full-time employment. Whether you dream of travelling the world, spending more time with family, or nurturing community projects, you need a nest egg to make it happen without enduring financial strain.

Retirement planning starts with understanding how much income you will need in your post-work era. While no single figure fits everyone, a typical strategy is to aim for a portion of your current earnings. If you anticipate active retirement with trips abroad or hobbies, you might need a higher share than someone envisioning a simpler routine. Budgeting for future healthcare costs is also wise, given that medical expenses can rise with age.

Your contributions to workplace or private retirement schemes represent one of the simplest ways to prepare. Some employers match a percentage of your contributions, and ignoring this benefit is akin to leaving free money on the table. When such matches exist, aim to contribute enough to receive the full match before allocating funds to other investment vehicles. Remember, this portion accumulates over the course of your career, so small, consistent contributions over decades can balloon into a substantial sum by your final working years.

Beyond formal schemes, you can explore personal investment accounts earmarked for retirement. You may opt for tax-efficient vehicles, depending on your region's regulations, to keep a larger slice of returns for yourself. These might include certain types of ISAs or IRAs, where the tax advantages can speed up the compounding effect. The aim is to have your retirement funds working quietly in the background, growing while you focus on your daily life and career progression.

Some people delay saving for retirement, feeling that their current responsibilities carry higher priority. Yet, each year that passes without making a start potentially robs you of compounding gains. If you begin at 25 and invest modestly but consistently, you often surpass someone who starts a decade later and contributes more aggressively. Time acts as a multiplier, so every year you wait is a missed opportunity for greater growth.

You will also want to recalibrate your strategy as you move closer to retirement. Early in your working life, you can tolerate more volatility by focusing on growth-oriented assets such as shares. As the retirement date nears, shifting toward more conservative holdings can protect the wealth you have accumulated, lessening the impact of a potential market downturn. This rebalancing act guards against last-minute losses that could harm your carefully built nest egg.

Ultimately, retirement readiness reflects respect for your future self. By devoting part of your income to retirement plans, you give yourself the gift of choice later. Perhaps you will keep working in some capacity, not out of necessity but for fulfilment. Maybe you will move to a coastal town and finally learn new skills. With a secure financial buffer, your decisions are driven by desire rather than desperation. By starting now, no matter how small your contributions, you set the stage for a retirement filled with freedom and possibility.

7. Protecting What You Build: Insurance and Safeguards

After spending years building up your financial house, savings, investments, property, or even a business, you need robust protections in place. Unexpected events can strike with little warning, from accidents and illness to property damage, leaving you vulnerable. Insurance, far from being an afterthought, stands as your financial shield, ensuring life's emergencies do not dismantle the wealth and stability you have worked so diligently to establish.

Different types of insurance address different risks. Health insurance safeguards you from overwhelming medical bills. Life insurance, meanwhile, secures loved ones in the event of your passing, offering them a financial cushion. Property insurance protects against disasters that could ravage your home or prized possessions. For car owners, vehicle insurance is not just mandatory in many places; it defends you from the financial repercussions of collisions or theft.

You might feel tempted to avoid insurance premiums, viewing them as sunk costs that do not yield visible returns unless something goes wrong. However, that is exactly why they exist: to soften the blow of misfortune. The alternative is facing an avalanche of expenses when tragedy strikes, wiping out years of careful saving. Once you see insurance as risk management rather than wasted money, the investment in consistent premiums becomes more palatable.

Apart from traditional insurance, you can set up additional safeguards. An extended emergency fund, beyond the standard three to six months of expenses, can shield you from extended job loss or unforeseen financial crises. You might also consider legal measures, like drawing up a will or establishing a trust, to ensure your wealth is directed according to your wishes. Taking the time to articulate these details spares your loved ones from confusion or disputes later.

Your career can also benefit from protective measures, like income protection insurance that replaces a portion of your earnings if you are unable to work. This sort of policy is especially relevant for those without substantial sick leave or who work in fields prone to accidents. Even business owners can look into insurance that covers interruptions, property damage, or liabilities arising from daily operations.

Occasionally, you will see unscrupulous offers or believe you need every form of insurance under the sun. While being underinsured is risky, being overinsured means your monthly premiums could weigh you down. Strike a balance by carefully assessing which risks are most relevant to your life and finances. That might mean a robust health plan for a family with children or comprehensive property coverage if you own valuable real estate.

When done wisely, these protective measures do more than mitigate risks. They foster peace of mind, letting you focus on progress rather than living in fear of a life-altering setback. Insurance and related safeguards are not the glamorous side of personal finance, but they form a crucial line of defence. They ensure that a stroke of bad luck does not undo your financial achievements, allowing you to press ahead with confidence.

8. Navigating Taxes: Keeping More of Your Earnings

Taxes can feel like a labyrinth designed to siphon away your money. Yet, you have more power than you think to reduce what you owe, legally and ethically, ensuring that you keep a larger share of what you earn. Effective tax planning is not reserved for corporations or the very wealthy. By understanding applicable rules and allowances, you can structure your finances to be more tax-efficient, adding yet another layer of stability and opportunity to your financial life.

Start by examining your tax obligations in relation to how you earn your income. If you earn through employment, you might benefit from pension contributions taken pre-tax or from salary sacrifice schemes that reduce your taxable income. If you are self-employed, you have a different set of possibilities, such as deducting certain business expenses. In both scenarios, you can capitalise on legitimate allowances, everything from tax-free savings accounts to relief for charitable giving.

Record-keeping proves vital here. Receipts, invoices, and meticulous tracking of your financial activities can mean the difference between paying more tax than necessary or ensuring every allowable expense is claimed. While it may sound tedious, solid records are your defence if the tax authorities ask you to explain a deduction. Knowing you can back up each figure brings confidence, reducing the stress often tied to the annual tax return.

There is also the option of strategic timing. For instance, if you anticipate a higher income in the next tax year, you could accelerate certain expenses or pension contributions to the current period or vice versa. This approach is about mapping your known or likely earnings to take advantage of thresholds and cut-offs that significantly affect how much tax you pay. If you think about your finances in multi-year cycles, you can place yourself in more favourable tax positions.

Consulting a qualified tax adviser can be a wise move, especially if your situation involves multiple income streams, overseas earnings, or investments. These professionals might reveal angles you had not spotted, from optimising your business structure to applying for tax relief in lesser-known categories. While a consultation carries a cost, the potential savings can outweigh those fees, particularly if you are juggling large sums.

Still, do not fall into the trap of thinking that aggressive schemes or "quick fixes" are your golden ticket. Overly complex or suspicious arrangements can bring long-term problems, including scrutiny from tax authorities, penalties, or reputational damage. It is smarter to employ transparent strategies that comply with regulations than to skirt the boundaries for short-term wins.

Ultimately, taxes are part of life, but they need not drain your enthusiasm or finances. By knowing where each pound goes, harnessing available allowances, and staying aware of legislative updates, you can keep more of your earnings and maintain better control over your resources. This is yet another step in crafting a personal finance strategy that is both robust and adaptive, designed to help you flourish now and in the years ahead.

9. Real Estate and Other Avenues: Exploring Bigger Moves

With solid foundations, disciplined budgeting, and investment basics under your belt, you may look toward bigger arenas of wealth creation. Real estate often tops the list, as property ownership can provide not only a roof over your head but a potential asset that appreciates in value over time. Alongside property, you could explore other ventures, small businesses, peer-to-peer lending platforms, or alternative investments that offer fresh streams of income and diversification.

Real estate appeals because it is tangible. You can live in a home you own or rent out a property for recurring income. In favourable markets, your equity grows as property values rise and tenants cover your mortgage. Yet, property is not always a guaranteed windfall. Market downturns can shrink valuations, unexpected repairs can eat into profits, and tenants can sometimes pose complications. Approach real estate with the same diligence you apply elsewhere, do the maths, understand local markets, and factor in ongoing costs like maintenance and insurance.

If you are not ready for the responsibilities of being a landlord, you might explore other ways to tap into property's potential. Real Estate Investment Trusts (REITs) allow you to invest in property portfolios without directly purchasing or managing a building. You collect a portion of the rental income and potential value growth, though your returns vary with market conditions. This option suits those seeking exposure to property with less direct involvement.

Beyond real estate, your personal finance journey can encompass small business ownership. Maybe you have a skill or product you believe fills a market gap. Launching a side business or entrepreneurial venture can be lucrative if approached with thorough planning. You start small, test demand, and refine your offering. As the venture grows, reinvest profits wisely, aiming to create an entity that eventually stands independent of your day job. Being your own boss has pitfalls, like inconsistent earnings and higher stress, but success can open the doors to real wealth creation.

If you prefer less hands-on involvement, consider alternative investments like peer-to-peer lending platforms or certain commodities. Peer-to-peer lending lets you lend money to vetted borrowers, earning interest in return. Risk management is key: you diversify your lending across multiple loans to mitigate potential defaults. Likewise, commodities (gold, agricultural products, etc.) can serve as a hedge against inflation or economic turmoil, though their prices can be volatile.

In stepping into these bigger moves, caution is essential. While the upside can be higher, so can the complexities and risks. A thorough analysis, perhaps aided by professional advice, can help you avoid overextending your capital. Setting up clear objectives, whether monthly rental income or long-term capital growth, helps guide your decisions. The aim is to build a robust portfolio that stands on multiple pillars so a stumble in one sector is cushioned by stability in another.

As you venture beyond basic savings and investment products, keep your mindset grounded in facts rather than hype. Not every property deal is a bargain, nor is every business idea a goldmine. Yet, with careful research, you can create valuable additions to your wealth-building strategy. Real estate and broader avenues stand ready for those who have done the groundwork, are prepared to manage complexities, and appreciate the potential gains and pitfalls.

10. Sustaining Momentum: Adapting for Lifelong Prosperity

Reaching this stage in your personal finance journey means you have assembled a robust framework. You manage your money rather than letting it manage you; you keep debts under control, invest with intent, and guard against life's uncertainties. However, your work does not end here. Sustaining momentum requires consistent review, a willingness to adapt, and an ongoing commitment to learning.

Financial goals evolve. Perhaps you initially aimed to buy a home, but as time progresses, you start considering a second property for rental income or saving to assist an ageing relative. Your investments might shift to safer assets as you approach retirement, or you could channel more funds toward philanthropic causes. Staying flexible ensures your finances match changing life stages, ambitions, and family dynamics.

One effective practice is a periodic financial check-up. Schedule a time, maybe annually or semi-annually, to revisit your budget, investments, insurance, and retirement progress. Run through key questions: Has my income changed? Do I foresee major expenses in the next year? Is my portfolio too tilted toward one type of asset? Am I still comfortable with my risk level? This self-examination keeps your strategy aligned with reality and fosters the habit of continuous improvement.

Moreover, keep educating yourself. The financial world never stands still. Markets fluctuate, property trends shift, and governments revise tax laws. A new regulation could open up unexpected advantages, or an innovation could change how you handle your finances day to day. By staying curious, reading credible blogs, consulting professionals, or watching reputable presentations, you remain agile and well-equipped to navigate any shifts.

During this lifelong endeavour, do not lose sight of the importance of purpose. Money, once you have secured your essentials and future stability, can serve as a tool to enrich your life in non-material ways. It might fund a passion project, give you the chance to spend more time with loved ones, or help you make a difference through charity. As your financial health strengthens, your freedom to choose how you live increases. That sense of agency is one of the greatest rewards of sustained personal finance success.

At the same time, resist complacency. Even the most disciplined strategy can falter if you slip back into old spending habits, get seduced by high-risk speculative ideas, or overlook your safety nets. Prospering financially is less about a one-time sprint and more about an ongoing marathon. You cultivate resilience step by step, ensuring each financial decision aligns with your overarching vision for life.

By maintaining this momentum, you remain in the driver's seat, shaping your future according to your values. You leverage your finances to support goals that reach beyond your personal sphere, perhaps mentoring budding entrepreneurs, guiding family members on the path to fiscal responsibility, or investing in community projects. When you reflect on the journey, you realise this is about far more than figures on a balance sheet. It is about building the life you want, anchored in a sturdy foundation and propelled by clarity, determination, and a profound sense of financial empowerment.

Chapter 8

Career Planning for Future Leaders

If there's one truth to understand as you step into this chapter, it's that your future as a leader begins today. Career planning isn't something you casually think about or leave to chance; it's the roadmap that guides you towards becoming the leader you're capable of being. Whether you're just starting your journey or transitioning towards bigger roles, clear planning empowers you to take confident strides forward. By intentionally aligning your strengths and passions with a clear vision, you can craft a career that not only fulfils you professionally but also resonates deeply with your personal values.

Great leaders never find their roles by accident. They thoughtfully envision the impact they want to make, continuously sharpen their skills, and seize opportunities that move them closer to their goals. As you read through this chapter, you'll discover how to identify your natural strengths, set strategic milestones, and harness your passions to fuel your journey. You'll also learn why adaptability, lifelong learning, and strategic networking are not optional but essential components of successful career planning. The strategies you're about to explore will equip you with the confidence to become a future leader who leaves a lasting legacy, guiding others towards a brighter and more purposeful path.

1: Why Career Planning Matters for Leadership Potential

You hold more power over your professional journey than you might realise. Career planning is not a distant concept reserved for people with ironclad five-year plans; it is the strategic foundation that ensures you enter your field with clarity and progress in a direction that aligns with your values. By charting your path, you equip yourself with the tools to make purposeful decisions, stay focused on what matters, and cultivate leadership potential long before you assume a leadership title. Whether you are at the start of your working life or in the midst of a transition, the underlying discipline of planning can save you years of drifting and second-guessing.

Leaders do not simply appear at the helm. They often begin by defining the kind of impact they wish to have; then, they steadily develop the capabilities to achieve it. This does not happen by accident. It emerges from the daily decisions you make: seeking roles that build relevant skills, forging strong networks, and being ready to adapt when new opportunities align with your long-term vision. Think of individuals who rose from unknown backgrounds to leadership roles in innovation or public service; they did not float passively, hoping success would fall into their laps. They set out with a strategy for growth, remained open to fresh challenges, and refined their path with time.

Career planning matters because it allows you to anticipate changes in your field while remaining grounded in your strengths. If a certain industry evolves at breakneck speed, you want to be the person who saw it coming and aligned your progression with that wave. Instead of reacting frantically when major shifts occur, you will have a blueprint that helps you pivot gracefully. This proactive stance not only builds your credibility but positions you as someone who can guide others. Colleagues and mentors begin to notice your readiness to seize key moments, and this often leads to recommendations or collaborations you might never have expected.

Another key reason to plan your career is the confidence it instils. When you know the next step and have a sense of where you are headed, your self-assured manner reflects in job interviews, networking events, and day-to-day interactions. Other professionals gravitate toward those who speak with clarity about their aspirations. In turn, you strengthen your leadership presence well before you sit in executive meetings or direct large teams. This self-assurance becomes a magnet for the right opportunities.

Still, a plan must never be rigid. You should view it as a guiding map rather than an unchangeable script. You need a steady approach that also welcomes recalibration because every industry, from finance to technology, can pivot unexpectedly. The most effective leaders thrive on this dual nature: a vision anchored in purpose combined with adaptability. When you focus on purposeful career planning, you can identify when a detour will bring growth or when it deviates from your intended leadership goals.

In essence, career planning equips you to step forward with boldness. You become the architect of your professional trajectory rather than waiting for others to chart it for you. This foundation of strategy and foresight is indispensable for future leaders because once you claim responsibility for where you are headed, you position yourself to serve, guide, and inspire those who look to you for direction.

2: Identifying Your Natural Strengths

To excel as a future leader, you must first know what you do exceptionally well. Too many professionals wander through years of work without a clear sense of what makes them stand out. If you can pinpoint your strengths, you accelerate your path to expertise and gain a unique position in your chosen field. Whether those strengths are analytical thinking, persuasive communication, or creative problem-solving, understanding them allows you to steer your career intelligently.

Self-reflection is often the starting point. Look back on moments when you thrived. Were you coordinating a project? Solving a technical puzzle? Motivating a group? These instances contain subtle clues about your strongest attributes. It might feel daunting if you have not done it before, but shining a spotlight on those moments of peak performance reveals patterns. Document them, examine what skills you employed, and note which tasks felt both challenging and energising. Those tasks typically show where your greatest potential lies.

Another powerful method is to seek genuine feedback. Sometimes, others see your strengths more clearly than you do. Ask colleagues or mentors which tasks they believe you handle with finesse. When done thoughtfully, these conversations can uncover strengths you never credited yourself for. You might discover you have a knack for boosting morale in stressful settings or that you excel at finding cost-effective solutions. This external perspective can be invaluable, especially early in your career planning.

Leaders who rise quickly are those who harness their innate talents and refine them to a professional level. You can do the same by consistently practising the skills that position you as invaluable to a team. If you realise you communicate ideas compellingly, seize every chance to present in meetings, speak at small conferences, or pitch new ideas to senior colleagues. This constant exercise of your abilities not only polishes them but also signals your readiness for bigger responsibilities. Before long, your name becomes associated with that particular talent, and your reputation grows.

However, remember that no strength stands alone. A skilled communicator still needs organisational abilities; an analytical thinker still needs to build relationships. The best leaders blend their main strengths with a well-rounded professional toolkit. So, while you nurture your standout qualities, spend some time gradually enhancing your supporting skills. It does not have to be intensive all at once; small, steady efforts can transform you into a robust candidate for leadership roles.

Furthermore, identifying your strengths keeps you motivated in tough periods. Jobs and industries can shift, but your core abilities remain a reliable anchor. When new technology disrupts a sector, those who know their unique value can reposition themselves more smoothly. Meanwhile, people who have never explored their strengths may struggle to adapt. Your clarity becomes your advantage. You will be poised to say, "I thrive best in situations that allow me to use these talents," making it easier to spot which roles fit your potential.

To lead in a meaningful, impactful way, build your foundation on strengths that genuinely energise you. By acknowledging your strongest attributes early and investing in them, you place yourself in the best position to stand out. As your responsibilities grow, these strengths will guide you, help you innovate, and encourage you to push even further in your quest to shape your field.

3: Aligning Passions with Professional Goals

Pursuing a career solely for financial gain or external validation can leave you feeling restless and unfulfilled. True leadership potential arises when you align the work you do with the passions that drive you. When you tap into the deeper interests that spark energy in your daily life, your motivation intensifies, and you open a path to leading with authenticity. Without this alignment, even high-paying roles can feel hollow.

First, reflect on activities that captivate you beyond mere obligation. Perhaps you are drawn to mentoring young professionals, improving local communities, or pioneering eco-friendly solutions. These passions often develop naturally from personal experiences or deeply held beliefs. When you integrate them into your professional direction, you transform your career from a treadmill of tasks into a purposeful journey. This is what fuels your resilience: it is far simpler to devote extra energy to something that resonates with your values.

Aligning passion with professional goals does not mean ignoring practicality. You still need to evaluate market demand, sustainable income, and growth potential. However, when you identify an intersection between what excites you, what contributes to society, and what employers or clients need, you strike a powerful sweet spot. Leaders with this synergy typically stand out because their enthusiasm is palpable. Colleagues sense their conviction, and customers believe their message.

To align passion with your career, undertake targeted research. Find out how your interest area is evolving within your industry. If you are passionate about innovative software solutions, explore the latest technologies, attend specialised conferences, or connect with industry experts. Through this focused approach, you uncover niches or emerging trends that match your excitement, turning raw passion into tangible career pathways. Your pursuit of knowledge in that niche can then become a springboard for thought leadership because you will be at the forefront of developments.

Next, incorporate practical steps that integrate your passion into your daily work. Maybe you start a small pilot project within your company that addresses a community need you care about. Or you could volunteer your professional skills to a cause aligned with your interests. By doing so, you build experience and credibility in your chosen focus area. This not only enriches your CV but shows decision-makers you can produce results where you have genuine commitment. Employers value those who display initiative and a deeper sense of purpose, as it often translates into strong performance and loyalty.

Keeping your passions at the forefront also boosts your leadership appeal. People are drawn to leaders who demonstrate genuine purpose because it signals integrity. You become more persuasive without having to force your viewpoints. Your excitement is evident through your tone and work ethic, inspiring others to rally behind the same vision. This sense of shared mission can unify teams, spark creativity, and enhance overall morale.

Ultimately, aligning passions with professional goals merges practicality and meaning. You will still face hurdles, routine tasks, and market shifts. Yet when your career direction echoes your core motivations, you bounce back more quickly from setbacks. You will persevere through late nights or challenging projects because you recognise the deeper reason behind your efforts. In this alignment, future leaders find their greatest drive, forging paths that not only benefit themselves but also uplift the people and causes that matter most.

4: Short-Term Milestones and Long-Term Vision

Every robust career plan balances short-term achievements with a broader sense of direction. Without clear short-term milestones, your long-range goals can remain airy and intangible. Conversely, if you fixate only on immediate targets, you risk losing sight of the overarching trajectory that propels you toward leadership. Finding the harmony between near-term progress and far-sighted vision is essential for sustainable growth.

Short-term milestones serve as stepping stones. These could be completing a certification in a sought-after skill, leading a small project at work, or delivering a successful presentation in front of stakeholders. They are the tangible checkpoints that affirm your development is on track. When you achieve them, you gain momentum, bolster your confidence, and send signals to peers and managers that you are serious about advancement. However, it is vital to ensure these milestones feed into your ultimate leadership goals rather than becoming random tasks driven by immediate convenience.

A strong long-term vision, on the other hand, provides the enduring framework for everything you do. Visualise where you would like to stand in five or ten years; this might involve heading a department, launching your own enterprise, or becoming a leading expert in your field. This overarching vision shapes your choices. If you aim to spearhead a division that focuses on sustainable products, you might take on short-term projects that bolster your knowledge in environmental research. If you plan to create a groundbreaking tech start-up, your interim milestones could centre on programming, product design, or business strategy.

It is also beneficial to review and adjust your goals periodically. Industries evolve, economic conditions shift, and unexpected personal interests may emerge. By revisiting your short-term and long-term objectives every six months or annually, you maintain relevance. This prevents you from clinging to outdated targets. Instead, you can update your path while preserving the essence of your vision, ensuring flexibility without losing your fundamental direction.

For instance, if your original target was to secure a managerial role within three years, but your organisation reorganises, and a new department emerges that better aligns with your evolving interests, you can pivot your milestones accordingly. This kind of agility shows others that you remain steadfast to your core vision yet adaptable to changing landscapes, a hallmark of effective leadership.

Short-term milestones also keep you accountable. It is easy to say you aspire to be a respected leader in the finance sector. It is more meaningful to decide that within the next six months, you will pass a relevant professional exam or successfully manage a complex finance project for your firm. This measurable progress clarifies your next steps and gives you an honest gauge of how close you are to meeting your vision. If you miss a milestone, you can investigate the reasons, correct course, and regain momentum.

A symbiotic relationship links short-term milestones and long-term vision: the small wins feed the bigger dream, while the dream keeps those small wins meaningful. Together, they craft a career plan that is both concrete and aspirational. You have a reason to persevere through daily hurdles because each action ties into a future that you can see, aspire toward, and progressively shape. This balanced approach ensures your leadership ambitions gain the structure necessary to become reality rather than remain faint wishes.

5: Building Expertise Through Lifelong Learning

In a world that rewards those who adapt swiftly, you cannot rely on a static body of knowledge from your university years or entry-level training. The pursuit of expertise demands perpetual growth. Future leaders distinguish themselves by their commitment to ongoing education, whether through advanced courses, reading widely, or learning on the job. When you approach learning as a lifelong habit, you remain relevant, sharpen your decision-making, and set an example for those who look up to you.

One core element is cultivating curiosity. Leaders who embrace curiosity do not feel threatened by new technology or emerging methodologies. Instead, they treat these developments as chances to strengthen their skill set. Picture someone who started in marketing long before social media took off. If that individual dismissed social platforms, assuming they were irrelevant, they would quickly fall behind. In contrast, a curiosity-driven professional would immerse themselves in the shifting trends, picking up digital marketing tactics and mastering analytics tools that might intimidate others.

Your commitment to lifelong learning can take various forms. You might enroll in specialised online programmes that deepen your technical abilities or refine your leadership approach. You can read extensively, choosing books and journals related to your field as well as topics that broaden your horizons. Forums and professional communities allow you to exchange insights with peers, while seminars and conferences connect you with thought leaders you might not encounter otherwise. Blending these methods ensures you never stagnate.

Another advantage of continuous education is how it underpins adaptability. Industries pivot swiftly, and if you remain locked in outdated practices, you will struggle to guide your organisation through change. Leaders who remain curious are typically the first to spot fresh trends, swiftly incorporate them, and steer their teams toward new opportunities. This helps you build a reputation as a forward-thinking professional, someone people trust when they spot the next wave of industry evolution.

Continuous learning also reshapes your mindset, encouraging humility. The more you discover, the more aware you become of gaps in your knowledge. This humility fosters an environment where your peers and subordinates feel comfortable sharing feedback or challenging ideas, knowing you are open to growth. It also nurtures your resilience. Mistakes can happen, but if you are committed to learning, setbacks transform into lessons that strengthen your future performance.

Above all, your choice to be a lifelong learner sets you apart in recruitment or advancement opportunities. Hiring managers and decision-makers often place significant value on those who show evidence of recent skill enhancement. Displaying credentials from recent courses or highlighting contributions to knowledge-sharing platforms signals you are not content with past achievements. Instead, you reflect a drive to grow in step with a rapidly changing world.

You are never too far along in your career to learn something new. It keeps your mind agile and your skill set marketable, but more importantly, it aligns with the spirit of leadership. When you show your team that continuous learning is the norm, you inspire them to pursue self-improvement. This collective embrace of growth can fuel an atmosphere of innovation and excellence, placing you in the perfect position to elevate everyone around you.

6: Strategic Networking for Career Growth

Far more than exchanging business cards, networking is about forging authentic, mutually beneficial relationships in your industry. You connect with people who spark fresh ideas, deliver timely advice, or share opportunities that align with your goals. Future leaders who understand the strategic importance of networking dedicate time and effort to building these connections, viewing them as invaluable assets. Whether it is building alliances with peers, seeking mentorship from seasoned figures, or collaborating with professionals in adjacent fields, your network can propel your career in ways formal qualifications alone rarely achieve.

Effective networking often begins with genuine curiosity about others. While it is tempting to fixate on what you might gain, the strongest bonds form when you show real interest in another person's viewpoint or challenges. By asking questions, actively listening, and offering support before you seek it in return, you establish goodwill and credibility. This dynamic forms the foundation of professional trust. For instance, if you meet a software developer while you work in product management, you might offer insight on product positioning or user feedback. In turn, that developer could later share developments in emerging technologies relevant to your future plans.

Digital platforms expand your reach exponentially. With professional social media sites or industry-specific forums, you can engage with experts thousands of miles away. Contributing thoughtfully to online discussions, sharing resources, or seeking clarifications can catch the attention of influencers in your niche. However, be mindful that authenticity matters; spamming people or making superficial connections might grant a fleeting benefit, but it rarely results in lasting relationships.

Yet face-to-face interactions remain potent. Conferences, workshops, and seminars offer a chance to converse in real-time, pick up subtle nuances, and build rapport through direct dialogue. When you approach these events with a clear sense of purpose, perhaps you are looking to learn about a new tool or discover potential collaborators; you can prioritise where you invest your energy. Following up promptly with new contacts, referencing a specific point from your conversation, sets you apart from those who hand out cards with no real interaction.

Networking is also about offering value. If you regularly attend events or forums, think of what you can provide your network, whether it is an introduction to a relevant contact, a resourceful article, or a thoughtful perspective on a trending topic. Over time, you develop a reputation as a connector and contributor. People respond positively to those who help without always expecting something immediate in return. This fosters reciprocal relationships. When you need guidance or an introduction, your network is much more willing to respond.

Leaders with robust networks can more easily pivot into new roles or industries, adapt to market disruptions, and gather a diverse pool of ideas. If your current role faces uncertainty, the connections you have cultivated might point you toward a more promising path. For major undertakings like launching a venture, your network can supply advice, referrals, and moral support. In essence, these relationships act as a professional safety net. By investing your time in honest, strategic networking, you create an environment that nurtures your leadership journey, guiding you toward increasingly impactful roles and projects.

7: Navigating Transitions and Overcoming Setbacks

No career path is immune to periods of uncertainty. You might face organisational restructuring, miss a promotion you believed was yours, or feel compelled to switch industries midway through your professional journey. These moments test your resilience and adaptability. Although setbacks can challenge your confidence, they are also prime opportunities for reflection, recalibration, and growth. Leaders who emerge stronger from difficulties are those who refuse to be defined by any single disappointment, instead using each hurdle as fuel for future successes.

Adaptability is key during transitions. You may have spent years honing your skills in a particular domain, only to find that technological innovations or market demands now call for something entirely different. Rather than view that shift as a crisis, you can treat it as an invitation to expand your capabilities. Embrace new learning, enrol in courses to refresh your skill set or shadow colleagues who excel in emerging areas. This not only broadens your professional horizons but also shows decision-makers that you are an asset with a can-do attitude in unpredictable climates.

Setbacks are a universal feature of ambitious careers, whether it is failing to secure a promotion or encountering a project collapse. The difference lies in how you respond. A leader who temporarily stumbles but maintains composure and uses the event to identify knowledge gaps can come back more formidable. By contrast, those who grow bitter or passive in the face of setbacks risk undermining their future. Reflecting on what went wrong, taking responsibility if applicable, and outlining a plan for improvement demonstrate maturity. Employers and colleagues often respect individuals who exhibit this level of introspection.

Building a reliable support system can also help you navigate transitions. This includes mentors who can offer guidance from their own experiences, peers who can share honest feedback, and mentees who might lend fresh perspectives. Sometimes, simply discussing your challenges out loud with someone you trust can clarify the next step. You might discover that your supposed dead-end is an indirect path to a more fulfilling area you had not previously explored.

Additionally, keep an eye on your mindset. Dwelling too long on disappointments can lead to inertia, undermining the proactive spirit you need for change. Shift your focus toward learning objectives: what new skills can you gain, which relationships might help you progress, and how can you use the experience gained from previous roles as a platform? Avoid tying your identity too firmly to a single employer or position. Instead, see your career as a journey with multiple chapters, each shaped by your response to challenges.

Finally, transitions often present a hidden gift: they can highlight what truly motivates you. If you lose a job in a field you were not passionate about, perhaps this is the moment to pivot toward something more aligned with your values or interests. If you are forced to relocate, you might discover a new network and environment that amplify your progress. By embracing these shifts, you stay flexible, relevant, and ready to lead in changing times. Your resilience becomes a beacon for others, showing them that adversity can spark fresh ambition rather than extinguish it.

8: Developing Leadership Skills for Advancement

While technical expertise can land you a role, leadership skills carry you further up the ladder. Prospective leaders must actively cultivate abilities such as strategic thinking, collaboration, decision-making, and clear communication. Too many employees assume they will automatically develop leadership qualities if they remain long enough in a company, but leadership requires intentional practice. If you deliberately strengthen these skills, you earn a reputation as someone who can handle higher-stakes responsibilities and lead teams effectively.

Start with self-awareness. By understanding your personal style, whether you prefer to delegate or maintain a hands-on approach, whether you thrive in large group settings or excel in one-to-one discussions, you can shape your leadership method. Self-awareness also helps you identify blind spots. For instance, if you notice you tend to micromanage, you can work on trusting team members to encourage ownership of tasks. Meanwhile, if you discover that you shy away from decisive action, you can push yourself to make timely calls.

Strategic thinking is another important quality. Future leaders do not limit their view to immediate tasks. They connect daily actions to overarching objectives, whether for the organisation or their career. You can practice this skill by studying how your industry evolves, brainstorming potential challenges, and mapping out how to address them. If you are in a role that lacks obvious strategic dimensions, volunteer for committees or cross-departmental projects that broaden your perspective. This willingness to engage at a higher level of planning positions you for growth when leadership spots become vacant.

Strong communication and interpersonal abilities are non-negotiable. Leaders cannot hide behind screens or jargon; they must inspire trust through clarity. You can refine this by seeking regular feedback on how you present ideas, whether in emails or meetings. Focus on empathy as well; this means truly listening when team members speak, reading non-verbal cues, and responding in a way that shows respect. Leaders who master this approach tend to create more cohesive teams with fewer misunderstandings and higher morale.

Decision-making is another arena where you can stand apart. Leaders do not procrastinate on tough calls; they gather relevant data and consult where needed but ultimately move forward with confidence. You can hone this skill in smaller ways: volunteer to coordinate a minor project that forces you to weigh options, set deadlines, and deliver results. As you become more comfortable, you can tackle bigger, riskier decisions. Over time, others will recognise your ability to stay calm under pressure, making you a natural choice for leadership posts.

Lastly, never assume leadership growth happens alone. Seek mentors, read books on leadership, and invest in training programmes that hone the precise areas you need to improve. By combining self-reflection with real-life application, you transform theory into tangible growth. Your consistent efforts not only make you a more effective teammate but also build a track record that decision-makers notice. In the long run, advanced leadership skills are the scaffolding upon which you build promotions and broader influence. They bridge the gap between a capable employee and a visionary figure who can guide teams, projects, or entire organisations to new heights.

9: Balancing Professional Ambition and Personal Fulfilment

High achievers often pour so much energy into their careers that their personal life or well-being suffers. That level of sacrifice might secure short-lived gains, but over time, it can breed burnout, strained relationships, and a diminishing sense of purpose. For future leaders, learning to balance professional ambition with personal fulfilment is a skill as critical as any technical or managerial competence. It ensures your success does not come at the cost of your health or long-term happiness.

The journey toward equilibrium begins with clear boundaries. If you allow work to spill into every aspect of your life, you erode your capacity to perform well. Sleep shortens, stress compounds and creativity falters. On the other hand, setting realistic limits, such as designated hours for emails or committing to weekly downtime, fosters discipline. You will be more present and efficient in the hours you do work, knowing that there is time set aside for rest. This boundary-setting also signals to colleagues or managers that your well-being and personal obligations merit respect, and they often reciprocate with greater understanding.

Prioritising personal fulfilment is also about knowing which pursuits refuel you. This might be spending time with family, practising a hobby that recharges your creativity, or simply taking regular walks to reflect. You become a more effective leader when your mind and body are revitalised. If you treat personal time as optional, you risk reaching a point where enthusiasm for your career dips and frustration takes over. Maintaining a routine that includes personal passions not only gives you fresh energy but can also spark new insights you might never discover in a purely work-centric environment.

Another dimension of balance is understanding when and how to delegate. Future leaders who try to shoulder every responsibility alone quickly hit a wall. Delegation is not about relinquishing control but about recognising that distributing tasks can free you to focus on strategic or high-level responsibilities. Furthermore, when you empower teammates, you foster professional development within your group. This shared leadership can reduce your workload and help you sustain a healthier pace without compromising on team productivity.

Staying attuned to your emotional well-being is also essential. If anxiety, impatience, or disillusionment creeps in, view it as a signal, not something to dismiss. Leaders who attend to their mental wellness, perhaps through regular exercise, structured downtime, or discussions with trusted friends, are better equipped to guide others. Ignoring these signals can result in emotional burnout or conflict that undermines your credibility. You cannot effectively guide a team if you are struggling to manage your own inner state.

Ultimately, striking the balance between ambition and personal fulfilment is a dynamic process. Demanding seasons will arise where you work late and push harder. However, these periods should be temporary, not your everyday normal. When you keep balance as a core principle, you preserve the vitality and perspective that enable you to excel for years, not months. You also model a more sustainable path for those around you, demonstrating that leadership can be achieved alongside a rich, multi-dimensional life. Through this measured approach, you create lasting impact in your career without neglecting the personal elements that keep you grounded and motivated.

10: Sustaining Career Momentum and Staying Adaptable

Even after you secure a leadership role or gather significant achievements, your journey is not over. Complacency can slow your growth or even derail it entirely. Sustaining career momentum involves continually scanning the horizon for shifts, proactively refreshing your skill set, and nurturing the qualities that brought you success in the first place. At the same time, adaptability remains your most reliable shield against market disruptions or strategic pivots within your organisation.

To sustain momentum, make regular self-assessments part of your professional routine. Every few months, ask yourself: Have I taken on new challenges recently, or have I stayed in a comfort zone? Are my tasks stretching my capabilities? If the answers are lacklustre, it might be time to seek fresh projects or responsibilities. You do not need to wait for an official promotion to remain dynamic. Propose new ideas, volunteer for cross-functional teams, and keep a lookout for areas that need innovation. When leaders stay curious, they seldom run out of ways to evolve.

Adaptability, however, does not come automatically. It requires mental agility and the willingness to pivot when new data arises. You might have planned to perfect one specialised skill, only to learn that the industry is shifting toward a different technology or methodology. Embracing this shift rather than resisting it keeps you ahead. For instance, if your field witnesses a surge in artificial intelligence solutions, an adaptable leader explores how to integrate AI-related knowledge into ongoing projects or even personal studies. Resisting change because you are comfortable with the familiar can lead to professional stagnation.

Another cornerstone of sustained momentum is reviewing and recalibrating your network. People who supported your growth at one stage might help you access different opportunities at another. Meanwhile, forging new relationships can open doors to projects or markets you have never explored. Periodically reach out, share updates, or schedule conversations with a range of contacts. This is not about using people; it is about staying connected in a dynamic environment where alliances often spark unexpected collaborations.

Additionally, maintain a habit of reflection. Record your successes and struggles, not as a way to dwell on the past but to glean lessons for the future. When you keep track of what worked, you refine best practices. When you note what derailed projects, you create a playbook of pitfalls to avoid. This cycle of learning ensures that even if you encounter similar hurdles, you will handle them more effectively next time.

Finally, keep your purpose at the centre of your career. Momentum can lead to busyness, and busyness can make you lose sight of what truly drives you. By periodically revisiting your core motivations, why you began this path, what legacy you hope to leave, you check if your current actions align with your deeper convictions. Leaders who stay anchored in purpose can adapt to external changes without compromising their authenticity. They find ways to innovate while staying true to the principles that shaped their leadership vision from the start.

By sustaining momentum and embedding adaptability into your thinking, you continue growing no matter how seasoned you become. This combination propels you beyond fleeting success, enabling you to maintain an enduring presence at the forefront of your industry. In an environment where everything can shift quickly, you remain agile, relevant, and ready to lead the way through whatever challenges tomorrow brings.

Chapter 9

Health and Fitness, Your Wealth

You've reached one of the most significant chapters of your life's journey, Health and Fitness, Your Wealth. In our fast-paced world, it's easy to forget that true wealth isn't just about money or possessions; it starts with how you feel every day when you wake up. Imagine your life filled with energy, strength, and mental clarity; this is not a distant dream but a reality within your grasp.

Your physical and mental well-being underpins everything you do, from pursuing your career ambitions to nurturing your personal relationships. The healthier you are, the better you can engage with life's challenges and seize its opportunities. Yet, health isn't about rigid diets or gruelling gym sessions; it's about creating sustainable habits that bring joy, purpose, and vitality into your everyday life.

In the pages that follow, you'll explore how simple, consistent movements invigorate your body and mind, discover nutritional strategies that fuel your ambitions, and learn the essential role of rest in replenishing your strength. You'll also gain insight into managing stress, overcoming common fitness hurdles, and creating routines that stick because they resonate with who you are and how you live.

Consider this chapter your personal guide to a richer, healthier, and more fulfilling life. Your body is the only place you truly live; it's time to treat it with the respect and care it deserves and, in doing so, unlock the greatest wealth of all.

1. Your Health, Your True Wealth

You are standing at the threshold of one of the most important decisions in your life: the decision to safeguard and enhance your health. People often speak of building wealth, yet genuine abundance means little if you are constantly low on energy or battling preventable illnesses. Your physical and mental vigour underpins every other pursuit. Strengthen it, and you elevate all aspects of your existence.

Think of health as something you treasure every day. You are not meant to feel sluggish or restricted in your movement. You are designed for strength, resilience and vitality. Your career prospects, personal relationships and self-confidence all flourish when you have consistent energy and stamina. When you respect your body and commit to nurturing it, you set yourself on a path of control, knowing that every domain of your life will benefit.

Cultivating health is not about chasing a perfect image or becoming obsessed with numbers on a scale. Rather, it is about finding practical ways to keep your body active, nourished and well-rested. Dwayne "The Rock" Johnson, for instance, has dedicated himself to a disciplined lifestyle that includes focused workouts and thoughtful nutrition choices. This way of living underpins his ability to switch between film sets and demanding fitness goals while retaining a commanding presence. His dedication is not merely about building muscle; it is a testament to how sustained health practices strengthen your mind as much as your body.

Imagine waking up feeling energised, free from nagging aches and with a clear mindset. That sense of freedom and motivation is truly priceless. It is a form of wealth that nobody can seize from you, provided you guard it with care and discipline. The demands of everyday life, career stresses, family responsibilities, financial pressures, can quickly erode your health if you ignore it. The good news is that you have the power to shield yourself from these damaging forces by prioritising daily routines that promote wellness.

Your mission is to acknowledge that your health is a precious form of wealth. You do this not through radical leaps but by establishing sustainable habits that compound over time. As you learn to plan nutritious meals, commit to movement that suits your lifestyle and schedule rest, you build a fortress of resilience. This foundation gives you the stamina to face challenges without feeling perpetually drained.

Remind yourself that outward success, no matter how large the salary or impressive the accolades, rings hollow when your body is constantly struggling. True wealth is the ability to move with ease, think clearly, rest deeply and feel confident in your own strength. When you adopt the mindset that your health is your most valuable resource, you unlock a powerful shift in how you make choices. Every meal, every hour of sleep and every moment of physical activity becomes an investment in a future that is strong and full of possibility.

In the next section, you will discover the importance of consistent movement and how it galvanises your body and mind, laying a sturdy base for lifelong vitality.

2. The Power of Consistent Movement

Movement is your lifeline to a stronger, more energetic existence. It is not about punishing workouts or punishing yourself when you miss a day. Instead, it is about understanding that consistent activity, in forms you find motivating, awakens your vitality. You have a remarkable body capable of far more than you might realise. By engaging in regular movement, you empower yourself to thrive rather than survive.

Consider David Goggins, a man who transformed himself from being overweight and directionless to becoming one of the most formidable endurance athletes alive. His journey shows that the human body when combined with disciplined training and mental grit, can break boundaries once thought unbreakable. While you do not have to replicate Goggins' extreme feats, you can draw inspiration from his mindset of relentless improvement. Challenge yourself a little more each time, and you forge a body that is ready for life's daily battles.

When you commit to consistent movement, you stimulate more than your muscles and joints. Physical activity releases endorphins that elevate your mood and sharpen your focus, giving you a mental boost. Many people overlook how effectively exercise counters stress and anxiety. When you sweat and push your body in a structured way, you relieve your mind of pent-up tension and replace it with clarity and renewed confidence. Whether it is a brisk walk, a run or a dance session, regular activity fills you with a sense of purpose.

Look at the many forms of movement available: Pilates to build core strength, boxing to release tension or recreational sports to spark friendly competition. You do not have to train like an Olympian to reap powerful rewards. Maybe your best path is a daily walk in the fresh air, soaking up the sun's energy and reminding yourself that you are alive and capable. What matters most is that you choose an activity you can sustain. Movement ceases to feel like a chore when it aligns with your preferences.

Aim for at least half an hour of moderate exercise each day, whether it involves cycling through your neighbourhood, playing a casual football match with friends or following along with a home workout. These consistent habits can become the backbone of your physical well-being. Rather than eyeing short-term goals alone, keep a broader perspective: you want a fitter body not only for the summer but also for long-term resilience.

Celebrate small wins throughout your journey. Perhaps one week, you walk a few extra minutes; the next, you notice your jeans fit more comfortably, or you can climb a flight of stairs without feeling breathless. Each incremental improvement is proof that your commitment pays off. Over time, these achievements accumulate, creating a stronger and more energised version of you.

Next, you will discover how to fuel that active body with the right nourishment so that your exercise efforts are matched by smart dietary choices.

3. Feeding Your Body with Purpose

Your body is a finely tuned system that depends on high-quality fuel to perform at its best. Whether you are sprinting, lifting, playing with your children or concentrating at work, the food you eat sets the tone for your energy levels and long-term health. When you learn to nourish your system well, you create the conditions for consistent performance and vitality.

Tom Brady, the legendary quarterback, is famous for his focus on nutrition. He credits his longevity to a diet built on nutrient-dense, unprocessed foods that sustain his demanding training schedule. While you may not be throwing footballs under stadium lights, you can still borrow from Brady's philosophy: a well-planned diet is not restrictive; it is strategic. Think of it as a solid plan for giving your body what it needs to function optimally rather than a rigid set of prohibitions.

What does this look like in daily life You might focus on fresh produce including colourful vegetables and fruits, lean proteins like fish or chicken and wholesome grains such as quinoa or oats. These choices are full of vitamins, minerals and antioxidants to support immune function and assist muscle recovery. By prioritising these foods, you shift from a mindset of denying yourself guilty pleasures to intentionally fuelling your aspirations. Rather than an endless list of foods you cannot eat, you have an abundance of flavourful, life-giving options.

Be mindful of portion sizes. Many people eat mindlessly, not realising how easily calories can exceed the body's needs. Pay attention to your hunger signals. It is perfectly acceptable to leave food on your plate if your body tells you that you have had enough. Likewise, if you feel real hunger, do not ignore it out of fear of overeating; instead, choose nourishing snacks like nuts, yoghurt or fruit. This balance ensures that your body always has the fuel it requires without being weighed down by excess.

Also, keep an eye on hydration. Your muscles and organs need adequate water to function well, and even mild dehydration can cause you to feel tired and drained. Sip water consistently throughout the day. If you find plain water dull, infuse it with slices of citrus, cucumber or berries to add flavour without chemicals or artificial sweeteners.

Remember that no single diet suits everyone. Bodies differ in metabolic rates, sensitivities and personal preferences. The key is to focus on whole foods, sensible portions and moderation in indulgences. You are not aiming for rigid perfection; you are building a sustainable approach to eating that promotes energy and resilience.

Nourishing yourself properly requires planning. That might mean setting aside time each weekend to prepare meals or learning simple, tasty recipes to help you avoid impulsive junk-food purchases. This planning gives you control, freeing you from last-minute decisions that leave you vulnerable to convenience meals lacking in nutrition.

As you fine-tune your dietary habits, you will find that nutritious food amplifies the benefits of your exercise regimen. Next, discover how sleep, the often overlooked pillar of health, is essential to your ongoing progress.

4. The Unsung Hero Called Sleep

Many people view sleep as a luxury, trimming it down to eke out extra hours for work or entertainment. You might tell yourself that fewer hours of rest will help you fit more into your schedule. In reality, depriving your body of adequate sleep undermines your vitality at the core. If health is your wealth, then sleep is the bank vault protecting that fortune from erosion.

Sleep is far from passive. As you rest, your brain removes toxins, consolidates memories and repairs the day's wear on your body. This process is vital for hormone balance, muscle recovery and cognitive sharpness. Roger Federer, one of tennis's greatest champions, routinely sleeps for ten or more hours every night. He attributes his long career partly to the restorative benefits of uninterrupted rest, which helps him stay agile and mentally alert. While you may not have a tennis star's schedule, adopting a consistent sleep routine can dramatically improve how you feel and function.

Aim for seven to nine hours each night. This is not an act of indulgence; it is a strategic choice to protect your most valuable resources: your energy, your clarity and your resilience. Lack of sleep throws your hormones off balance, leading to mood swings and cravings that derail healthy eating. It also sabotages your exercise progress since your muscles rely on deep sleep for recovery and growth. You might be pushing yourself at the gym or following a strict diet, yet poor rest can nullify many of those efforts.

If you struggle to settle down at night, start by creating a bedtime routine. Dim the lights and avoid screens before bed, as the bright light from devices can trick your brain into thinking it is still daytime. Perhaps read a few pages of an uplifting book or write in a journal to clear your mind. Keep your room cool and limit background noise so that you are not pulled from slumber by minor disturbances. A calm environment signals your brain that it is time to power down.

Consider the effects of caffeine or large meals close to bedtime. Stimulants can keep you wired, and heavy meals can make you feel uncomfortable when lying down. Aim to finish caffeine intake by late afternoon and have your final meal well before sleeping. A soothing cup of herbal tea can help you transition into a calm, restful mindset.

Guard your sleep zealously. Treat your bed as a sanctuary, free from distractions. When you wake up after a night of deep rest, you are setting yourself up for a more productive day, better emotional balance and the energy to meet your health and fitness goals. It is a form of self-respect to grant your body the rest it deserves.

Now that you have seen the critical role sleep plays, we will examine how stress can quietly erode your well-being and what you can do to keep it firmly under control.

5. Mastering Stress for a Stronger Body and Mind

Stress seeps into your life from many directions, often disguised as everyday busyness. You might carry tension in your shoulders from tight deadlines or restless thoughts that disturb your sleep. Though certain stressors are unavoidable, you can maintain your physical and mental strength by mastering stress rather than letting it master you.

Think of your health as a fortress. Stress is the force trying to breach the walls and undermine your defences. Excessive levels of stress trigger hormonal shifts, including the release of cortisol, which can sap your energy, hinder muscle recovery and weaken your immune system. Chronic stress also strains mental resilience, potentially fuelling anxiety or dampening your motivation. Left unchecked, stress can sabotage even the best exercise and nutrition plans.

Arianna Huffington famously collapsed from exhaustion early in her career. That wake-up call prompted her to overhaul her habits and embrace tools like mindfulness, meditation and prioritised rest. By tackling stress head-on, she shielded her overall well-being from the damage caused by unrelenting demands. Her transformation highlights what is possible when you stop dismissing stress as the cost of ambition and begin actively mitigating its impact.

One of the most accessible ways to alleviate stress is through mindful breathing. Inhale slowly, counting to four or five, then exhale for the same duration, focusing your attention on each breath. This simple act of controlled breathing soothes your nervous system, lowering cortisol and helping your mind re-centre. When performed regularly, these mini-sessions build a resilient baseline so that stress does not accumulate to dangerous levels.

Regular exercise is also a proven stress buster. A brisk walk or a session with kettlebells releases tension while releasing mood-lifting endorphins. Furthermore, engaging in activities you enjoy, whether gardening or painting, serves as a psychological break, allowing your mind to reset. Setting boundaries on work obligations, social commitments, and screen time preserves your energy for the pursuits that nourish you rather than drain you.

Another potent method for taming stress is to align your daily actions with your core values. When you understand what truly matters to you, you stop wasting energy on distractions that lead only to frustration. Each day, reflect on what you need to accomplish, but also how you can protect space for self-care and family time. This clarity prevents you from feeling stretched in too many directions at once.

You cannot eliminate every source of stress in your life, but you can choose how you respond to it. By weaving stress-management strategies into your routine, you shield yourself from the detrimental effects of chronic tension. Your body and mind remain strong, ready to handle challenges without depleting your energy reserves. This approach complements your exercise, nutrition and rest, forming a unified strategy to keep you in top form.

Next, you will learn how to build a fitness routine that stands the test of time, enabling you to remain active and determined on your path to lifelong health.

6. Crafting a Fitness Routine That Lasts

A short-lived burst of enthusiasm, followed by eventual burnout, is a common trap when attempting to ramp up your physical activity. You might throw yourself into an extreme programme, only to lose momentum when the novelty wears thin. To break that pattern, you need a fitness approach that integrates well into your life rather than turning it upside down for a few frantic weeks.

Jane Fonda is a prime example of longevity in fitness. Even into her eighties, she remains active, credits regular movement for her enduring vitality and encourages people of every generation to find a routine that suits their specific stage of life. Her philosophy is that consistency trumps short sprints of high-intensity effort. She has shown that a routine balanced between challenge and enjoyment can become a permanent part of your schedule.

Begin your sustainable fitness journey by assessing your current abilities and constraints. Are you juggling long work hours or looking after a family You must be realistic about how much time you can invest each day. Start small, perhaps with 15 minutes of focused exercise. If you have more flexibility, consider 30 minutes or an hour. Over time, your stamina grows, and you can increase your session length or intensity. The key is to build a baseline that does not feel unmanageable.

Variety is essential for longevity. Repeating the same activity daily can lead to boredom and plateauing results. Try mixing strength training, cardiovascular sessions and flexibility exercises. For instance, you could schedule a yoga session on Monday, a run on Wednesday and a strength circuit on Friday. This approach keeps your body guessing, stimulates multiple muscle groups and maintains your interest. It also reduces the risk of overuse injuries since different workouts stress the body in distinct ways.

Rest days matter more than many people acknowledge. You might believe that continuous daily training speeds up progress, yet constant exertion without recovery can result in setbacks like injury or mental exhaustion. Insert rest or lighter sessions into your schedule to allow muscle repair and keep your motivation high. Genuine progress requires balance, not a stubborn refusal to pause.

Track your progress to maintain momentum. Keep a journal or use a fitness app to log achievements such as distance covered, weight lifted or workout frequency. Observing improvements over time reinforces your belief that your efforts pay off. Celebrate these wins, however small, because they signal real growth. If your improvements stall, adjust your routine with new activities or slight increases in intensity.

Finally, recognise that real life will throw disruptions your way. Illness, family obligations or unexpected work demands can disturb your exercise plans. The solution is resilience. Resume your routine as soon as possible, adjusting if you need to. An all-or-nothing mindset is harmful; skipping a workout or two should not lead you to abandon everything. Long-term fitness is shaped by adaptability and patience, not inflexible perfection.

Now, discover how a strong body supports a healthy mind, ensuring that your overall well-being stands on a firm foundation.

7. How Physical Health Fuels Mental Well-Being

Physical fitness and mental health are deeply intertwined. It is easy to compartmentalise them, yet research shows how profoundly exercise, nutrition, and rest influence your emotional resilience. When you care for your body, you are simultaneously nurturing your mind.

Michael Phelps, the most decorated Olympian in history, openly shares his experiences with depression and anxiety. He attributes a large part of his mental wellness to his intensive training routine. Swimming is not just a career for him; it is a form of therapy. Phelps found that pushing himself physically helps him manage stress, silence self-doubt and maintain focus. His journey highlights a crucial lesson: regular, purposeful movement can be a protective shield against emotional turbulence.

When you exercise, your brain releases mood-enhancing chemicals known as endorphins. These chemicals can lift your spirits, reducing anxiety and counteracting low moods. Even a brisk walk outside can clear your mind and refresh your outlook. Meanwhile, if you spend too long in a sedentary slump, your mind may start to spiral into negative thinking. Physical stagnation breeds mental stagnation, making it more difficult to handle daily challenges.

Nutrition also plays a central role in mental well-being. The gut has its own nervous system and significantly impacts how you feel. Foods high in processed sugars or unhealthy fats can lead to erratic energy levels and irritability, affecting your mood. In contrast, a balanced diet rich in whole foods stabilises your energy and supports brain function, helping you tackle problems with greater calm.

Additionally, the restorative power of sleep is not limited to your muscles; it rejuvenates the brain. Adequate sleep fortifies your emotional balance, making you less reactive and more capable of responding rationally to stressors. Conversely, chronic sleep deprivation can escalate anxiety and make daily tasks feel overwhelming. You may find yourself snapping at loved ones or losing concentration at work, all stemming from your body's plea for proper rest.

Managing stress effectively is the final piece linking physical health to mental strength. Physical exercise, mindful breathing and consistent sleep lower the excessive cortisol levels that chip away at your composure. You become more patient, more empathetic and better equipped to handle life's ups and downs when you sustain healthy stress responses.

In essence, your body is not a separate entity from your emotions but a foundation that nourishes or hinders your state of mind. By valuing movement, nutrition and rest, you amplify your capacity to face adversity and remain mentally alert. This synergy between body and mind leads to clarity and self-assurance, equipping you to deal with everyday obstacles without feeling perpetually drained.

Next, we will tackle the hurdles that often stand in the way of achieving optimum health, exploring solutions to keep you on track when challenges arise.

8. Overcoming Common Obstacles on Your Health Journey

Pursuing robust health and fitness is fulfilling, yet you will encounter stumbling blocks. You might lose motivation, feel pressed for time or grapple with injuries. Understanding these hurdles and how to surmount them prevents you from abandoning your goals. Whenever a challenge threatens your progress, you have the chance to adapt and strengthen your resolve.

Simone Biles, a world-renowned gymnast, offers a powerful example of resilience. Despite facing injuries and immense scrutiny, she repeatedly returns to the mat with unshakable focus. Her story reminds you that setbacks, though frustrating, are opportunities to discover new strategies, whether by refining your technique or giving yourself the rest you need. Injuries require patience; pushing through pain can cause lasting harm. Instead, heed your body's signals and consult professionals when problems arise.

Time constraints are another significant barrier. Work demands, family obligations and unexpected errands can erode your exercise plans and disrupt healthy eating. The solution often lies in rethinking your schedule. Instead of insisting on a single long workout, split it into short sessions throughout the day. Ten minutes of focused exercise in the morning and again in the evening can still bolster your fitness over time. Planning meals in advance or preparing ingredients beforehand enables you to grab nutritious options quickly, rather than opting for fast-food items when you are busy.

Lack of motivation can creep up on you if you do not see rapid results or if life's daily stresses diminish your enthusiasm. Reignite your motivation by visualising why you started in the first place. Remember the energy levels you yearn for, the clothes that fit comfortably or the freedom of moving without strain. Sometimes, teaming up with a friend or a local fitness group can add accountability, making you feel part of a supportive community. Celebrating small wins, like your first three-kilometre run, reinforces your sense of accomplishment and keeps you encouraged.

Plateaus can also dampen your spirit when progress stalls and the scale, mirror or performance metrics remain unchanged. Rather than interpreting this as defeat, see it as your body's way of telling you it is ready for something new. Introduce a different exercise: switch the treadmill for a rowing machine or swap your usual workout for a circuit routine. Similarly, consider minor adjustments to your meals, focusing on nutrient density. These strategic shifts jolt your body out of stagnation and restart your momentum.

Lastly, be prepared for life's curveballs. Travel, family emergencies and social commitments will test your adherence to a health routine. Embrace flexibility, not rigidity. On holiday, pick active excursions or mindful meals. When life demands your time unexpectedly, do what you can, however modest, and avoid the trap of assuming you have failed altogether. Resilience involves adapting rather than giving up.

With the ability to sidestep or reduce these obstacles, you become equipped to continue your health journey. Up next, explore the power of embracing outdoor activities and sports to diversify your routine and invigorate your spirit.

9. Exploring Outdoors, Embracing Sports

Stepping outside for physical activity offers a refreshing break from indoor routines. When you run, cycle or hike in natural surroundings, you soak in sunlight and breathe in fresh air, both of which enhance your mood and overall well-being. Research suggests that exercising in green spaces reduces tension and increases motivation, leaving you feeling energised and mentally revitalised.

You might recognise Sir Ranulph Fiennes as a prime example of pushing boundaries in nature. Called the world's greatest living explorer, he has led expeditions across polar ice caps, scorching deserts and treacherous waters, all powered by sheer determination and a bond with the outdoors. While you may not be crossing Antarctica, you can still discover a taste of that same spirit by engaging in local outdoor pursuits, trail walks, weekend treks or even team sports on open fields. These experiences nurture both your body and your sense of wonder.

Outdoor activities come with unique benefits beyond indoor workouts. Natural landscapes often involve varied terrains such as hills or uneven paths, forcing your muscles to adapt in ways that a treadmill session might not. This challenge can improve balance and coordination. Exposure to sunlight also helps your body synthesise vitamin D, essential for bone health and immunity. The experience can feel less monotonous since each outing can present new sights and sounds.

You could also explore a sport that resonates with you. Cricket, tennis or football fosters a sense of camaraderie and injects an element of fun. Playing in a team can sharpen your social skills, teach cooperation and provide a welcome change from solo workouts. If organised sports feel intimidating, try joining a casual local league or gathering a few friends for a friendly match. It is not about winning trophies; it is about staying engaged while reaping the fitness rewards.

Of course, being outdoors means taking precautions. Dress suitably for the weather, keep hydrated and remain aware of your surroundings. If you decide to venture into more demanding settings, mountainous regions or long-distance cycling routes, take time to build up your endurance and consider practising with shorter sessions first. Gradual progression ensures that you enjoy your adventure without causing undue strain or risking injury.

When you embrace nature or pick up a sport, you are adding vitality to your life. The fresh environment sparks your enthusiasm, and you are more likely to be consistent in these activities. There is something undeniably liberating about feeling the ground beneath your feet and the breeze on your face, reminding you that fitness can be a joyful pursuit rather than a chore. The outdoors and sports broaden your perspective, encouraging you to push limits with a spirit of curiosity and play.

Now, we turn to the impact of modern technology on health and fitness. You will learn how to harness its advantages while avoiding the pitfalls that might hamper your progress.

10. Transformational Stories: Real People, Real Results

Nothing motivates like witnessing real-life success stories of those who have reshaped their lives through determined health and fitness efforts. When you hear about individuals who faced obstacles yet emerged stronger, it reinforces the belief that you can achieve remarkable results, too. Every person's journey is unique, yet the lessons are universal.

Joe Wicks, known as The Body Coach, started as a personal trainer without much recognition. Through a relentless commitment to making nutrition and fitness accessible, he turned his platform into a global sensation. While the online workouts and meal plans he shares have helped countless people improve their health, his underlying message is what truly resonates: consistency and simplicity beat crash diets and short-lived boot camps every time. His own transformation from an unknown trainer to an influential health leader highlights how sustained effort makes a profound impact.

Likewise, Dame Kelly Holmes overcame multiple injuries and personal struggles on her path to Olympic glory in the 1500 and 800 metres. At one point, she nursed stress fractures in both legs, yet she never surrendered her dream. Her achievements demonstrate that genuine progress often involves setbacks, mental battles and plenty of patience. She eventually claimed double gold at 34, proving that determination and resilience make age and adversity less limiting than many assume.

Meanwhile, many ordinary individuals share equally meaningful stories, even if they do not earn headlines. Perhaps a mother of three who prioritised morning runs so she could maintain enough energy to keep up with her children. Or a retiree who started a daily walking group to stay connected and fend off loneliness. These personal victories illustrate how your environment, previous setbacks or even your age do not have to be permanent barriers.

Key themes emerge from these transformations. First, discipline does not mean perfection. Both high-profile athletes and everyday heroes often fall off track, but they realign themselves swiftly, never straying too far from their goals. Second, having a community or supportive circle, be it an online group or close friends, eases the burden of going it alone. Third, a sense of purpose fuels consistency; when you link your health goals to something deeper, whether performing better at work or setting an example for family, you are more likely to persist.

These stories remind you that health is not merely about aesthetics. It is about proving to yourself that you are capable of more than you thought possible, physically and mentally. Each time you choose to move, eat healthily or rest properly, you write your own success story. The victories might be incremental at first, but they add up to a powerful transformation in how you feel, act and view your potential.

As we end this chapter, let the lessons of these real-life accounts echo in your mind. Your health journey is not a short sprint; it is a lifelong marathon that rewards dedication, resilience and optimism. These qualities, once cultivated, can enrich every dimension of your life, reminding you daily that your health is indeed your wealth.

Chapter 10

Communication: Your Leadership Tool

In your journey as a leader, nothing is more powerful or transformative than your ability to communicate effectively. Words carry weight, and how you deliver them can either lift your team to new heights or leave them disconnected and uncertain. Communication isn't merely about transferring information from one person to another; it's about forging connections, building trust, and inspiring action. When you master the art of genuine communication, you tap into a strength that will elevate your leadership and solidify your influence.

Throughout this chapter, you'll uncover how to use communication not only to clarify your vision but to energise your team and foster true collaboration. You'll see how legendary leaders have used words with precision, sincerity, and authenticity to inspire nations, steer companies, and change lives. By mastering both what you say and how you say it, you'll create an atmosphere of openness, trust, and mutual respect. This isn't about impressive speeches or clever writing; it's about speaking truthfully, clearly, and intentionally so that your words resonate deeply and produce lasting results.

1. Why Communication Matters for Leaders

Effective communication is the force that underpins every successful leader's legacy. You might have a brilliant strategy and a competent team, but if your words fail to connect, you will struggle to rally your people or influence those around you. Communication goes far beyond relaying facts. It involves energising others, winning trust, and creating a bond that fosters cooperation. When you speak or write with clarity, you help people latch on to your vision; when you truly listen, you show them you value their insights. In leadership, these elements cannot be separated from the task of motivating individuals to achieve common goals.

Winston Churchill's wartime leadership is a fitting example of how communication can galvanise a nation. Churchill's speeches were not passive recountings of events; they were calls to courage, laced with sincerity and delivered in a measured tone that instilled both hope and resilience. He did not flood his audience with unnecessary complexity. Instead, he selected phrases that captured the essence of perseverance. His communications carried an undercurrent of conviction, making listeners feel they were an indispensable part of the mission. What you can learn from Churchill is that your ability to move hearts begins with sincerity, clarity, and a keen sense of timing. You do not need dramatic theatrics; you need language that rings true.

Communication also drives trust. People follow leaders they trust, and that trust often emerges when they feel heard. To achieve this, you must be prepared to engage with genuine interest. That includes showing empathy, maintaining appropriate eye contact, and demonstrating consistent follow-through on what you say. This is as vital in a conference room as it is on a shop floor. Whether you are addressing a room full of executives or having a one-on-one meeting with a team member, your willingness to communicate honestly builds relationships that withstand pressure.

Such honest discourse must go both ways. Talking is only half the equation. If you fail to make space for feedback and questions, you risk alienating those who have vital contributions. Instead of delivering top-down pronouncements, invite open dialogue. Ask for opinions, then act on the insights shared. This builds a cycle: you communicate your vision, you let others share their experiences, and together, you refine the direction. It also cements your credibility because people see you are not hiding behind pompous speeches or ignoring their concerns.

To commit to clear communication, refine your messages until they are concise, and adapt them to the people you are addressing. Doing so eliminates the danger of confusion. Speak with conviction, and do not let filler words dilute your point. Don't drown your listeners in complicated jargon; instead, value straightforward language. Let them see you believe every word you say.

You have the responsibility and privilege of setting the tone for how people relate to each other. Communication is not an afterthought or an optional extra. It is at the very heart of leadership. Embrace it, hone it, and watch the transformative effect it has on your team's trust, alignment, and morale.

2. Mastering Verbal Expression

Verbal communication may appear simple, utter words, and someone hears them. Yet you know that is rarely enough to drive real impact. In many cases, your team or audience remembers how you spoke more than the raw content of your statements. Were you rushed? Did your words convey passion or gloom? Were you repetitive or straight to the point? When you speak, you have an opportunity to project your vision with conviction. Doing this well means paying attention to tone, pacing, and the structure of your words. Verbal expression is about giving weight to each phrase so that your listeners walk away with a clear and compelling understanding of your message.

One powerful illustration is Ronald Reagan, often lauded as "The Great Communicator." Reagan's speeches were direct and heartfelt. He had a knack for painting images that made national policy resonate on a personal level. His approach combined optimism, straightforward vocabulary, and an unwavering tone that conveyed belief. He did not overcomplicate his language. You, too, can learn from this: speak in a style that reflects your natural self while considering your audience. If you try to sound like someone else or slip into language that feels unnatural, your authenticity suffers. Authenticity resonates far more than any carefully rehearsed script.

A strong delivery requires intentionality. Think of your favourite public speakers; they breathe at suitable intervals, pause to let important ideas land and maintain measured pacing. When you rush through your words, your core points get lost. If you mumble or fill every gap with "um" or "er," your authority shrinks. Instead, let silence be your ally. A brief pause can highlight a key statement. Your listeners will lean in, sensing the importance of what you're about to reveal.

Knowing your audience helps you shape your message. A technical briefing for engineers can hold more complex terms, but if you address volunteers who know less about the subject, adapt your language to avoid confusion. This is not about watering down your material but making sure you guide your audience to keep up without feeling patronised. When you match your speech to the group's knowledge and concerns, you bridge gaps in understanding and keep them engaged.

Another dimension of verbal mastery is emotional resonance. Hard facts have their place, but humans respond powerfully to stories and vivid examples. If you want to rally your team, inject relevant stories that show why your goal matters. Share a small success story about a colleague whose improvement demonstrates how your strategy makes sense. Show others the human face of your objectives. This helps them imagine how they, too, can play a part.

Finally, you must rehearse. While spontaneity has its moments, rehearsal ensures you know your material well enough to deliver confidently. Practising your verbal delivery can reveal clumsy phrases or unclear sections. You can correct them before anyone else hears them. When you step up to speak, aim to be clear and purposeful. Verbal expression, when honed, can transform a mundane announcement into an inspiring charge.

3. The Silent Edge of Nonverbal Cues

You communicate beyond words every time you step into a room. Your stance, gestures, facial expressions, and even the tilt of your head all signal messages to those watching. While you might plan your spoken remarks meticulously, your nonverbal behaviour can reinforce or undermine what you say in seconds. If your voice projects warmth but your posture radiates impatience, people pick up on the mismatch. Nonverbal communication can be a secret weapon or a hidden minefield for leaders.

Take Margaret Thatcher, the former British Prime Minister often dubbed "The Iron Lady." Known for her poised posture and controlled gestures, she exuded authority and composure. Even when she faced tough questioning, her upright stance and unwavering gaze signalled confidence. She rarely needed to shout; her demeanour handled much of the work. By contrast, a slouched figure or continuously shifting eyes broadcast tension and uncertainty. It's not about pretending. It's about aligning your outward signals with your real convictions so your presence feels authentic and self-assured.

Maintaining eye contact is a particularly powerful nonverbal tool. A leader who rarely looks people in the eye comes across as distracted or dishonest. On the other hand, a steady but respectful gaze suggests openness and credibility. The key is moderation. You don't need to lock eyes until it becomes intimidating. Look at someone long enough to show genuine focus before moving on, especially in group scenarios where multiple people need your attention.

Body language also includes the position of your arms and hands. Crossed arms often read as defensive or standoffish, regardless of your words. Meanwhile, open hands and palms can indicate sincerity. When you gesture while explaining an idea, it should look natural, not forced. If your arms wave around erratically, the emphasis may overshadow your point. Keep your hand movements purposeful: emphasise the moment a central idea emerges, but don't overdo it until it distracts from the message.

Your facial expressions count as well. Smiling at the right moments conveys warmth and puts others at ease, but a smile that pops up at the wrong time (like when discussing something serious) can erode credibility. Watch how your face reacts as you listen. Do you appear irritated or bored? Perhaps you're unaware of a slight frown or a rolling eye. People notice fleeting expressions and draw conclusions from them. If you find yourself scowling unintentionally, you might be sending signals that clash with your intended message.

To harness nonverbal communication, it can be helpful to record yourself speaking or get feedback from a colleague who observes you in action. You can then notice any disconnect between what you say and how you look while saying it. Through honest feedback and a little self-awareness, you can refine your body language until it supports, rather than sabotages, your words. The silent edge is a powerful part of leadership. It's often the unspoken details, not the big speeches, that shape how others perceive you.

4. How to Listen and Build Trust

Leaders often get spotlighted for oratory gifts, but your listening ability is equally, if not more, crucial. Listening fosters trust. When team members see you give your complete attention, their confidence grows, and they feel safe to share their thoughts. Good listening is the bedrock of healthy communication: you show respect, gather insights, and prove that everyone's voice counts.

Picture a town-hall meeting where a manager fields employee questions. If the manager repeatedly interrupts or rushes to find quick fixes, the employees' trust wanes. By contrast, a leader who sits forward nods genuinely and asks clarifying questions before replying creates a setting that encourages honest dialogue. That team leaves the meeting feeling respected and empowered, even if final decisions remain the same. The difference is they have been heard.

Listening is not a passive activity. It demands your full engagement. You must switch off your mental noise, those opinions forming in your head as you half-listen, and be present in the moment. If you multitask, it sends a signal that you rank your conversation partner lower than your smartphone notifications or your list of tasks. Even if you believe you can juggle them all, the other person senses your divided focus. That robs the conversation of the authenticity trust needs to flourish.

Empathy is central to real listening. You do not have to agree with every idea. However, you should aim to see issues from the speaker's angle. Ask them open-ended questions, like "Help me understand how you came to that conclusion." This approach invites further explanation, breaks down guard walls, and offers deeper knowledge about the speaker's viewpoint. It also reassures them that you take their words seriously.

Paraphrasing is another effective technique. After they finish, reflect back on your interpretation of their message: "So you're saying that these new shifts are affecting your family responsibilities, did I understand that correctly?" This clarifies possible misunderstandings and shows you care enough to restate their points. Equally important is your follow-up, which might be an action you take or a piece of relevant information you share later. These gestures prove you haven't neglected what they told you.

Don't wait until a quarterly review or formal event to exercise your listening skills. In a quick hallway chat or a five-minute phone call, make the same effort to tune in fully. The more consistent you are, the more people trust that their words truly matter. Over time, this fosters an atmosphere in which people dare to share their best ideas or voice concerns without fear of dismissal. That honest feedback loop propels a team to high performance because people feel genuinely appreciated.

When you listen, you receive more than data. You give people the confidence to take ownership, to step forward and innovate, knowing that their leader values their input. Mastering the art of listening is a huge leap toward building a trustworthy, high-functioning team that meets challenges head-on.

5. Communication Styles that Drive Results

Each person has a preferred communication style shaped by upbringing, personality, and experiences. As a leader, part of your role is recognising these styles, both your own and those of people around you, and adapting so messages are received as intended. Common categories include passive, aggressive, passive-aggressive, and assertive styles. While none of us are confined to a single style at all times, you often have a default pattern that surfaces under pressure. Learning how to shift from less effective habits to more assertive, respectful patterns can elevate both your personal brand and your team's outcomes.

A passive communicator may hesitate to speak up or share opinions directly, hoping to avoid conflict. They might appear agreeable but carry underlying frustrations. Such leaders can struggle when firm decisions are needed, leaving others uncertain about directions. On the opposite end, an aggressive communicator is apt to dominate conversations and may use confrontational language to push their agenda. Although aggression can temporarily show force, it often destroys trust and morale. People may comply for fear of repercussions but give minimal genuine support.

Passive-aggressive styles are trickier. This might involve sarcasm, backhanded remarks, or agreements made but never properly executed. A leader who resorts to this approach fosters tension behind the scenes. People interpret the signals as manipulative or two-faced, which sows mistrust. None of these three styles are conducive to a healthy, productive environment.

The assertive style, however, is widely regarded as the ideal balance, helping you voice your viewpoints and requests while respecting others. An assertive communicator speaks with clarity, stands by their convictions, and remains open to feedback. This fosters mutual respect because people see honesty delivered with courtesy. Although every scenario is different, the leader who employs assertiveness sets a tone of openness and fairness. This approach can be particularly helpful in negotiations or conflict resolution.

You can train yourself to shift closer to assertiveness. If you have a habit of passivity, start by speaking up in low-stakes moments, volunteer an idea or share a concern earlier than you normally would. If you lean towards aggression, practise pausing to ask, "Is my tone or language overshadowing the message?" Passive-aggressive tendencies can be tackled by addressing issues directly rather than through sideways comments.

A helpful technique is noticing the results your communication yields. Do your direct reports leave discussions feeling guided, or do they seem anxious? If you suspect the latter, re-evaluate your style. Strive for clarity in each exchange: present your stance, invite the other perspective, and find common ground. The outcome is not about proving who's right; it's about reaching an actionable resolution. When you master an assertive style, you stimulate creativity, reduce misunderstandings, and encourage others to step up. The energy shifts from a power struggle to a collaborative partnership, where the real winners are the projects and the team spirit.

6. Becoming Assertive While Staying Respectful

Stepping into assertiveness can feel daunting if you're used to either avoiding confrontation or bulldozing your way to outcomes. Many think that you either let people walk over you or you become pushy. Yet assertiveness sits squarely in the middle: you can speak your mind without diminishing the other person's worth. It's about standing firm for your needs or decisions while making space for someone else's viewpoint. Mastering this equilibrium often starts with clarifying your priorities and boundaries. By doing so, you approach discussions knowing what you stand for and how flexible you can be.

Imagine you run a small team, and a member frequently ignores agreed deadlines, causing delays in the wider project. A passive approach might see you quietly picking up the slack, building frustration that never surfaces until you explode. An aggressive style might lead you to publicly scold them, humiliating them and possibly souring the team climate. The assertive path would be to have a private conversation, clearly outline the missed deadlines' effects, and invite the person to explain their challenges. You firmly insist on accountability while remaining open to solutions. This approach is respectful yet unmistakable in its stance.

Respectful assertiveness hinges on using "I" statements rather than blameful language. Compare "You never do what's asked" to "I've noticed tasks aren't completed on time, and it's creating backlogs for the rest of us." The second phrasing points to the issue without attacking the individual's character. It also sets the stage for collaboration: "Let's figure out how to fix this." This method reduces defensiveness because you avoid labelling them; you focus on the behaviours and consequences. You then propose a path forward, giving them ownership of their response.

Tone is equally important. A calm, steady tone conveys confidence. If your voice is too quiet or wavering, you may appear unsure. If it's too loud or harsh, the other person may feel threatened. Aim for an even pace, articulate your words, and hold a posture that aligns with the seriousness of the topic. Keep your shoulders relaxed, maintain balanced eye contact, and refrain from fidgeting. If you sense yourself tensing up, take a short pause to regain composure. Slowing down can prevent you from veering into aggression or retreating into passivity.

Assertiveness also involves a willingness to accept feedback. If you expect others to respect your needs, you must display the same willingness. When they share their perspective, listen sincerely. You could discover valuable information, for instance, maybe they have constraints you were unaware of. That insight can help you adjust and find workable solutions. An assertive approach is not a monologue; it's a conversation that respects both sides. This balance establishes a working climate where people feel comfortable voicing issues before they balloon. They know you will handle concerns directly but fairly. Over time, your leadership reputation grows, and your team learns to engage in honest, result-focused communication.

7. Persuasion and Public Speaking

Public speaking can be a thrilling opportunity or a dreaded chore. As a leader, you'll often speak to groups, pitching ideas, outlining strategies, or rallying people around new initiatives. Effective public speaking is about persuasion, convincing others to share in your vision or at least give it serious thought. Your confidence on stage or behind a podium sets the tone for how your message lands. If you appear timid or hesitant, your audience wonders if you believe your own words. Conversely, a strong, well-paced delivery can kindle the crowd's enthusiasm.

One of the finest examples is Martin Luther King Jr., whose "I Have a Dream" speech stands among history's greatest orations. King's measured cadence, evocative language, and fervent conviction captured the hearts of thousands that day and millions since. Granted, you might not have such a monumental cause at every presentation, but the structure of clarity, emotional appeal, and unwavering commitment applies to any scenario, be it unveiling a quarterly plan or addressing an industry conference.

Preparation is non-negotiable. You can't speak persuasively if you're still guessing your own data. Structure your talk around a simple skeleton: an opening that hooks attention, a concise explanation of the key problem or idea, and a conclusion that energises the room. If relevant, weave in a brief story or a personal anecdote that exemplifies the difference your proposal can make. Stories stick in the mind far longer than abstract concepts. They connect the intellectual with the emotional, giving life to your main points.

Eye contact and body language, which we covered earlier, remain crucial. Scan the audience, don't stare at a single individual or note card, and keep your posture upright. Aim for an even pace: not so slow that people lose interest, not so fast that they struggle to follow. Your voice should carry a sense of authority. Speaking too softly suggests insecurity while shouting can feel confrontational. Listen to good speakers, whether through recordings or live events and adapt their strengths to your style, not to imitate them but to refine your own approach.

If you're dealing with public speaking nerves, a proven tactic is visualising success. Before you step on stage, picture yourself delivering an impactful talk, hearing the applause, and seeing nods of understanding. This mental rehearsal can reduce anxiety and boost your composure. Another method is to start with a brief pause before diving into your first words. That small moment allows you to gather your energy and settle instead of rushing in breathlessly.

In the end, the success of your talk is measured by whether your audience grasps and remembers your message. Persuasion occurs when they not only understand what you said but also feel a spark to act or change their perspective. When you connect your facts, passion, and structure cohesively, you stand a strong chance of influencing the decisions and emotions of those who hear you speak.

8. Writing to Influence and Lead

Though public speeches grab headlines, the written word remains a cornerstone of leadership communication. Emails, proposals, memos, and articles carry your message beyond spoken interactions. Clear writing influences how others perceive your expertise and organisation. It also becomes a permanent record of your thought processes. When you draft a written message, you must be aware that each sentence reflects your professionalism and your mission's essence.

Communication: Your Leadership Tool

Lee Iacocca, the visionary behind Chrysler's revival, was renowned for his succinct and compelling memos that rallied employees to turn the company around. The trick was not flamboyance but clarity. He wrote in plain language yet chose words carefully to emphasise urgency and align everyone behind a shared objective. You can do the same. A well-structured message is easier to follow, fosters trust and clarifies responsibilities.

Begin by determining your goal. Are you informing, convincing, or calling for action? If your email is to update staff on procedural changes, keep it tight. State the change, how it affects them, and the date it takes effect. If you need approval or buy-in, present a concise argument that answers potential questions. Include reasons why your recommendation matters and steps for how they can engage. In short, let the reader see your logic, then help them know precisely what to do next.

Structure is key. A strong subject line or title signals your main topic. A short opening paragraph states the purpose. Subsequent paragraphs expand on details, supporting facts, or instructions. Conclude by reiterating the action or summarising the significance. When your structure flows logically, readers can scan for the sections that matter to them or read in full if they want more depth. In any case, they won't be lost in rambling explanations.

While you might occasionally need formal language, do not bury meaning under ornate phrases. Jargon can alienate those without insider knowledge. Keep your wording crisp. Rather than bury crucial points halfway through a paragraph, place them where they stand out. If you must present a list of items, lead in with a line explaining each item's relevance.

You do not want your text to feel overwhelming or poorly organised.

Proofreading is non-negotiable. Spelling errors and grammar missteps make you seem careless, particularly if you hold a senior position. Find a systematic way to check your work; reading it aloud can help catch awkward rhythms or repeated phrases. Asking a colleague to read a sensitive memo can highlight any unintended tones or missing elements.

Lastly, be mindful of emotional cues in writing. Without vocal inflections or facial expressions, your words might sound harsher or colder than intended. Use respectful language and a courteous sign-off. If you need to address a sensitive topic, like a performance issue, choose your words with empathy in mind. Writing to influence is about clarity, brevity, respect, and purpose. Mastering these elements amplifies your leadership voice and helps your plans take root even when you are not physically present to explain them.

9. Bridging Cultural Gaps

In a world where teams often span multiple countries or regions, your communication challenges expand. Differing languages, cultural traditions, and communication norms can introduce complexities that test your leadership capacity. Yet, if you handle these differences well, you can form a cohesive team enriched by varied viewpoints. If you handle them poorly, misunderstandings can derail progress and disrupt trust. Cultural awareness is not about becoming an expert in every tradition but about approaching differences with respect and a willingness to adapt.

Communication: Your Leadership Tool

Imagine you have team members based in London, Tokyo, and New York. A single approach to delivering feedback might not fit all. In some cultures, direct feedback, though polite, may be common. Elsewhere, people might communicate critiques in roundabout or softer ways to prevent embarrassment. If your style is blunt, you risk offending those who interpret frankness as aggression. Conversely, if you dance around an issue with a more direct culture, they might see it as dishonesty. By knowing and respecting these distinctions, you can adjust your tone accordingly, preserving harmony without weakening your message.

Listening becomes even more valuable here. Invite team members to clarify how they prefer to communicate concerns. Some might prefer detailed documentation, while others may find lengthy documents cumbersome. A few might gravitate towards personal conversations rather than group discussions. This knowledge should shape your strategy so everyone feels included rather than subjecting them to a one-size-fits-all method. This is not about pandering but about meeting individuals where they are so the entire team remains effective.

Language barriers can also complicate matters. If English is not a colleague's first language, be mindful to avoid idiomatic expressions or slang that they may not recognise. Offer to repeat or rephrase points in simpler terms. Doing so saves them from feeling embarrassed or left behind. If you are in a position where people speak multiple languages, encouraging them to use translation tools or providing translated summaries of key documents can make a big difference. Small gestures that acknowledge linguistic hurdles can boost morale and productivity.

Cultural differences can also appear in nonverbal cues. Eye contact, personal space, and acceptable forms of address can vary widely. While one culture might see persistent eye contact as a sign of trust, another might regard prolonged staring as aggressive. Remain observant and willing to shift your approach. Adaptation does not erode your authenticity. Instead, it shows that you respect your colleagues enough to treat them in ways that resonate within their cultural framework.

Remember, bridging cultural gaps is an ongoing process. Learn from each interaction and remain humble. Ask for input on how you can improve cross-cultural communication. When you set the example of open-mindedness and courtesy, your team is more likely to follow. Ultimately, the effort you invest in understanding cultural nuances repays itself in stronger, more united collaboration that taps into everyone's strengths.

10. Resolving Conflict through Clear Dialogue

No matter how skilled you are, conflicts arise. Varying personalities, clashing priorities, and misunderstandings can rapidly escalate if left unaddressed. As a leader, it falls on you to guide disputes toward resolution without damaging trust. This is not about avoiding conflict altogether but about knowing how to navigate differences swiftly and fairly. Effective communication stands as your primary instrument to calm tensions, reveal true concerns, and map out a positive route forward.

Visualise a scenario where two high-performing colleagues disagree on how to allocate limited resources. Each believes their project deserves priority. If you ignore the tension, it might flare into open hostility, with each party undermining the other. Alternatively, you can call a meeting where everyone states their perspective. Your job is to keep the discussion on topic and free from personal attacks. A well-handled debate can reveal creative compromises that neither side had spotted alone, often strengthening team unity rather than weakening it.

Begin by giving each person a fair chance to articulate the root of the conflict. This includes acknowledging any underlying personal or emotional factors that might be amplifying the dispute. Ask clarifying questions such as, "What outcome would you see as ideal?" or "How does this affect your ability to meet goals?" By prompting them to focus on the broader impact and potential solutions, you steer the discussion away from blame games. You must remain neutral, refraining from taking sides prematurely.

Offer empathy but remain solution-oriented. Phrases like, "I understand your frustration; let's see how we can fix this," show you do not dismiss their feelings. Summarise each side's points to confirm understanding: "So you need these funds because your campaign deadline is tight, while the other side requires them to maintain service quality. Is that correct?" Re-stating shows you are listening, and it diminishes the chance of confusion. Then encourage brainstorming: "What are all possible ways we can use these resources effectively for both needs?"

When you facilitate respectful dialogue, team members sense your fair-mindedness. This increases their willingness to reach a compromise. Sometimes, you might suggest a temporary pilot approach, splitting resources or adjusting timelines to balance both priorities. If you must decide alone, do so after hearing all parties thoroughly. Deliver your choice clearly and explain your reasoning so no one suspects hidden agendas.

Finally, confirm the new plan and any follow-up tasks that will keep everyone on track. This approach, though more time-consuming than delivering a decree from on high, ensures buy-in. People who see that their ideas were thoughtfully examined are more likely to accept outcomes, even if those outcomes are not exactly what they initially hoped for. Conflict resolution done well can build stronger bonds and reveal better ways to collaborate, turning friction into a catalyst for improvement rather than a persistent sore point.

Chapter 11

Flow: The Key to Peak Performance

Every day, you face a battle between productivity and distraction. Your responsibilities pile up, and interruptions relentlessly tug at your attention. Yet, within this chaos, there's a powerful state of mind called flow that offers a path to extraordinary performance. Flow isn't a mysterious phenomenon reserved solely for elite performers or artists; it's a tangible mental state where your skills perfectly align with the task at hand. Imagine becoming so engrossed in your work that time disappears, stress fades away, and every action feels effortless. This chapter is your roadmap to understanding and intentionally accessing this profound state to elevate your performance across all areas of life.

Psychologist Mihaly Csikszentmihalyi first identified the concept of flow, defining it as the sweet spot where challenge meets capability. When you're in flow, you're neither overwhelmed nor bored; you're energised, completely focused, and deeply engaged in what you're doing. Consider the example of Usain Bolt, who described how he would tune out distractions and feel completely connected with the moment during his historic sprints. When Bolt spoke about these races, he wasn't merely describing athletic achievement; he was highlighting the transformative power of being fully present and immersed in one's task.

Flow matters profoundly because it not only elevates your performance but enhances your overall satisfaction and resilience. When you emerge from a state of deep focus, you're left feeling fulfilled, energised, and ready to face new challenges. Cultivating flow regularly demonstrates that your potential often lies untapped, waiting patiently to be unlocked. Whether tackling complex projects at work, learning new skills, or engaging in physical activities that match your abilities, flow is accessible and waiting for you.

In the pages that follow, you'll explore the science behind flow and uncover practical methods for achieving and sustaining this powerful state. You'll learn how ordinary tasks can become extraordinary experiences, transforming your approach to work, relationships, and personal goals. Ultimately, embracing flow is your gateway to heightened creativity, resilience, and genuine fulfilment, a powerful tool for redefining success on your terms.

1. The Meaning of Flow and Why It Matters

You stand at a crossroads between productivity and distraction each day. On one side, you have your ever-expanding to-do list; on the other side lurks every possible interruption. When you tap into flow, you position yourself for peak performance. Flow is not a random stroke of luck, nor is it reserved for elite athletes. It is the state where your mind and skill converge perfectly, and you feel so immersed in the task that time fades away. This chapter is about harnessing that power deliberately so you can excel in all you do.

Psychologist Mihaly Csikszentmihalyi introduced the concept of flow, describing it as the mental sweet spot where the difficulty of a task meets your ability. You neither

Flow: The Key to Peak Performance

feel overwhelmed nor bored; you feel energised, focused, and at one with your efforts. Usain Bolt spoke candidly about these moments during his record-breaking sprints. When you witness a champion like Bolt talk about tuning out noise, stress, and distractions, he is describing complete immersion in the present moment. In such a state, your entire being is directed toward the target, every movement seamless.

Why does flow matter to you, though? First, it boosts your achievement levels. You will discover a dynamic surge in energy, enabling you to handle tasks more efficiently. Second, flow is associated with greater satisfaction. When you finish a session of deep focus, you walk away fulfilled, not drained. Third, cultivating flow supports mental resilience. Knowing you can achieve such concentration in your work or hobbies reminds you that your potential often lies dormant, waiting to be activated.

You do not need to be a professional athlete or a creative genius to access flow. You have the capacity to experience it, whether you are tackling a challenging project at the office, learning a musical instrument, or even engaging in physical exercise that matches your level of skill. The key is to approach your tasks with clarity, focus, and a suitable level of challenge. When you focus on tasks just beyond your comfort zone, you stretch your abilities and feed your curiosity. That state of expansion is precisely where flow can flourish.

Recognising the significance of flow is essential because it offers you a fresh perspective on how to engage with life's demands. Instead of viewing each day as a random list of chores, you begin seeing tasks as opportunities for deeper engagement. Flow becomes more than a fleeting high; it becomes a skill you can train yourself to reach. This chapter will guide you through the science and psychology of flow, shedding light on conditions that spark flow and methods to sustain it. Embrace the possibility that you can transform ordinary tasks into peak experiences and revolutionise how you approach work, relationships, and personal goals.

Ultimately, flow is your gateway to elevating both performance and happiness. It is a path that promises deeper creativity, increased resilience, and a profound sense of accomplishment. Once you unlock flow, you equip yourself with a powerful tool that can reshape your outlook on any pursuit, fuelling a life defined by motivation, mastery, and authentic enthusiasm.

2. The Science Behind Flow and Its Mental Rewards

You may think flow is merely a mystical concept, but it has deep scientific roots. Researchers have spent decades analysing why your brain feels so entirely absorbed in certain activities. Flow sits at the intersection of neuroscience and psychology, activated when you meet a meaningful challenge with sufficient skill and intense focus. This balance sparks a unique chain reaction in your brain, releasing chemicals like dopamine, a reward signal that encourages you to keep going.

Dopamine is not merely about pleasure; it reinforces the behaviours leading to that feeling of accomplishment. When you take on a challenging task, and you succeed step by step, your brain sends these reward signals, making you want to continue. This cycle propels you into a deeper focus. You are not chasing frivolous distractions; you are hooked on the satisfaction of improvement. In this state, your stress levels can drop dramatically. Studies published by the

Flow: The Key to Peak Performance

American Psychological Association reveal that people who frequently experience flow report higher levels of life satisfaction because a flow state provides a brief, welcome escape from daily worries. All your mental bandwidth directs itself toward the task at hand, leaving minimal space for anxiety or self-doubt.

Aside from the mood boost, your cognitive abilities also benefit. In flow, your prefrontal cortex, which is responsible for self-criticism and conscious doubt, becomes quieter. This temporary hush can free your mind from negative chatter. You gain an enhanced sense of clarity, creativity, and problem-solving capability. The less mental noise you have, the easier it is to see connections and solutions you might otherwise miss. This shift fosters a distinct sense of control and confidence in your abilities.

Of course, your mindset influences whether you enter flow. People who push their limits regularly develop a capacity to find that sweet spot between comfort and panic. Think of an artist like Pablo Picasso. He immersed himself in painting for hours, losing track of time and surroundings. His relentless drive to master new techniques sustained this immersion. Athletes do the same by training at the edge of their current skill level, forcing adaptation. In everyday life, you can replicate this by consistently stretching your capabilities in meaningful ways, perhaps learning a musical piece that challenges you or tackling a complex project at work.

Importantly, flow is self-reinforcing. Each experience encourages you to seek more, creating a positive cycle. You feel accomplished and energised, which boosts motivation for future tasks. This psychological loop can elevate your resilience. If you have had a taste of flow, you know you have the capacity to achieve a high level of focus. During setbacks, reminding yourself of those experiences can rekindle your confidence.

In sum, flow is not fantasy or hype. It is the result of complex chemical processes in your brain, guided by specific psychological conditions. When your challenge and skill align, you ignite an experience that elevates your mood, sharpens your mind, and inspires your best performance. As you understand the science, you equip yourself to seek these states deliberately, creating a cycle of mental growth and fulfilment.

3. Essential Conditions for Tapping into Flow

There are certain universal conditions that help you experience flow. These are not optional; they form the bedrock of the flow state. Without these pillars, you risk slipping into boredom or anxiety, neither of which cultivates peak performance. By deliberately arranging your tasks, environment, and mindset, you create the conditions necessary for deep immersion and enhanced productivity.

One key condition is having clear goals and immediate feedback. If you begin a task without direction, your mind drifts. You might do a bit of the task, dabble in distractions, and then return without making real progress. Instead, when you start with a crystal-clear objective, such as finishing a specific chapter of writing or achieving a precise performance metric, your mind fixes on that target. Pair this with timely feedback, and you have the immediate information needed to adjust your efforts. For instance, a tennis player receives immediate feedback from the ball's bounce and trajectory, helping refine the next shot. Similarly, if you are writing software code, short test runs give you instant data on which parts are succeeding and which need correction. This quick loop of action and response keeps you engaged.

Another essential condition is the delicate balance between challenge and skill. Think of it as a scale. If a task is too easy, your mind wanders. If it is too difficult, you become stressed. Flow emerges when you set a task slightly beyond your current level, compelling you to push your limits without feeling crushed. You remain in a focused, energised state because the goal is tough enough to excite you yet attainable enough to keep you motivated. Olympic gymnast Simone Biles exemplifies this balance. She continues to raise her routines' difficulty in proportion to her growing ability, sustaining a level of challenge that captivates her fully.

A distraction-free environment is also essential. In a world with countless pings, pop-ups, and instant messages, you must protect your attention. Deep flow often requires extended blocks of uninterrupted work. This does not mean you must lock yourself in a silent room for hours. It means you should minimise unnecessary intrusions: mute notifications, set boundaries with colleagues, or work during periods when interruptions are least likely. Some individuals find success by practising time-blocking, allocating a chunk of the day to immersive work, then taking scheduled breaks to handle communication.

Finally, self-confidence plays a role. Flow is fragile. If you start doubting yourself mid-task, your attention is no longer fully on what you are doing. Self-criticism disrupts concentration, leading to anxiety or the urge to quit. You can strengthen your belief in your abilities by preparing meticulously, practising beforehand, and reminding yourself of previous accomplishments. When you do feel self-doubt creeping in, pause, breathe, and refocus on the step in front of you.

By aligning these conditions, clear goals, immediate feedback, a balanced challenge, a distraction-free environment, and confidence, you set the stage for flow. Through thoughtful preparation and an understanding of these fundamental building blocks, you give yourself the greatest chance of reaching that state of optimal focus and fulfilment.

4. The Transformative Benefits of Living in Flow

When you immerse yourself in flow, you do more than boost your output. You create a ripple effect that enhances almost every aspect of your life. The first, and perhaps most obvious, benefit is improved performance. Your productivity often skyrockets because you become fully absorbed in the present task. Free from niggling doubts or outside diversions, your concentration intensifies, and you handle complex tasks more efficiently.

That heightened performance often translates to stronger confidence. Nothing affirms your abilities like completing a complicated project under focused immersion. You see first-hand that you have what it takes, raising your self-assurance for future challenges. This accumulation of small victories fuels a belief that you are capable of mastering tough tasks. Think of a basketball player like LeBron James, who finds that zone during a critical match. The calm confidence that emerges on the court is not merely a personality trait; it is a by-product of flow. Each well-executed play reinforces trust in his own skills, creating a cycle of achievement and self-belief.

Flow: The Key to Peak Performance

Another key advantage is the reduced stress and anxiety that come from being present. Ironically, working extremely hard in a flow state does not drain you the way haphazard multitasking might. The deep focus helps you avoid those draining mental loops of worry. Because flow blocks out irrelevancies, it also lowers the cortisol associated with scattered thinking and frantic tasks. Your mental health can stabilise, and you can experience a calmer perspective on challenges. Indeed, many high-performers claim that stress melts away once they reach flow, replaced by an invigorating sense of purpose.

Furthermore, flow often unlocks deeper creativity. Freed from the constraints of self-criticism or second-guessing, your mind may discover unconventional solutions or fresh angles. Writers sometimes describe a feeling that the story is emerging on its own, as though they are mere vessels for the narrative. In that moment, the usual internal censors are muted, allowing ideas to flow freely. This creative surge is not limited to traditional arts. Engineers, scientists, and anyone working on intricate problem-solving can witness new insights when fully immersed in their work.

Additionally, the satisfaction you gain from flow goes beyond fleeting pleasure. It contributes to a long-term sense of fulfilment. Achievements born from a flow state are memorable because they result from your most authentic effort. You do not feel you succeeded by accident, nor do you see it as purely luck-based. Instead, you recognise how your skill and focus combined at the perfect moment. This recognition bolsters your internal drive, encouraging you to seek more tasks that cultivate flow and keep the cycle of growth in motion.

In essence, living in flow can revolutionise your relationship with work and personal challenges. You gain an enhanced capacity for productivity, a robust self-confidence, a calmer mental state, a spark of creativity, and a rich, lasting sense of accomplishment. These outcomes combine to elevate your life, both professionally and personally, making the pursuit of flow a worthwhile and transformative endeavour.

5. Flow and Creative Excellence: Unlocking Innovation

Creative breakthroughs often surface when your mind roams freely, unbound by rigid constraints. This is why flow and creativity share an intrinsic connection. When you are in a flow state, you direct all your concentration toward a chosen activity, yet your mind remains expansive and flexible. This is not an intellectual contradiction; it is a unique mental harmony. You work with fierce clarity while maintaining the freedom to explore unexpected ideas.

Observe how Lin-Manuel Miranda composed the acclaimed musical Hamilton. His creative process involved submerging himself in historical texts, hip-hop influences, and unwavering dedication to lyrical detail. In those moments of intense writing, he was not merely ploughing through lines; he was entirely immersed. This allowed for sharp creative leaps and a compelling blend of historic narrative and modern rhythm. Flow gave him that uninterrupted lane to conceive fresh rhymes, unexpected structures, and emotional resonance, qualities that might have been stifled if he had been disrupted by self-doubt or continuous distractions.

From a neurological standpoint, creativity in flow emerges because you turn down your inner critic. That internal voice that questions every stroke of paint or every sentence vanishes when you are engrossed in the task. You become receptive to experimental ideas, letting them evolve without fearing immediate judgment. The result is often a more daring, emotionally charged output that resonates deeply with others.

However, unlocking this synergy between flow and creativity is not automatic. You must strike a balance between familiarity and novelty. If you cling to the same formula or environment for too long, your mind drifts into autopilot, reducing the element of creative spontaneity. Conversely, if you try something wildly beyond your skills or domain knowledge, you might become overwhelmed. The ideal approach is to approach tasks that are challenging but still within your grasp, ensuring that your creative exploration feels exhilarating rather than crushing.

Rituals can help. Some artists, writers, and problem-solvers maintain specific routines before diving into their creative flow. This might include listening to certain music, meditating for a short period, or tidying their workspace. While these rituals can seem trivial, they serve a psychological function: signalling to your mind that it is time to enter a focused, immersive state. Once you associate a ritual with that mindset, you can slip into flow more reliably.

When you cultivate flow for creative tasks, you discover a level of innovation that remains elusive in a distracted or self-conscious mental space. Your work becomes imbued with genuine inspiration because you operate in a zone of heightened intensity and curiosity. You are not labouring through forced brainstorming; rather, you tap into a wellspring of inventiveness that arises from within. This alignment between deep focus and imaginative freedom is the bedrock of creative excellence.

Ultimately, whether you are composing a piece of music, designing a new gadget, or formulating a fresh marketing campaign, flow can be your golden ticket to innovation. It pushes you to combine skill with an openness to novelty, granting you the confidence and mental latitude to explore and refine daring concepts that stand out in a crowded world.

6. Entering Flow on the Job: Fostering a Peak-Performance Workplace

In your professional life, flow can be the difference between dragging yourself through tedious tasks and thriving in a role you genuinely enjoy. When flow surfaces at work, it energises you, turning routine responsibilities into opportunities for deep engagement. This is not an abstract ideal; it is a practical approach to enhancing team spirit, fostering innovation, and elevating quality. Whether you manage a team or work independently, creating a flow-friendly environment can produce a dramatic impact on performance and satisfaction.

To begin, it is essential to match roles and responsibilities with each person's skill level and interest. People are more inclined to experience flow if they find their tasks sufficiently challenging and aligned with what they do well. If someone is overqualified, boredom seeps in. If they feel out of their depth, stress escalates, which undermines concentration. In an ideal arrangement, each team member is tasked with assignments that stretch abilities without being impossible. Managers can set up regular one-to-one check-ins to assess how employees feel about their workload and the difficulty of their tasks, adjusting as skills develop.

Clear objectives also pave the way for flow at work. It is hard to lose yourself in a state of deep concentration if you do not understand why you are doing what you do. By defining goals, both short and long term, you allow yourself or your team to channel efforts more precisely. Imagine a software engineer coding without any real sense of the end objective. That engineer may slip into mechanical routines without true engagement. In contrast, if the aim is specified to build a user-friendly feature within a certain timeframe, there is a measurable outcome to target. That clarity sharpens focus and can lead to flow.

Minimising interruptions is another crucial factor. Open-plan offices, while encouraging collaboration, often bring a barrage of distractions. You might get interrupted for quick questions, casual chats, or notifications. While human interaction is important, it is beneficial to create zones or time blocks where deep work can unfold without intrusion. Professionals like Cal Newport have popularised methods such as "deep work blocks," where you turn off your phone, sign out of messaging apps, and set an away status so colleagues know you need uninterrupted time. This approach helps maintain a mental state conducive to flow.

Additionally, an atmosphere of trust is vital. If you constantly worry about micromanagement or punishing attitudes toward mistakes, you cannot dive into flow. Fear stifles creativity and risk-taking. Instead, supportive leadership fosters an environment where you feel safe experimenting, provided you learn from any missteps. Regular feedback, delivered constructively, helps you adjust quickly without undermining your morale. When trust and autonomy are woven into a company's culture, employees have the freedom to immerse themselves deeply in their responsibilities.

A flow-friendly workplace is not about working longer hours; it is about entering a heightened state of engagement. By aligning tasks with skill level, setting clear objectives, allowing minimal distractions, and nurturing trust, you create the space where flow thrives. This leads to improved performance, job satisfaction, and a shared sense of purpose that energises everyone involved.

7. Confronting Barriers: Overcoming the Enemies of Flow

Your path toward flow is rarely smooth. You may have the right goals and an excellent work setting, yet obstacles such as self-doubt, digital distractions, and outside pressures threaten to derail you. Identifying these common barriers and developing strategies to move past them is crucial if you wish to sustain flow and maintain your best performance.

One glaring barrier is the intrusive nature of modern technology. Phones ping with notifications, colleagues send instant messages, and social media beckons at every turn. Each alert pulls you from immersion, snapping your focus and making it harder to return to that zone of flow. To combat this, you can set strict boundaries. Switch your phone to silent, schedule your message-checking times, and inform peers when you are in an immersion period. Even short disruptions can break the flow cycle, so protective measures matter.

Another hurdle is mental clutter, which covers all forms of nagging worry, racing thoughts, and self-criticism. When your mind is swamped with negativity or fear, you struggle to sustain the concentration necessary for flow. You might be partway through a task and abruptly question your competency or recall an unresolved issue from earlier. To handle this, mindfulness techniques work wonders. Simple breathing exercises before you begin can calm your mental noise, preparing you for deeper focus. Over time, reminding yourself that it is normal to have stray thoughts helps you acknowledge them without letting them take over.

External pressure also threatens your flow state. This can come from deadlines or from expectations set by colleagues, family, or even yourself. While some level of pressure is helpful for motivation, excessive stress can elevate anxiety to the point where flow is unattainable. You might feel paralysed by the stakes, worried that each move could lead to failure or criticism. The key is to reframe these pressures. Turn them into challenges, not threats. If you see them as opportunities to test your growth, you maintain a healthier mindset. Setting smaller milestones within larger deadlines also makes a massive project more manageable.

Finally, consider the role of your physical state. Insufficient rest, poor nutrition, or lack of exercise can dampen your capacity to concentrate. If your body is fatigued or undernourished, your brain's ability to engage in deep focus declines. Therefore, treating your body well by sleeping adequately, eating a balanced diet, and staying active lays the groundwork for mental performance. The synergy between physical and mental well-being is powerful, and many top performers credit consistent self-care for their capacity to hit flow states regularly.

Confronting these barriers requires both discipline and self-awareness. You must identify the distractions and mental hurdles that most often disrupt you, then create personalised strategies to mitigate them. By doing so, you safeguard your focus, increase the likelihood of entering flow, and fortify your resilience against the storms of modern life that threaten your most productive and gratifying mental state.

8. Flow as a Gateway to Lasting Fulfilment

Flow is not a temporary trick to boost your output for a single assignment. It can become a cornerstone of a life lived with purpose and satisfaction. When you taste the depth of engagement that flow brings, you find a renewed sense of direction. Achievements secured through this intense focus do not merely tick boxes; they enrich you with a sense of mastery and genuine pride. More significantly, repeated experiences of flow weave an overarching narrative of fulfilment, echoing through both your professional pursuits and personal growth.

Yo-Yo Ma, the celebrated cellist, embodies this principle. When playing, he immerses himself so completely in each piece that external pressures fall away. Time can vanish, and what remains is pure devotion to the music. This experience has driven his career and personal contentment. He does not perform merely to impress; he plays because the immersion itself is nourishing. You can apply a similar mindset to your own endeavours, seeking tasks, crafts, or challenges where your entire being feels awakened.

Over time, you realise that flow fosters a journey towards self-mastery. As you intentionally push your limits, you begin to see continuous improvement as a gratifying adventure rather than a punishing chore. Each time you achieve flow, you confirm you can handle something that once felt intimidating. This incremental expansion of your skill set enhances confidence in a lasting manner. You start to believe more deeply in your potential and become more open to facing new challenges that stretch your abilities.

Moreover, flow experiences can rejuvenate your emotional landscape. Many individuals cite that regular immersion in meaningful tasks serves as an antidote to the daily stresses of modern living. Whereas shallow tasks or mindless scrolling leave you restless, flow offers a form of mental refreshment. You come out of these deep dives not exhausted but energised, carrying forward a sense of contentment that spills into other areas of your life. This phenomenon can strengthen relationships, boost self-esteem, and heighten your sense of connection to your aspirations.

There is also a cumulative effect. As you accumulate flow experiences, you begin to structure your life around them. You might shift your schedule to carve out protected blocks of time for your main pursuits or transform your environment to reduce friction when starting a task. These changes might appear small day by day, but they add up to a profoundly more fulfilling lifestyle. You no longer regard challenging tasks as hurdles to be reluctantly cleared; instead, you see them as gateways to another enriching episode of flow.

This path leads to deeper fulfilment because your motivation springs from within. External rewards like praise, promotion, or financial gain become secondary to the intrinsic joy you find in the process. Your confidence strengthens as you witness yourself performing at new heights, and you nurture a belief that your potential is far from fixed. You become the architect of your peak moments, forging a reality where deliberate practice, curiosity, and self-trust combine to form the tapestry of a deeply fulfilling life.

9. Practical Routines and Habits for Flow

Flow thrives under certain routines and habits that foster focus and engagement. Crafting these practices into your daily schedule gives you a structured approach to prompt deeper immersion in whatever you do. While flow can sometimes appear spontaneously, setting up a reliable system makes it more predictable and frequent.

Start with time-blocking. If you routinely jump between emails, phone calls, and various tasks every few minutes, it is nearly impossible to slip into flow. By assigning a specific window, say 90 minutes, to one crucial activity, you signal to your mind that this period is sacred for deep focus. Support this by silencing notifications and letting others know you are unavailable. When that time block ends, take a break to move around, refresh your mind, and then either return to the same task or begin another. Adopting this rhythm can dramatically increase your chances of entering flow.

Another habit is goal segmentation. Large projects can feel overwhelming, making it tough to reach a state of relaxed concentration. Break tasks into smaller milestones. Each segment becomes a mini-challenge, offering clear goals and quicker feedback. The act of completing these increments feeds your sense of progress, sustaining motivation. In creative fields, for example, you might structure your progress so that you focus on brainstorming for a set time, then drafting, then revising. Each stage delivers distinct feedback, enabling you to keep your engagement high.

Also, introduce a preparatory ritual. You might brew a specific type of tea, straighten your workspace, or do a brief mindfulness exercise. These small signals nudge your brain into knowing it is time for focused work. Many authors and composers, for instance, have famously used such rituals. Ernest Hemingway wrote at daybreak, while Beethoven took a careful coffee ritual each morning. Over time, these actions become a cue for your mind to transition into deep engagement.

Physical well-being is also paramount for consistent flow. Regular exercise keeps your energy balanced, reducing sluggishness. Sleep quality influences your ability to concentrate for extended periods. A body that is well-rested and energised sets the stage for mental acuity. Even short stretches or walks can break mental stagnation, clearing your head and returning you to your task with renewed vitality.

Lastly, keep track of your flow instances. Reflect on days when you felt that time dissolved and your performance soared. Note the conditions, time of day, environment, mood, and the nature of the task. By analysing these elements, you glean insights into what triggers your flow most reliably. This knowledge enables you to replicate the circumstances and refine them over time, making flow less an accident and more a component of your daily routine.

When you incorporate these routines, time-blocking, segmenting goals, pre-work rituals, and physical self-care, you stack the odds in favour of achieving flow regularly. You move from hoping for a magical moment of focus to deliberately engineering a mental space conducive to absorption. The more frequently you step into flow, the greater your accomplishments and the richer your sense of purpose.

10. Bringing It All Together: Your Path to Peak Performance

You have explored how flow can turbocharge your creativity, productivity, and sense of fulfilment. The question that remains is how to apply it across the various dimensions of your life. Misty Copeland's journey to becoming a principal dancer at the American Ballet Theatre did not hinge on raw talent alone. It was sustained periods of deep focus, rigorous discipline, and an unwavering pursuit of meaningful goals. Richard Branson may be famed for entrepreneurship, but his breakthrough moments arrived when he submerged himself in building businesses free of small distractions.

Translating these lessons to your life means approaching every endeavour as an opportunity for deep immersion. Cultivating a mind primed for flow involves acknowledging distractions, scheduling tasks that align with your skills, and pushing your limits so you do not stagnate. Yes, you must navigate everyday responsibilities, chores, emails, social obligations, but you can carve out sacred blocks of time where you operate at full capacity, shielded from trivial interruptions.

As you do so, remember that flow is not reserved for the workplace or high-stakes competitions. You can find it in hobbies, volunteer efforts, or personal development. Imagine deciding to learn a new language. If you set goals slightly beyond your comfort level and practise with full involvement, you can find flow in each lesson. The same logic applies to cooking a complex recipe, painting your first canvas, or refining your guitar techniques. By nurturing flow in these arenas, you develop a broader sense of satisfaction that goes beyond career achievements.

Still, flow demands consistent effort and experimentation. You may fail to achieve it in early attempts if the tasks are too hard or too simple. Reflect on each experience, adjust your approach, and refine your skills. Over time, you will discover that you can access flow more readily and feel more confident stepping into unfamiliar territories. Flow grows in tandem with your resilience, forging a mindset that embraces challenges instead of shrinking from them.

Ultimately, pursuing flow is not about chasing perfection. It is about striving for that intersection between your ability and ambition. When you align your tasks, mindset, and environment to foster flow, you unlock your peak performance, where each action feels purposeful and rewarding. Life no longer appears as an endless string of mundane responsibilities but as a series of opportunities to enter a state of profound engagement. That sense of immersion and mastery, repeated over time, can reshape your personal and professional narrative.

Embrace the methods outlined in this chapter, set clear goals, match your skill to the challenge, reduce distractions, build flow-friendly routines, and track your achievements. By doing so, you create fertile ground for a richer, more focused, and triumphant life. Flow becomes a guiding principle, enabling you to push your boundaries and cherish the process. As you commit to living in flow, you step into the realm of ongoing growth, heightened creativity, and the unshakeable conviction that your best work emerges when you are fully present, leaning into challenge with passion and confidence.

Chapter 12

The Power of Gratitude

You've come a long way on your journey to creating a prosperous and balanced life. Now, as we turn to Chapter 12, you're about to unlock one of the most impactful practices for personal transformation: gratitude. Gratitude isn't simply about saying 'thank you' or acknowledging kindness; it's a powerful mindset that shifts how you see the world and experience your daily life. When you genuinely embrace gratitude, every ordinary moment holds the potential for extraordinary joy, and every challenge becomes an opportunity for deeper growth.

In this chapter, you'll learn how gratitude can profoundly reshape your perspective, helping you focus on abundance rather than scarcity. You'll discover that it's more than a fleeting feeling; gratitude can become the bedrock of your emotional health, the cornerstone of your relationships, and a shield during life's storms. By consciously weaving gratitude into your daily routine, you'll transform how you interact with the world, fostering stronger connections, reducing stress, and cultivating genuine happiness.

As you embark on this chapter, open yourself to the possibility that a simple shift in perspective, choosing gratitude daily, could be one of the most transformative choices you ever make.

1. A Transforming Perspective: Embracing Gratitude

The Power of Gratitude

You hold within you the power to completely shift how you see your circumstances, and that power is gratitude. It might sound simple: thanking life for what you have, appreciating the warmth of a morning sunbeam, or feeling glad for a friend's support, but these small acknowledgements can transform your outlook. By actively embracing gratitude, you nurture a perspective that emphasises growth and hope rather than lack or frustration. Instead of fixing your gaze on regrets or unmet desires, you direct your thoughts towards what has bloomed and prospered in your life.

Think of your mind as fertile ground. Whichever seeds you water most will become the strongest plants. If you keep watering the seeds of discontent, they will flourish and crowd out everything else. On the other hand, by consistently watering seeds of gratitude, you allow optimism to take root. This shift is not about pretending your challenges do not exist; rather, it involves recognising that even in adversity, small beacons of goodness can still shine brightly. When you focus on these positives, you tap into a well of mental resilience that can steady you in life's storms.

Another remarkable aspect of gratitude is its effect on your sense of purpose. When you wake up and actively look for reasons to be thankful, you start identifying hidden opportunities and subtle gifts in ordinary moments. Many people overlook these daily treasures because they are too occupied with stress. By switching your mindset to notice the good, you remind yourself that you have the agency to shape your narrative. You are not denying reality; you are choosing to highlight the parts of it that uplift and strengthen you.

Over time, this consistent highlighting of what is positive makes you more open-hearted. You begin to see that life need not be perfect to hold moments of genuine joy. Even if certain areas of your life are not going as planned, acknowledging what you do have shifts you from a reactive stance to a proactive one. Rather than feeling drained, you feel energised and resourceful. Gratitude transforms your frustrations into lessons, your mistakes into stepping stones, and your long waits into seasons of growth.

It is also important to note that gratitude fosters deeper connections. The more aware you are of how someone's kindness, time, or presence has enriched your day, the more likely you are to reciprocate. Relationships flourish in this environment of mutual appreciation. By letting people know you see their efforts and value them, you create a welcoming atmosphere that draws in genuine support and respect.

Embracing gratitude is not a one-time declaration; it is an ongoing commitment to see the world with clarity and hope. As you strengthen this perspective, you will discover that your mind becomes a stage for possibility rather than defeat. This sets a powerful tone for how you navigate challenges and how you nurture your sense of well-being. Let this spirit of thankfulness guide you to the next step, where you will learn how gratitude goes beyond a passing feeling and establishes a firm foundation for your mental and emotional health.

2. The Foundation of Gratitude: How it Shapes Your Wellbeing

You are the architect of your mindset, and the quality of that mindset shapes your well-being. Gratitude underpins this structure, acting like the bedrock on which you build not only your emotional resilience but also your physical health. When you consistently practise gratitude, you do more than utter polite words; you create a fortified inner world where stress is better managed, conflicts are resolved more calmly, and everyday pressures feel more bearable.

From a psychological standpoint, gratitude alters how your brain processes experiences. Instead of clinging to disappointments or fears, you train yourself to recognise elements that uplift you. This shift in focus reduces your body's stress responses. Prolonged stress has the power to undermine immune function and interrupt healthy sleep patterns, whereas a grateful mind calms these responses. The moments you feel genuinely thankful, perhaps when a friend calls to check on you or when you are able to enjoy a cup of tea in peaceful silence, send signals to your nervous system, telling it to ease tension and allow equilibrium to return.

You will also find that this foundation of gratitude influences your relationships. By consciously appreciating the qualities in others, whether it is their humour, empathy, or willingness to lend an ear, you bring out more of those attributes in your interactions. When people feel noticed and appreciated, they become more open, more trusting, and more inclined to collaborate. Disagreements, though still present, take on a more constructive tone because there is a shared understanding that the relationship rests on mutual respect.

Moreover, gratitude shapes your decisions. When you recognise the good that already exists in your life, you become less prone to impulsive pursuits of external validation. You will likely see a decrease in the frantic chase for possessions or status symbols. Instead, you will find yourself drawn to pursuits that hold deeper meaning, experiences that speak to your soul rather than merely stroke your ego. This shift can lead to wiser financial choices, more thoughtful career moves, and a more balanced approach to how you invest your time.

In many ways, gratitude is the lens that adjusts your vision of life. Even when you face genuine hardship, you can still pick out threads of positivity, whether it is a valuable lesson you have learned or a sign of inner strength you did not realise you possessed. This does not erase pain or invalidate struggles, but it does remind you that life is never entirely bleak. There is always some glimmer of hope or growth you can harness.

When you view gratitude as a foundation, you treat it as a non-negotiable aspect of daily life rather than a casual afterthought. It is akin to maintaining your home's foundation: you invest time and energy into ensuring it remains strong and stable. As you continue to reinforce this core of appreciation, you will begin to notice a profound resilience taking shape within you. From this solid ground, you can more confidently explore the ways gratitude can reshape your mindset, equipping you to break habitual patterns that no longer serve you.

3. Shifting Your Mindset Through Gratitude

You might be familiar with the idea that your thoughts influence how you feel and behave. Gratitude amplifies that truth by guiding you towards perspectives that foster optimism, perseverance, and ingenuity. When you deliberately shift your mindset to focus on thankfulness, you dismantle habitual patterns of negativity. This shift does not demand a wholesale denial of real-life challenges; rather, it gives you a better vantage point from which to address them.

Changing mental patterns can be daunting. Negative thinking can become second nature, particularly if you have grown used to dwelling on worries or regrets. Yet the moment you remind yourself to pause and ask, "What blessings can I spot in this situation?" you disrupt the spiralling narrative of doom. It might be as straightforward as saying, "I am grateful for the chance to learn from this mistake," or "I appreciate having someone who cares enough to offer tough feedback." Each time you do this, you chip away at the assumption that life is primarily a series of disappointments.

As you shift your mindset, you will find that gratitude diminishes the intensity of day-to-day stresses. Responsibilities at work or conflicts in personal relationships may still arise, but gratitude lends you a calmer lens for interpreting them. Where you once saw a setback as a complete catastrophe, you might now perceive it as a lesson or even an invitation to become more adept at problem-solving. By acknowledging what is still going right, even amid setbacks, you regain control over your mental state. This controlled perspective keeps you from feeling swept away by adversity.

Moreover, this mindset shift nurtures your creativity and capacity for innovation. When you focus on lack or obstacles, your thinking can stagnate, stuck in an unproductive loop of complaints. However, by paying attention to even the smallest positives, you create a mental environment where fresh solutions can emerge. Gratitude inspires you to think, "There is a kernel of hope here; how can I expand it?" or "This avenue might open a new door if I look at it differently." Innovators in every field often remark that their breakthroughs occurred when they stayed receptive to possibilities. Gratitude primes you for this openness.

Shifting your mindset also influences those around you. When you maintain gratitude as your default stance, you become the person who spots overlooked merits in a project or the one who encourages others not to lose heart. Instead of pulling people down with cynicism, you lift them up with constructive perspectives. Over time, this habit of highlighting hidden positives can become a cultural norm in your circle or workplace. Collective morale gets a boost, and collaborative successes become more frequent.

Adjusting your worldview through thankfulness does not come without effort. It may feel strange at first, perhaps forced, because negativity or criticism can be a strong force of habit. Yet, with repetition, gratitude becomes second nature. You learn to greet challenges without immediate defeatism, seeing them rather as temporary hurdles. This new vantage point paves the way for integrating gratitude into practical routines, ensuring it is woven seamlessly into your daily life.

4. Integrating Gratitude Into Each Day

You are best served by embedding gratitude in your daily life so it no longer remains a fleeting sentiment but becomes a reliable companion throughout your routine. This conscious incorporation starts the moment you wake up. Imagine taking a quiet moment before you grab your phone or leap out of bed to reflect on something good in your life. Perhaps you recall that you have a supportive friend, a roof over your head, or even a skill you have been able to improve. This mental note sets a more hopeful tone for the day, reminding you that there are positive aspects you can appreciate.

Carrying gratitude into the rest of the day calls for thoughtful yet straightforward practices. If you usually rush through your breakfast, try pausing to recognise that you have nourishment. When you go to work, you might mentally thank yourself for having employment or for having the determination to keep searching if you are in between jobs. Such simple acknowledgements do more than make you feel temporarily better; they sharpen your awareness of everyday gifts. By noticing these gifts, you grow more present, which in turn helps you stay grounded when stress threatens to derail your calm.

Another way to integrate gratitude is by sharing it with others. Speaking up and expressing genuine thanks can shift the tone of a conversation or relationship. If a colleague helped you with a task or a family member took care of a chore you dreaded, articulate your appreciation. This does not have to be a grand speech. A brief, heartfelt acknowledgement can spark a ripple effect of goodwill. That spark can inspire them to pass on a kind gesture to someone else, forming a chain of small, uplifting acts.

Journalling is also a powerful means to cement gratitude in your everyday life. Set aside time, perhaps in the evening, to write down a few positives from the day. They can be simple: "I solved a tricky problem" or "I had a pleasant walk in fresh air." Over time, these entries accumulate into a record of how your life contains moments of brightness, even if it feels ordinary or demanding. Reading past entries can rekindle appreciation you felt previously, reinforcing the idea that challenges, no matter how persistent, do not blot out every ray of light.

Of course, sustaining these habits takes effort. The rush of daily obligations might push them aside if you are not deliberate. Try anchoring these small habits to existing routines. For example, use the first sip of morning tea as a trigger to think of one person you are thankful for. Or set a phone reminder mid-day to pause and acknowledge what is going well. These mini reflections prevent you from sleepwalking through life's daily motions. Instead, they awaken a deeper sense of reverence for your experiences, no matter how mundane. As you strengthen these habits, your relationships will begin to feel the impact of a grateful heart, illuminating how gratitude draws people closer together and fosters a sense of unity.

5. Deepening Bonds With Gratitude

You will notice a remarkable improvement in your connections once you consciously nurture gratitude in how you relate to others. Relationships are seldom free from tension, personalities clash, misunderstandings happen, and life can pull people in different directions. Yet gratitude acts as a bridge, reminding you to see someone's good intentions or positive traits even if you disagree with them.

When you approach relationships through a lens of thankfulness, you shift the dynamic from one of expectation to one of appreciation. If you reflect on what someone contributes, a listening ear, a shared laugh, or guidance in a tough moment, you soften any inclination to focus solely on their flaws. The more you recognise a person's efforts or kind gestures, the more you anchor the relationship in mutual respect. This dynamic fosters loyalty and goodwill, turning even brief interactions into opportunities to connect meaningfully.

Expressing gratitude directly to others can breathe new life into relationships that have grown distant or strained. A sincere "I value what you did for me" or "Your presence really makes a difference" can be enough to open a dialogue that was once blocked by resentment or bitterness. Gratitude brings a measure of humility to your interactions: you recognise that another person's kindness or labour contributed to your own well-being, which softens pride and invites empathy.

In workplaces, gratitude can elevate team spirit. A manager who regularly acknowledges team members' contributions creates an atmosphere where employees feel seen and motivated. Likewise, colleagues who show appreciation for one another's roles in group projects cultivate trust and reduce friction. Instead of obsessing over credit or territory, people unite around shared achievements. This unity can boost productivity, cut down on conflict, and lead to greater job satisfaction.

Family relationships also flourish under gratitude's influence. It is easy to take relatives for granted when you have known them all your life, but a conscious effort to notice their positive qualities can remind you of why they matter. That might look like thanking a sibling for their unwavering support or telling a parent how a small lesson they taught you years ago continues to guide you. These acknowledgements transform mundane family routines into cherished moments, fostering a sense of belonging.

Recognising the good in people does not mean you overlook unhealthy or harmful behaviours. Rather, it helps you approach problems from a place of understanding rather than hostility. When you begin with a foundation of appreciation, you can tackle differences with composure. You are less likely to hurl accusations and more likely to express concerns in ways that encourage resolution.

Through gratitude, you revitalise the connections that sustain you. Whether it is your oldest friend or a colleague you rarely speak to, looking for the good in people shifts your interactions from transactional to enriching. Next, you will see how gratitude stands firmly by your side in moments of turmoil, acting as a shield against despair and a source of quiet courage.

6. Standing Tall in Hardship: Gratitude as Your Shield

You will inevitably face hardships, whether they arrive as sudden loss, prolonged stress, or unexpected changes that rattle your routine. During such times, gratitude becomes a powerful shield, not to block the reality of pain but to soften its blow. Instead of viewing adversity as a crushing force, you begin to interpret it as a challenge you can confront armed with the stabilising force of a grateful heart.

Gratitude refocuses your perspective. If you are grappling with a job setback, you might think, "At least I still have certain resources that can help me pivot," or "I am thankful for the supportive contacts I have built over time." In moments of health struggles, you can find meaning in the people who stand by you or the healthcare professionals offering aid. This is not a naive pursuit of silver linings; it is a conscious recognition that even in the shadow of difficulty, there are points of support and kindness you can draw strength from.

Moreover, gratitude fosters resilience. Resilience is the ability to bounce back and keep moving forward despite obstacles. When you consciously look for aspects to be thankful for, you lessen the likelihood of being overwhelmed by despair. This shift can help you maintain a clear mind, making it easier to assess solutions or make level-headed decisions. For instance, you might say, "I am grateful I have the freedom to try a different approach," or "I appreciate this wake-up call to reorder my priorities." By embracing the lessons embedded in hardship, you grow more resourceful, determined, and compassionate.

Another way gratitude serves as a shield is by preventing negative emotions from stacking on top of one another. When a challenge arises, fear or frustration can snowball into bitterness. Gratitude interrupts that spiral by directing your attention to something hopeful or instructive. You learn to see adversity not as an endless pit but as a temporary roadblock that may even have a hidden lesson. Your shield of gratitude does not guarantee the road ahead will be smooth; it simply ensures you are not stepping onto it with defeat in your heart.

In building this resilience, you become an example to others who may also be struggling. Your ability to remain poised sends a message that it is possible to endure hardship without succumbing to cynicism. This does not mean ignoring your pain or brushing off real problems. Rather, it means anchoring yourself in an attitude that fosters courage, perseverance, and compassion. You become less likely to lash out or surrender to hopelessness and more likely to persevere with dignity.

Even the bravest among us can feel lost in times of crisis, but gratitude lightens that burden. It gently reminds you that life contains more than the current storm. By harnessing this shield of thankfulness, you build a stable foundation for navigating challenges, which is particularly vital in professional contexts, where your capacity to handle stress can make or break team morale and productivity.

7. Elevating Professional Environments With Gratitude

You spend a substantial portion of life in your professional sphere, making it a prime setting to harness gratitude for substantial benefits. Whether you lead a team or contribute within a group, expressions of genuine appreciation can transform office dynamics. When employees feel their efforts are noticed, they become more engaged, collaborative, and solution-oriented. Gratitude generates the trust needed for efficient teamwork and can spark creativity by making people feel comfortable sharing new ideas.

Leaders who cultivate a culture of gratitude often find that their teams become more cohesive. By highlighting an individual's strengths, you encourage others to look for what is admirable in their colleagues instead of zeroing in on flaws. This shift sets a constructive tone: tasks are accomplished with collective energy, and responsibilities are shared more willingly. Companies that prize gratitude see lower employee turnover because people want to remain in an environment where they feel respected and seen. The payoff is more than a warm atmosphere; it includes higher productivity and often better financial performance.

Gratitude also promotes healthy communication in challenging scenarios. Workplace conflicts usually arise from misunderstandings or unacknowledged efforts. When you, as a manager or teammate, make it standard practice to thank individuals for their input, particularly during conflict resolution, tensions can dissipate faster. You show that even in disagreement, you recognise the value the other person brings. This approach fosters compromise rather than entrenched hostility. People are more inclined to seek mutually beneficial outcomes when they sense that their contributions are appreciated.

In addition, gratitude fosters resilience in the face of professional setbacks. Projects do not always go as planned; sometimes, the market shifts or a key client pulls out unexpectedly. In these moments, frustration can run high. However, acknowledging what still works, perhaps a team's adaptive ability or certain resources that remain available keeps morale from crumbling. By focusing on these positives, you create the possibility for new strategies and innovations to emerge out of the ashes of disappointment.

Take a moment to think about your own work environment. Imagine if you regularly made it a point to thank colleagues for small gestures: a timely response to an email, a thorough bit of research, or a supportive comment during a meeting. These acknowledgements cost you nothing yet can yield extraordinary returns in goodwill. Over time, this habit of notice and praise spurs others to follow suit, evolving into a culture of mutual support.

Lastly, gratitude feeds professional growth on an individual level. When you appreciate the learning opportunities in each project, you stop seeing obstacles as dead ends. Instead, they become stepping stones for acquiring knowledge and refining your skills. As you develop, you can then pass on the same mindset to new hires or colleagues, perpetuating a positive cycle. The workplace becomes not just a site of tasks but a community built on respect, empathy, and the pursuit of collective excellence. This sets the stage for more personal methods of integrating gratitude, such as keeping a journal, which can anchor your progress in this uplifting mindset.

8. Gratitude Journals: A Path to Growth

You can greatly strengthen your grateful outlook by adopting a consistent journalling practice. A gratitude journal is not simply a ledger of random, fleeting thoughts; it is a structured space where you reinforce your habit of recognising life's positives. When you write down reasons to be thankful, no matter how trivial they might seem, you transform gratitude from a vague, occasional notion into a personal discipline that grows day by day.

To begin, dedicate a short window each evening, or whenever suits you, to reflect on your day. You might recall that a friend sent you a reassuring message or that your morning commute was surprisingly smooth. Recording these observations does more than create a record of pleasant moments; it realigns your thinking towards what enriches your life. In times of stress, revisiting these entries provides evidence that not every day is overshadowed by challenges. You see that your life offers supportive people, small victories, and resources that sustain you.

Beyond this emotional uplift, a gratitude journal can sharpen your focus on self-improvement. Perhaps you note how a co-worker's suggestion streamlined your process or that your healthier eating habit gave you an energy boost during a busy afternoon. Recognising these factors in writing helps you connect the dots between what you appreciate and how you are evolving. You begin to see patterns: maybe better sleep or an honest talk with a colleague often correlates with a more productive day. These insights guide you to make conscious adjustments that continue fostering gratitude and its benefits.

Moreover, journalling helps counteract negativity bias, which is the human tendency to dwell on setbacks or distress. Your mind might fixate on the one mistake you made or the one rude remark you received, even if many decent things also happened that day. By documenting positives in a journal, you give them the prominence they deserve. This gradual rewiring of your mental habits makes it harder for negativity to monopolise your thoughts. The journal stands as a tangible reminder that goodness is ever-present, even amid a few stumbling blocks.

To keep this practice engaging, allow yourself creative freedom. Some days, you might write detailed paragraphs describing how a specific event made you feel. Other days, a simple list of bullet points will suffice, though if you plan to use bullet points, you can introduce them by explaining that you are about to list particular areas of gratitude, then revert to standard writing. Either way, the method you choose should resonate with you, making it more likely you will stick to the routine.

Over time, your journal entries become a potent record of how a grateful outlook transforms your mindset. It also becomes a testament to how you have tackled hardships without losing sight of what you treasure. Such transformation provides tangible evidence that gratitude is not a passive, occasional emotion but a deliberate, life-enhancing practice. Next, you will learn how this ongoing dedication to thankfulness can uplift your emotional state and bring you closer to a deeper sense of contentment and joy.

9. Unbreakable Ties Between Gratitude and Happiness

You likely recognise that a happy life is not defined by complete absence of problems, but by the capacity to maintain perspective, resilience, and hope. Gratitude directly fortifies these qualities. By regularly affirming what is good in your life, you feed the positive emotions that form the essence of happiness, things like contentment, joy, and an overall sense of life satisfaction.

One reason gratitude is so closely linked to happiness is that it shifts your mental spotlight away from what is lacking to what is present and meaningful. Human nature often leads you to dwell on the next big ambition or the next upgrade you believe will solve all your woes. Yet the moment you acknowledge that you have experienced small joys or that certain relationships bring you genuine warmth, you create a lasting sense of fulfilment. That is not to say you should not aim higher; it means your pursuit of new goals is accompanied by an appreciation for what you already have rather than solely driven by dissatisfaction.

Gratitude also boosts your happiness by promoting healthier comparisons. Instead of constantly measuring yourself against those who appear to have more, you start noticing that you do have good resources, a supportive friend, a stable living situation, or simply enough energy to tackle today's tasks. This mindset weakens envy and jealousy, allowing you to focus on personal growth rather than what others possess. As you find reasons to be satisfied with your life, your sense of self-worth rises, fuelling greater confidence and motivation.

Moreover, happiness flourishes in an environment of strong social connections, and gratitude is a potent tool for building those connections. When you consistently thank people for their support, ideas, or kindness, they feel acknowledged and valued. This fosters deeper bonds, which are essential for emotional well-being. Over time, these strengthened ties form a safety net; you know that you can depend on these relationships in both celebratory times and more trying moments.

The Power of Gratitude

Neurological studies have shown that repeated acts of gratitude and corresponding feelings of happiness can literally rewire parts of your brain. Through these repeated patterns, the mind becomes more inclined to pick up on positive experiences and store them. Essentially, gratitude primes you for happiness by ensuring you filter the world through a lens of appreciation. When bumps arise, you rebound more swiftly because your baseline mindset is oriented towards what is salvageable rather than irretrievably lost.

All of this suggests that gratitude and happiness feed into each other. The more you practise gratitude, the more reasons you find to be happy. That boosted happiness, in turn, encourages a grateful spirit, which enables you to see life's blessings even more vividly. This cycle fortifies your mental and emotional health. As you continue to cultivate gratitude in this manner, you will naturally look to real-life instances of how gratitude has brought about transformative outcomes in individuals across diverse backgrounds and circumstances.

10. Real-Life Triumphs: Gratitude in Action

You have seen how the power of gratitude operates on a conceptual level, but nothing is more convincing than real-life stories of people who embraced gratitude and achieved remarkable growth. It could be the person who overcame personal setbacks by focusing on what remained positive or the business leader who turned a failing venture around through sustained trust and appreciation among team members. These stories illustrate that gratitude is not reserved for those living in ideal conditions. Rather, it finds its true power in everyday challenges, guiding individuals to step beyond despair and into new possibilities.

Picture an entrepreneur whose initial plans disintegrated, leaving them on the brink of shutting down. Instead of stewing in bitterness, they acknowledged the unwavering support of a few loyal customers, the resilience of a small but dedicated team, and the rare opportunity to start fresh. By focusing on these elements, they rediscovered their vision, pivoted the business model, and ultimately built a venture more attuned to the market. Customers and employees alike sensed the shift; they felt genuinely valued, which bolstered loyalty and collaboration. Gratitude, in this instance, was the catalyst for reinvention.

Then there is the individual who battled a health crisis and could have easily succumbed to self-pity. Rather than indulging in despair, they turned their attention to what their body could still do, the genuine concern of friends and family, and the expertise of dedicated medical staff. This mindset allowed them to approach treatments with courage, enabling a stronger recovery and a deeper sense of empathy for others going through similar trials. In this person's story, gratitude played a quiet but decisive role in fortifying both physical and emotional well-being.

In family environments, gratitude has saved relationships on the verge of collapse. Tensions may arise from everyday disputes or deeper emotional wounds, yet a consistent effort to notice each other's redeeming qualities can bridge the gap where anger once festered. Thankfulness can diffuse blame and encourage discussions that focus on reconciliation rather than animosity. Each expression of appreciation, no matter how small, sends a subtle message that you value the other person's presence in your life, paving the way for understanding and forgiveness.

Professionals who habitually practise gratitude often become role models in their workplaces, illuminating how sincere acknowledgements can uplift morale and foster harmony. Employees who witness their manager or colleague praising small accomplishments or cooperating with grace often feel prompted to replicate that behaviour. Over time, the entire organisational culture shifts, demonstrating a collective devotion to respect and support. Under such conditions, conflicts become less destructive and more about collaborative solutions.

These tangible examples underscore how gratitude moves beyond concept and seeps into the fibres of daily existence, promoting second chances, renewed connections, and enduring strength. As you reflect on these stories, notice how they share one common thread: gratitude was never passive; it was the active decision to focus on what was alive, hopeful, or worthy of nurturing. This choice, repeated over time, shaped profound personal and communal transformations. Now, step forward and bring your gratitude practice to life, knowing that every day offers you an opening to harness this life-changing perspective.

Chapter 13

Embracing Change

Life is full of transitions, some welcomed, others unexpected, but each shift holds the promise of growth and opportunity. Change often feels like stepping into unknown territory, sparking feelings of uncertainty or apprehension. However, when you learn to lean into these moments rather than resist them, you discover strength you never knew existed, and doors open to experiences richer than you've imagined.

In this chapter, you'll explore why change, though unsettling at times, is a fundamental part of life and personal development. You'll delve into how your mind navigates the unfamiliar, recognise ways to overcome the fears that accompany new beginnings and gain practical strategies for adapting with confidence. By embracing change, you position yourself to not only survive life's inevitable twists and turns but to thrive because of them.

1. Why Change is Inevitable

Change surrounds you, shaping each stage of your life and challenging you to evolve. From shifts in technology to personal milestones, change arrives unannounced, and no one remains untouched by its effects. You may try to postpone it, ignore it, or even resent it, but change stands firm as an inevitable constant. Accepting that nothing remains fixed forever allows you to face life with eyes wide open rather than clinging to what feels safe. In this opening section, you will see how the inevitability of change informs every dimension of your journey and sets the stage for personal advancement.

When you deny that change is permanent, you risk stagnation. You might hold on to routines or situations that served you once but no longer align with your present needs. Imagine refusing to learn a new work process or resisting health recommendations that promote longevity. The world marches forward, and refusing to move along can leave you out of touch and unfulfilled. Recognising that change is guaranteed is the first step in learning to harness it rather than letting it disrupt your plans.

Consider your earliest memories. Change appeared in your life when you entered school or relocated with your family. You might have felt uncertain, but these shifts brought opportunities to make new friends, learn different subjects, and discover hidden talents. Later in life, you continue to face transitions, such as starting a fresh career path or adjusting to altered personal circumstances. Each development broadens your horizons and moulds you into a person of depth and resilience. Far from being an unwelcome guest, change often ends up being the catalyst that pushes you to step into the next phase of your life.

Despite the fact that change can feel unsettling, embracing it serves your best interests. When you approach life's transitions with a flexible mindset, you build an internal environment that is ready for growth. Think of a tree bending in strong winds; rather than snapping, it adapts to the gusts, roots digging deeper while its trunk remains strong. In a similar way, acknowledging that change is woven into every experience helps you remain open and grounded when life's winds blow.

You have likely noticed how new technology can reshape entire industries almost overnight. Businesses that fail to adapt soon become obsolete, while those that welcome innovation flourish. This lesson holds true in your personal life as well. Change can be a force that clears outdated ideas and opens a clear path toward better relationships, clearer priorities, and renewed motivation. When you treat change as a natural occurrence, you release your grip on the past and create space for a more fulfilling future.

In short, change remains an unwavering presence in your life. You can protest, hesitate, or even deny it, but acknowledging its unstoppable nature paves the way for wisdom and growth. The chapters that follow will show you how to align yourself with change rather than be swallowed up by its force. It is here, at the start, that you set the tone for how you will meet every transition. As you delve deeper into these pages, you will uncover ways to harness the energy of change to strengthen your resolve and enhance your path.

2. The Psychology of Change

Understanding why change can unnerve you begins with exploring how your mind processes unfamiliar territory. Change stirs a mixture of emotions: anticipation, anxiety, curiosity, excitement. Your brain is designed to seek safety, scanning for threats to protect you from danger. A pending transition can register as a possible threat, leading you to feel tense or hesitant, even if the change itself promises a positive outcome. By looking into how your mind perceives shifts in your environment, you can discover coping methods that keep you steady.

You might have experienced the initial alarm that arises when a routine alters abruptly. Perhaps your workplace changed operating procedures, or you received news that your daily schedule would be rearranged. Your stress level can spike because you are leaving what feels familiar. Yet the same part of your brain that triggers caution can also spark excitement when the novelty includes elements of reward. For instance, if a new job offers better work conditions or if a house move brings you closer to loved ones, your brain recognises potential benefits and starts to associate change with opportunity rather than fear.

Central to the psychology of change is understanding that perceived threats often overshadow potential gains. Evolution primed you to respond to threats with heightened vigilance, guaranteeing survival. However, modern shifts are usually not life-and-death matters but revolve around transitions in career, health, or relationships. When you learn to interpret signals that your mind sends, those pangs of nervousness or the impulse to retreat, you can pause and rationalise your emotional responses. Instead of becoming paralysed, you can channel that energy into constructive problem-solving.

One effective strategy involves reframing your internal dialogue. When faced with a shift, you might find your thoughts veering toward worst-case scenarios or self-criticism. Replace those reactions with affirming statements and reminders that change is expected in a thriving life. For example, if you catch yourself thinking, "This new role will be too overwhelming," challenge it by asking, "Which skills do I already have that will help me excel here?" This mental pivot from doubt to confidence empowers you to look for ways to succeed rather than reasons to falter.

Another dimension of the psychology of change is the concept of neuroplasticity, the brain's ability to adapt and reorganise itself. New experiences, when met with consistent effort, can rewire neural pathways, effectively teaching you to become more adaptable. If you lean into an unfamiliar undertaking, the repeated exposure to slight discomfort transforms into familiarity. In essence, by walking toward what you fear, you retrain your mind to find comfort within new surroundings.

Ultimately, understanding how your brain and emotions react to impending shifts allows you to approach change with readiness instead of dread. By becoming aware of your instinctive caution and learning to guide it, you shift from a place of anxiety to a space of deliberate engagement. This psychological awareness then paves the way for you to embrace every season of life, trusting that your mind is flexible and your capacity for resilience is far greater than you once believed.

3. Overcoming Fear of Change

Fear of change often grows out of a desire to protect what you already know. Stepping into the unknown stirs up the thought: "What if things get worse?" This leads many individuals to tolerate less-than-ideal circumstances, clinging to familiarity rather than risking the uncertainty of a new path. Yet when you continually avoid even minor transitions, your life can become small, and you miss out on the rich experiences that lie beyond your usual routines.

The first step to overcoming the fear of change is to examine why you feel threatened. Are you worried about failing if you take on a new challenge? Do you distrust your ability to adapt if life's scenery shifts? Pinpointing these underlying beliefs reveals how many of these anxieties lack a true foundation. You might discover that the worst outcome you fear is not as drastic as you initially assumed. Moving forward in the face of your misgivings can lessen the grip of fear.

Another essential tactic is to start with small, controlled changes to build confidence. This approach mirrors the way you gradually develop muscles through increasingly difficult exercises rather than a sudden strain. If you dread relocating to a new city, you could begin by visiting the area for a short stay, familiarising yourself with local amenities and noting the positives. By taking modest steps, you prove to yourself that adaption is within your reach, and you will be more prepared to face a larger move down the line.

Additionally, acknowledging the genuine risks associated with avoiding change can shift your mindset. Suppose you remain in a job that provides no growth, hoping stability alone will protect you. Over time, the lack of progress can weaken your potential and erode your motivation. The cost of never exploring fresh opportunities can outweigh the temporary discomfort of learning new skills or adjusting to a different environment. Recognising that fear of change can lead to stagnation may galvanise you to choose the brave option.

You also benefit from assembling a supportive network of people who encourage you to face your fears rather than reinforcing them. Friends who highlight your strengths and express faith in your capabilities can uplift you when doubts arise. If you sense yourself succumbing to old concerns, these allies can remind you of your track record in confronting challenges. Their assurance, combined with your own determination, acts as a safety net, allowing you to venture further than you would on your own.

Ultimately, fear of change is a deeply human reaction, yet it does not have to dominate your decisions. When you look closely at your anxieties, test them with incremental steps, and rely on a community that believes in your potential, you can turn dread into excitement. Your willingness to push beyond the boundary of what feels comfortable not only diminishes fear's hold on you but also opens up the life you are capable of building. Freed from the shackles of "what if," you can see that, more often than not, the unknown is brimming with fresh possibilities.

4. Strategies for Adapting to Change

Adapting to change demands more than accepting that it exists. You also need practical strategies that help you navigate the unexpected. While readiness begins in your mind, tangible methods solidify your ability to cope with new realities. By understanding and applying effective strategies, you can minimise disruption and sustain momentum when life shifts. This subheading explores specific tactics you can employ to position yourself for smooth transitions.

One approach involves setting short- and long-term objectives that clarify what you aim to accomplish amid changing circumstances. When you shape a goal, be it finding new employment, adjusting to a restructured household, or embarking on a health regime, you create a roadmap. With that sense of direction, you are less likely to feel lost or overwhelmed since each step serves a defined purpose. You transform unpredictability into structured action that leads you forward.

Time management is another powerful tool for successful adaptation. Under pressure, you might find yourself rushing or misplacing priorities, which heightens the sense that everything is spinning out of control. Planning ahead, batching tasks, and setting aside blocks of time to concentrate on pressing matters can anchor you in the midst of flux. For instance, if you need to reskill for a changing job market, dedicating a set schedule to courses or reading ensures you make steady headway without becoming swamped.

Flexibility in your mindset is crucial as well. Holding onto past methods can be reassuring, but it may stifle your ability to recognise emerging opportunities. You might think, "I have always done it this way," only to realise that an updated procedure or viewpoint is now more appropriate. A flexible attitude means you welcome alternative ways of doing things, even if they challenge your usual habits. This openness often reveals unexploited possibilities that would remain unseen if you insisted on rigidly following old routines.

Networking stands out as yet another way to adapt. Engaging with peers or mentors who have navigated changes similar to your own can speed your learning curve. These relationships give you direct insight into what works and what does not, saving you wasted effort. For example, if you are relocating to a new area, connecting with people who have made a similar move can give you valuable tips for settling in quickly. When you share experiences, you gain support, reassurance, and fresh viewpoints, all of which bolster your confidence in uncertain territory.

Finally, reflect on your progress. In periods of upheaval, it is easy to focus on what remains to be done and ignore how far you have come. Adapting to change is a cumulative process, with each milestone bridging the gap between where you started and where you want to be. By periodically taking stock of your achievements, however minor, you reinforce the belief that you can handle what comes next. This self-awareness keeps you engaged in the journey and stops you from slipping into complacency.

When you employ practical strategies, you are not merely hoping for the best; you are actively shaping your path. Equipped with goals, time-management tactics, flexibility, supportive networks, and regular self-evaluation, you can approach the twists and turns of life with assurance. Uncertainty will always exist, but with the right strategies, you can walk through change with a firm stride, ready to leverage whatever arises.

5. The Role of Change in Personal Growth

Growth rarely emerges from the comfort of the ordinary. It typically follows the decision to move in a fresh direction, propelled by changes that stretch your existing capabilities. Though you may crave stability, the process of personal development relies on a certain level of instability that prompts you to grow beyond current limitations. When you choose to welcome the transformations taking place, you step into a phase of expansion that might otherwise remain hidden behind your established routines.

Imagine you have always pictured yourself as someone lacking an adventurous spirit. Then, a spontaneous opportunity to travel arises, and a friend invites you on a journey to unfamiliar places. At first, you hesitate, clinging to the stable lifestyle you know. But if you embrace this chance, you discover resources within yourself: adaptability, courage, and curiosity. By the time you return, your perspective has shifted, and you no longer confine yourself to old labels. Change unlocked fresh facets of your identity.

In the realm of professional development, the presence of change is similarly pivotal. When industries evolve due to technological advances or market shifts, resisting these transitions often means falling behind. Those who adapt gain skills that set them apart, whether through retraining, diversifying their portfolio, or widening their network. While the process can be demanding and uncomfortable, it polishes your talents and reveals potentials you never thought you held. Embracing new trends or requirements encourages you to refine your approach, propelling you further than a static environment ever could.

Change also offers a wake-up call for your relationships. Sometimes, you do not detect underlying imbalances until you face a major life shift like relocating, changing careers, or stepping into parenthood. These turning points test the bonds you share with others, highlighting the strength of your support systems or revealing weaknesses. Challenges might intensify if the people around you struggle to accept new facets of who you are becoming. Paradoxically, this tension can give you the impetus to communicate more openly, cultivate deeper connections, or move on from relationships that no longer serve your growth.

Moreover, change compels you to practise resilience and reflection. Without moments of upheaval, you might drift along in a passive manner. Confronting significant alterations in your life, such as a medical diagnosis or a financial setback, forces you to confront your priorities and evaluate your choices. These periods act as catalysts for meaningful transformation, pushing you to re-evaluate long-held assumptions and find clarity on what truly matters. In responding to these prompts, your character strengthens, and your perspective widens.

Every chapter of your personal growth story involves moving from who you have been to who you can become. Change is the turning page that ensures your story is not stuck but continually unfolding. Although uncertainty may tempt you to retreat, your real strength arises when you trust the growth that change has the power to spark. Through acceptance and deliberate action, every phase of your life can serve as an invitation to deepen your sense of self, connect more genuinely with others, and align your day-to-day existence with an ever-evolving vision of what is possible.

6. Making Major Life Changes: A Step-by-Step Guide

Major life changes, such as changing careers, relocating to an unfamiliar area, or shifting family dynamics, carry multiple layers of complexity. Tackling these large shifts can seem daunting, leaving you caught between excitement and apprehension. However, when you break them down into manageable steps, the path becomes far less intimidating. This structured approach prevents you from feeling engulfed by the enormity of your undertaking.

Step one is clarifying your intention. Ask yourself why this change matters and what you hope to achieve through it. Without a guiding principle, your motivation can fade when setbacks emerge. Write down a concise statement, such as, "I am changing my career to find greater purpose and financial stability," or, "I am relocating to improve my family's quality of life." This intention will be your anchor, especially when you run into unexpected obstacles.

The second step is conducting thorough research. The aim is to build a strong knowledge base that will reduce anxieties and highlight realistic goals. For a career shift, dig into job market trends, speak with professionals in the sector, and identify the qualifications needed. If you are preparing to move, examine housing costs, community resources, and local culture. While total certainty remains unattainable, informed decisions minimise unwelcome surprises and boost your confidence in forging ahead.

Once you have gathered sufficient information, move on to step three: creating a tangible plan. This involves sketching out phases, timelines, and budgets. For instance, if you are transitioning into a new profession, you might plan to gain a certification within six months, apply for positions during the next two months, and aim to start in your new role by year's end. If you are moving, you might establish a timeline for securing housing, organising removal services, and informing necessary parties of your new address. Translating your intentions into concrete tasks helps you stay organised and quell the feeling of being overwhelmed.

Step four focuses on preparing yourself mentally and emotionally. Major changes often trigger stress or doubt, so it is wise to set up support systems early. This might include confiding in a mentor or counsellor, leaning on friends who have faced similar transitions, or joining groups where you can exchange experiences. Engaging in activities that nurture your well-being, like regular exercise, journaling, or mindfulness, can also stabilise you during turbulent phases.

Finally, execute your plan one milestone at a time. Celebrate each achievement, regardless of how small, to keep your morale high. When obstacles surface, revisit your original intention to remind yourself why you embarked on this journey. Adjust your plans if necessary, but do not allow setbacks to cast doubt on your overall direction. Steady progress is more valuable than attempting giant leaps that might prove unsustainable.

By applying these step-by-step measures, you transform an overwhelming venture into a navigable process. Along the way, you hone your problem-solving abilities, nurture emotional resilience, and inch closer to a future that aligns with your hopes and aspirations. Major changes may still present hurdles, but with structured planning and a firm grasp on your motivations, you can advance decisively and with self-assurance.

7. Navigating Change in the Workplace

Workplace change, be it a technology overhaul, a new management approach, or a structural reorganisation, can unsettle the calmest teams. You might feel lost when a once-familiar environment pivots toward novel processes or expectations. However, by recognising how to navigate these shifts effectively, you set yourself apart as someone who remains steady in the face of transformation. Far from viewing transitions as disruptions, you can interpret them as avenues for achievement and influence.

First, maintain open channels of communication. When senior leadership unveils new initiatives or reconfigures departments, rumours and speculation often fill in the blanks. Rather than allowing uncertainty to grow, seek accurate information. Attend any scheduled briefings, read internal memos thoroughly, and ask direct questions when points remain unclear. Accurate knowledge keeps anxiety at bay and equips you to respond intelligently.

Next, focus on cultivating adaptability. Instead of resisting every change, search for the advantages. Perhaps a new project management system eliminates tedious manual tasks, freeing you to engage more meaningfully in strategic thinking. As you highlight these benefits to colleagues as well as yourself, the shift feels less like a burden and more like an upgrade. Remember: your mindset sets the tone for your reactions. If you remain rigid, you close off potential progress. If you stay adaptable, you expand your capacity for creativity and leadership.

Furthermore, strengthen your skill set. When your sector or organisation is in flux, upskilling becomes a non-negotiable asset. Whether learning to use advanced software, mastering data analytics, or refining communication abilities, every enhancement to your knowledge base strengthens your positioning. By proactively meeting the workplace's new demands, you transform uncertainty into personal improvement and professional recognition.

Collaboration plays a huge part in easing transitions at work. Changes can fragment teams if people feel threatened or overlooked. Aim to be the colleague who encourages cooperation and mutual learning. If new policies baffle your teammates, offer assistance. When the environment is uncertain, unifying around common objectives can transform potential chaos into group resilience. You build camaraderie by ensuring that no one feels left behind.

Finally, do not forget self-care. Workplace adjustments can carry emotional tolls, from frustration at having to learn fresh systems to worry about job security. Protect your mental well-being by maintaining boundaries, taking breaks, and sharing concerns with a trusted mentor or HR representative. Recognising stress signals early allows you to address them before they escalate, and it also sets a helpful example for others who might be struggling silently.

Workplace change does not need to derail your career or your morale. By staying informed, welcoming adaptability, strengthening your skills, and leaning on (and offering) collaborative support, you can transform any shake-up into an opening for advancement. The next time your organisation revises its strategy or revamps procedures, see it as an invitation to show your leadership potential. When you practise calm, resourceful engagement with change, you develop a professional agility that prepares you for further steps along your career path.

8. Change as an Opportunity for Innovation

Innovation thrives where stability and novelty intersect. When your environment undergoes dramatic change, it can feel destabilising, yet those same circumstances allow you to generate fresh insights and creative breakthroughs. A new reality gives you the chance to shed outdated assumptions and build solutions better suited to emerging conditions. Once you train yourself to look for openings rather than obstacles, you unlock a mindset that can place you at the forefront of progress.

In business, inventors and entrepreneurs often seize opportunities created by large-scale shifts. One individual might see a gap in the market after major regulatory updates; another may devise new services to accommodate shifts in consumer expectations. This type of resourcefulness comes from recognising that change, far from being a threat, can highlight areas ripe for innovation. You can apply this logic in your own profession or personal life by focusing on what demands improvement or reimagining.

Innovation is not restricted to technology or business ventures; it touches every aspect of life. A personal health challenge, for example, might inspire you to find novel methods to manage your wellness. You could develop a new exercise regimen suited to your limitations, refine your eating plan to prioritise certain nutrients or join a support network that keeps you motivated. By responding creatively,

Embracing Change

you develop approaches that not only solve your immediate concerns but may also spark insights beneficial to others.

A helpful habit for leveraging change into innovation is questioning long-accepted norms. Ask yourself, "Why have I been doing things in this manner, and is there a more efficient or fulfilling path?" This might prompt you to streamline a process at work, rearrange your living space, or adopt fresh communication methods in your relationships. Sometimes, your new approaches become standard practice if they consistently outperform what was in place before.

Another route toward generating novel ideas involves collaboration with diverse perspectives. When circumstances shift, different minds bring different angles, forging solutions that a single viewpoint could easily miss. Gather input from colleagues, friends, or even online forums that tackle related problems. You might spark the best idea in a brainstorming session with people who share your vision for improvement yet bring different skill sets to the table. This synergy transforms uncertainty into collective ingenuity.

Moreover, give yourself permission to experiment without the fear of failing. Change is by nature experimental; you are navigating unfamiliar ground, and small missteps can pave the way to valuable revelations. Trial-and-error fosters adaptability, which in turn strengthens your capacity for innovating. This is where a growth-oriented mindset proves especially important, encouraging you to learn rapidly from setbacks and refine your approach.

When you reframe change as a launchpad for innovation, you transcend passivity and become an active shaper of outcomes. Whether it is organisational restructuring, societal shifts, or personal transitions, adapt by innovating. Modify, test, and keep your eyes trained on what can be rather than lamenting what no longer is. By embracing new possibilities, you channel disruption into creativity that enriches both your world and the lives of those around you. In this sense, innovation stands as a dynamic, positive ripple that emerges when the waters of life are stirred.

9. Building Resilience for Change

While adaptability helps you pivot in the face of change, resilience ensures you remain robust throughout the entire journey. Resilience is your ability to bounce back when challenges strike, to recover after setbacks, and to maintain forward momentum even under adversity. Without resilience, you might crumble as difficulties pile up. Cultivating it involves preparing your mindset, habits, and support systems so you can stay grounded in uncertain times.

A cornerstone of resilience is self-awareness. You need to recognise signs of strain in your emotional and physical health. Whether you notice persistent fatigue, increased irritability, or loss of enthusiasm, these indicators suggest that you need to recalibrate. Instead of pushing yourself to breaking point, take deliberate pauses to rest or engage in restorative activities, such as reading, mindful walks, or creative pursuits. By listening to these early signals, you preserve your energy reserves, making it more likely you will endure through extended periods of upheaval.

Another component is keeping your sense of purpose vivid. When you know the underlying reasons for your actions, you carry a compass that guides you through confusion. For example, if you are working tirelessly to expand a business, remain mindful of the deeper motivations; perhaps you seek to offer better solutions for customers or provide greater stability for your family. That clarity of purpose acts as a steady hand, holding you on course when unexpected hurdles appear. It reminds you that challenges are stepping stones rather than dead ends.

Resilience also involves strengthening your supportive network. Friends, family, mentors, or peer groups can provide both tangible and emotional aid. You do not have to handle every twist and turn alone. Talking about your struggles or brainstorming solutions with those who care about your wellbeing can lighten the load. They may suggest new perspectives or resources that can change your outlook. Simply knowing you have people in your corner can diminish the weight of uncertainty, giving you a sense of shared strength.

A practice that further nurtures resilience is celebrating progress along the way. Each time you adapt to a small change, note that victory. Each moment you solve a fresh challenge, commend yourself for learning. These acknowledgements serve as building blocks for your overall confidence. As your resilience grows, you become more willing to take calculated risks, seeing that past difficulties did not break you but enriched your capacity to cope.

In addition, adopting a flexible mindset is critical. Rigid thinking makes you vulnerable, as you might cling to old methods or preconceived timelines that no longer match reality. With a flexible approach, you shift when the environment demands it. This does not imply lacking principles; rather, you are open to multiple paths that can lead to the same ultimate goal. Resilience thrives on the willingness to pivot while holding onto your underlying aims.

When viewed collectively, these habits, self-awareness, purpose, supportive relationships, acknowledgement of small wins, and a flexible mindset form the scaffolding of resilience. They let you navigate changes not as catastrophes but as part of life's ongoing story. You gain confidence to step forward, trusting your ability to manage whatever arises instead of fearing the next wave that might wash over you.

10. Inspiring Stories of People Who Embraced Change

Throughout history, many individuals have defied personal limits by embracing change in ways that appeared radical to onlookers. Their stories show that you can use life's twists to forge new identities and pioneer uplifting transformations in the lives of others. Although no two journeys are the same, each example highlights a willingness to step beyond comfort and confront the unknown with determination and hope.

Think of a well-known athlete who started off modestly, lacking early signs of stardom but brimming with drive. Through unwavering training and readiness to adopt new methods, they grew into a record-breaker, redefining the limits of their sport. Or picture a successful business figure who initially faced multiple setbacks or bankruptcies but pivoted by developing products or services that aligned with shifting market demands. Their clarity of mission and refusal to cling to outdated strategies illustrate the power of forging ahead when external conditions alter.

You may also recall stories of individuals who changed the direction of scientific or humanitarian progress by challenging the status quo. One might have spotted a neglected need for affordable healthcare and responded by establishing initiatives that brought medical services to remote regions. By recognising an unfilled gap in how things were handled, that person channelled a desire for innovation into tangible, lasting benefits. The thread binding these narratives is not luck; it is the readiness to approach each turn of fate as a doorway to something greater.

In your own life, you have likely encountered people who personify the positive impact of embracing change. Perhaps a friend switched careers after decades in a single field, finding renewed purpose and success in an area they had once dismissed as unrealistic. Another might have tackled a health crisis by studying alternative wellness paths and emerged with knowledge that revolutionised how they and their community think about self-care. By championing flexibility and an open heart, they carved out new roads in their personal evolution and, in many cases, uplifted others as well.

Let their experiences serve as your reminder that change is neither an ending nor an enemy; it is a nudge from life toward growth, creativity, and transformation. Resistance to change may delay progress, but daring to face it head-on can produce extraordinary outcomes. Each story you encounter, whether from history or your own circle, underscores that the realm of possibility expands each time you choose to adapt. The secret lies not in having perfect foresight but in refusing to treat unexpected turns as dead ends.

Chapter 14

The Art of Time Management

In today's fast-paced world, where commitments pile up and demands constantly tug at your attention, mastering your time is not just beneficial; it's essential. You've likely felt the stress of juggling work responsibilities, family time, and personal goals, often feeling like there are never enough hours in the day. But the truth is, everyone has the same 24 hours; it's how you manage those hours that sets you apart.

This chapter dives deep into the transformative skill of effective time management, showing you how to take control of your most valuable asset, time. You'll discover practical strategies that go beyond simple scheduling, empowering you to prioritise what truly matters, sharpen your focus, and conquer procrastination. Whether you're aiming for professional success or personal fulfilment, learning the art of time management will help you move from constant stress to calm productivity, enabling you to build the meaningful, balanced life you desire.

Let's explore how to master your days with intention, purpose, and clarity, one mindful moment at a time.

1. Time: Your Greatest Asset and Why It Matters

You live in an era where every hour seems to race past with alarming speed. The bulk of your commitments, work demands, family responsibilities, social events, can feel overwhelming if you don't learn how to allocate your time with intention. Recognising time as your most valuable resource is not a trivial observation. It's the truth that underpins every triumph you'll achieve. Money can be replenished, and possessions can be replaced, but the hours you spend today are gone forever. This realisation is your first awakening to the importance of deliberate time management.

Yet time management goes beyond the mechanics of scheduling. It's a disciplined mindset that ensures you direct your energy toward tasks and goals that matter. You'll witness people who seem to accomplish far more than others in the same 24-hour window; that's not luck. They have discovered how to harness their time effectively, eliminating the needless distractions and focusing on endeavours that yield the highest impact. You can do the same by cultivating a conscious relationship with every moment you have.

Excellence in any domain, from business success to personal well-being, can be traced to individuals who have mastered the art of managing their days. They understand that time is finite, so they guard it with genuine care. They're not intimidated by deadlines or workloads because they've put systems in place to handle them. Adopting that perspective empowers you to move from a state of reacting to one of strategising. Think of your hours as resources in your command, ready to be invested in building the future you desire.

You may already sense the difference between existing in a hectic scramble and operating from a place of calm focus. When you seize control of your time, you discover that calm focus is possible even in demanding situations. This calmness forms a foundation for clear decision-making.

Instead of fumbling through hurried days, you'll direct your energy to projects that bring genuine results. By measuring your time like currency, you decide which areas are worthy of investment and which ones drain you without offering any lasting benefit.

Maintaining awareness of time's value pushes you to use it with purpose. It becomes easier to step away from meaningless activities, the endless scrolling or idle chatter that contribute little. Instead, you'll direct yourself toward actions that serve your goals. You'll sense the benefits in both your professional and personal life because the discipline of time management doesn't stop in your office. It shapes every choice you make, from the tasks you take on at work to the leisure pursuits you plan to rejuvenate your mind.

As you embark on this journey, hold onto the truth that time is your partner in creating the life you want. Cherish it, use it intelligently, and never forget that it's slipping away each second. Embrace the discipline that time management demands, for it grants the freedom you need to pursue meaning, creativity, and high achievement. When you look back, you'll be glad you devoted your hours wisely rather than allowing them to slip from your grasp.

2. The Power of Prioritisation and Focus

You live in a sea of choices every single day, some trivial, others life-changing. The constant challenge is determining which choices merit your limited time. This is where prioritisation steps in. It's the art of selecting what requires your immediate energy, ensuring you direct your focus toward goals that propel you forward. When you master the skill of prioritisation, you avoid the trap of scattering your efforts on tasks that offer minimal returns.

The Art of Time Management

To begin prioritising effectively, you must identify what truly matters. Reflect on what you want to accomplish this week, this month, or this year. Are you aiming to elevate your career, grow a venture, or strengthen personal relationships? The moment you clarify these key objectives, you know which tasks line up with them. In doing so, you filter out activities that drain your time without contributing to your overarching purpose. Many people feel overwhelmed partly because they have not defined what they must achieve. Without that clarity, every request or suggestion from others can hijack their hours.

With priorities established, focus becomes your ally. Genuine focus is laser-like attention on a single objective, unbroken by the constant tug of countless distractions. Rather than juggling multiple undertakings, you pour your energy into one significant task at a time. This intense concentration yields higher-quality work and accelerates progress. Instead of achieving shallow outcomes across many tasks, you produce deep, meaningful results in the tasks that count most.

However, prioritisation isn't just about deciding which projects to tackle; it's also about determining what to set aside. This is often the more difficult part since you might feel obliged to say yes to every request that lands on your desk. But every time you accept a commitment that doesn't match your bigger goals, you dilute the resources, time, mental energy, motivation, that could propel you forward. The discipline to say no when something isn't aligned with your priorities becomes a powerful guardrail, preserving your time for what matters.

Once you master prioritisation and adopt unwavering focus, the benefits ripple across your life. You discover that you can accomplish tasks more quickly while maintaining high standards. You also experience a deeper sense of satisfaction because your efforts are tied directly to your aspirations. Gone are the days of frantically rushing and ending each day with a nagging sense of unproductivity. Instead, you'll close your day knowing you invested your hours where they have the greatest impact.

To maintain momentum, revisit your priorities often. Circumstances shift, new opportunities emerge, and previous commitments may become irrelevant. A regular review, weekly or monthly, keeps you in tune with your direction. If your bigger vision evolves, adjust your short-term tasks to remain in sync with that grander aim. This adaptability ensures that you stay on a steady track, no matter how dynamic life becomes.

Your ability to focus on what truly counts will elevate you beyond the common struggle of aimless busyness. By prioritising smartly, you stand firm against distractions and progress toward your goals with a clear mind and relentless determination.

3. Planning and Scheduling for Maximum Productivity

A robust plan acts as the map leading you toward desired results. Without it, you may wander from one task to another, reacting to problems rather than steering your own direction. When you master planning and scheduling, you transition from passively responding to daily surprises to proactively shaping your work and leisure in line with your goals. This deliberate planning approach is transformative, giving you clarity about what you'll handle each day and when.

The Art of Time Management

Begin by mapping out your objectives for the near future, then break these objectives into tangible milestones. These milestones form the backbone of your short-term actions. Whether it's writing a series of articles, building a side project, or organising a major event, clear milestones give you stepping stones toward completion. When you distribute these milestones on a calendar, you avoid that last-minute scramble and reduce stress. You'll know precisely which segments of a project to complete each week, ensuring steady progress without overwhelming bursts of panic.

Among the most powerful scheduling methods is time blocking. This technique requires you to assign a specific task or type of work to each block of time in your calendar. For instance, you might devote the first two hours of the morning to creative work that demands deep concentration, then dedicate midday to routine tasks that need less mental horsepower. By systematically assigning tasks to distinct windows, you safeguard your most alert hours for the activities that have the greatest impact.

To refine your scheduling further, factor in your energy levels. Some people thrive in the early hours of the day, while others reach their peak in the late afternoon. Identify your natural rhythm and align the most intensive tasks with your highest energy periods. This strategy amplifies your output and minimises wasted effort spent fighting against your body's preferences. Embracing how you naturally operate is a subtle but invaluable tactic in maximising your productivity.

Life, of course, is not all about professional tasks. Creating time blocks for personal pursuits, family interactions, or even reflective breaks can help you preserve balance. When each block has a clear purpose, whether it's writing a business proposal or reading a novel for pure enjoyment, you ensure that your schedule respects the breadth of your responsibilities. This balanced approach counters burnout and enriches all areas of your day.

By adhering to a thoughtful plan and schedule, you foster consistency. You'll maintain a regular rhythm of accomplishment, day after day, because your tasks are mapped and feasible. Knowing what to tackle next frees your mind from the constant worry of planning on the fly. You can instead devote your focus to the specific project at hand, which improves your results. Over time, these scheduled blocks compound into significant achievements, reinforcing that your disciplined approach pays off. As you see projects come to fruition through structured planning, you'll gain confidence to extend this technique across every area of life that requires your attention and diligence.

4. Conquering Procrastination: Strategies for Swift Action

Procrastination is a stubborn opponent standing between you and your best performance. You've encountered those moments when starting a task feels like pushing a boulder uphill. Perhaps you know what needs doing but can't bring yourself to begin. Conquering procrastination isn't about lecturing yourself to "do better." It's about adopting practical tactics that lower the barriers to immediate action.

One effective method is the two-minute rule. If a task can be wrapped up in under two minutes, replying to an email, filing a document, or sending a quick update, handle it at once. This breaks the habit of pushing small tasks aside until they balloon into an intimidating backlog. The quick triumph of completion also gives you a mental boost, which can carry over to more substantial tasks. Think of it as priming your mind with small wins that dispel inertia.

However, your real battle might be tackling bigger tasks that can't fit into two minutes. In such cases, break them down into digestible segments. If the thought of writing a ten-page report feels daunting, decide to write the first paragraph or outline the main points. When your mind sees a smaller, achievable goal, it's less likely to resist. Momentum builds from each completed segment, turning a monumental project into a series of more approachable steps.

You'll also benefit from creating accountability. If you work alone, share your goals with a friend or mentor who can check on your progress. If you function within a team, openly declaring your next deadline makes you feel responsible not only to yourself but also to those around you. This gentle pressure can move you to act even when you'd rather dawdle. It's not about inviting criticism; it's about embracing social support that encourages timely action.

Another tactic is to address the emotional side of procrastination. Often, you delay tasks because you dread the discomfort of getting started, worry about making mistakes, or fear the outcome. Acknowledge these feelings without letting them dictate your behaviour. You might remind yourself that the first draft of any work can be refined later or that mistakes are part of the learning process. By reframing the activity, seeing it as an opportunity rather than a burdensome obligation, you soften resistance.

A final note is to keep your workspace conducive to action. If your environment is littered with distractions, it's all too easy to divert your attention. Turn off unnecessary notifications, isolate yourself from social media, or find a quiet place where you can focus. Equally vital is ensuring you have the tools and information needed before you start. Removing trivial obstacles prevents you from using them as an excuse to postpone work.

When procrastination rears its head, don't view it as a moral failing but as a signal. It tells you that a task has become too big or too vague or that you're avoiding a potential discomfort. By applying practical techniques, small tasks, accountability, reframing your perspective, and an organised environment, you'll stand a better chance of moving forward promptly and reclaiming the hours you might otherwise lose.

5. Sharpening Your Focus in a Distracted World

Your modern environment assaults you with beeps, pop-ups, and endless streams of digital content. These distractions can unravel your productivity before you realise it. Mastering focus in this context isn't a simple wish; it's a skill that sets the stage for excellence. Eliminating mental clutter means you can channel your intelligence, energy, and creativity toward the tasks that truly matter.

To begin, confront the biggest culprit: your digital devices. Your phone or computer can become a productivity weapon or a time sink, depending on how you govern it. When you face critical work requiring deep concentration, switch your device to silent mode and disable alerts that tug your attention away. Build a habit of checking emails or messages at set intervals rather than responding every time your device buzzes. By taking charge of your environment, you shield your mind from a barrage of distractions.

Another potent focus enhancer is single-tasking. Multitasking is often praised, but in reality, the human brain performs best when it tackles one task at a time. When you juggle multiple projects, your mind wastes energy switching between them, leaving you drained and less effective. In contrast, immersing yourself in one undertaking leads to faster completion and superior quality. You also experience less stress because your mind isn't pulled in conflicting directions.

Protect your mental energy by taking deliberate breaks. Pushing through fatigue can erode the very concentration you aim to sustain. A short pause, stepping outside, stretching, or taking a few deep breaths gives your mind a chance to reset. After the break, you're ready to resume with renewed clarity. Remember that breaks are not idle time but strategic resets that keep your focus robust across a long day.

Physical environment also plays a key role. If your workspace overflows with random items or leftover clutter, it visually reminds you of unfinished tasks. This mental noise can chip away at your concentration. Rearranging your workspace, removing the unneeded objects, and only keeping the essentials can work wonders for your ability to keep your eyes on the task at hand. An orderly environment soothes the mind, fostering an atmosphere where deep concentration can thrive.

Lastly, manage your internal chatter. Self-doubt or racing thoughts about unrelated issues can be as disruptive as external noise. Writing down concerns on a notepad can free your mind to focus on the immediate job, knowing you can address those issues later. If anxious thoughts persist, quick mindfulness techniques, slow, measured breathing, or briefly closing your eyes to centre yourself can quiet that mental storm.

In an age saturated with diversions, consistent focus is your secret weapon. By taking command of your devices, embracing single-tasking, scheduling purposeful breaks, creating a tidy workspace, and soothing any internal turmoil, you cultivate an environment where your focus becomes unstoppable. Guard that attention zealously and direct it toward your most meaningful undertakings. You'll not only accomplish more, but you'll also feel more at peace and in control of your own life.

6. Harnessing Time Management Tools and Technology

The technology at your fingertips can either undermine your productivity or elevate it to new heights. Rather than letting apps and devices become time traps, you can deploy them as allies in managing your schedule, tracking goals, and streamlining daily tasks. Learning to filter through the myriad of options is your first step in leveraging technology for better time management.

Start by examining which tasks consume the bulk of your time. Do you struggle with scheduling meetings, organising tasks, or remembering deadlines? Identify the areas where you need the most support, then find a tool that tackles that issue directly. For instance, if your calendar is always in chaos, you might benefit from a digital scheduler that auto-syncs across your devices. If to-do lists are your weakness, an intuitive task management app can help you break down large projects into smaller tasks with deadlines and reminders.

However, technology is only as effective as your discipline in using it. A sophisticated task manager won't serve you if you ignore notifications or fail to review your tasks daily. Integrate these tools into your routine, checking them as consistently as you would glance at a clock. One method is to open your task or calendar app every morning and evening, reviewing priorities for the day and assessing what remains. This keeps you aligned with your goals and wards off that sense of drifting.

Beyond scheduling and task management, apps that track your time can unearth insights about where your day truly goes. By measuring how long you spend on websites or applications, you can spot patterns of distraction. Once you see how quickly a few minutes here and there on social media add up, you'll be motivated to set boundaries. Some platforms allow you to impose time limits on certain apps, nipping mindless scrolling in the bud.

You can also adopt collaborative tech solutions if you manage or work within a team. Shared boards or project management tools enable everyone to see ongoing tasks, deadlines, and responsibilities, reducing miscommunication and saving time lost to repeated status updates. When every team member has a transparent view of priorities, it fosters accountability and prompts quicker issue resolution. However, keep an eye on the number of communication platforms you use, as toggling between multiple tools can undo the advantages of digital collaboration.

One word of caution: adopting too many tools at once can sabotage your efforts. There's a temptation to test every new productivity app you discover, which might lead you to spend more time exploring technology than getting your tasks done. Choose one or two tools that directly address your biggest challenges and master them before branching out.

Used judiciously, technology is a driving force behind efficient time management. It minimises manual tasks, clarifies priorities, and helps you track progress. The key is not to be dazzled by the possibilities but to pick tools aligned with your needs and then employ them consistently. When technology works for you, rather than dictating your actions, you'll see a marked improvement in how you manage your precious hours.

7. Balancing Work and Leisure for a Fulfilled Life

Your professional ambitions may be massive, but genuine fulfilment demands more than unending labour. While setting and pursuing big goals is essential, your overall quality of life hinges on striking a balance. Ignoring your personal sphere leads to burnout, strained relationships, and an empty sense of success. On the other hand, leaning too heavily into leisure without building a meaningful career path can yield dissatisfaction and financial precariousness. The sweet spot lies in a rhythm that respects both your drive for achievement and your need for enjoyment and rest.

The first step toward this equilibrium is granting leisure the importance it deserves. Instead of viewing relaxation as a luxury earned only when you're finished with every task, treat it as a core component of daily living. Schedule breaks or recreation just as you would schedule a client meeting, ensuring it occupies a stable place in your routine. This mindset acknowledges that you must recharge to remain productive, creative, and emotionally healthy.

Make your leisure time genuinely restorative. Passive activities like channel surfing might fill an hour, but they do little to refresh your mind and body. Seek pursuits that spark enthusiasm, teach you something new, or keep you physically active. Whether it's taking dance classes, gardening, or exploring local trails, find leisure activities that excite or calm you. Those experiences will reinvigorate you far more than aimless scrolling or background TV noise.

Spending time with people you care about is another powerful route to a balanced life. Whether it's sharing a relaxed dinner with family, catching up with friends, or engaging with a local group of like-minded individuals, strong relationships nourish the soul. Carve out space to meaningfully connect without the distraction of notifications or to-do lists. Such moments remind you of your roots and foster belonging, two elements that buffer you against burnout.

Striving for balance doesn't mean you avoid hard work. It means you approach it strategically, giving your peak energy to your priorities while granting yourself rightful space to decompress. There will be periods when work intensifies, like tackling urgent deadlines, and your leisure time might shrink temporarily. The key is to return to equilibrium once those intense phases pass. The long-term reward of that rhythm is resilience, motivation, and sustained overall well-being.

Monitor your mental and physical indicators to gauge whether you're drifting off-balance. Chronic fatigue, loss of enthusiasm for projects you once enjoyed, or frequent frustration can signal the need to recalibrate. Reflect on your daily or weekly routine, adjusting either your schedule or your leisure pursuits to bring back harmony. Such fine-tuning demands honest self-awareness. Even a small shift, like dedicating a half-hour of quality reading or exercise daily, can dramatically boost your sense of overall fulfilment.

Balance is not a rigid formula but an ongoing dance, changing as your life circumstances evolve. Your objectives, relationships, and personal interests all shape where that equilibrium sits. By respecting both productivity and rest, you position yourself for long-term success in every area of life. You'll also discover that your best ideas, your creativity, and your energy to tackle formidable challenges often emerge once you've honoured your own need for rejuvenation and pleasure.

8. Navigating Time Management in a Fast-Paced Digital Age

Your world teems with instant communication, endless notifications, and a continuous flood of information. This digital revolution offers astonishing possibilities, but it also poses a fresh challenge: managing your time when distractions multiply and blur the line between professional and private life. Adapting the timeless principles of efficient time management to these modern realities is essential if you aim to stay productive and balanced.

The root of the problem often lies in the always-on nature of digital technology. Work can spill into your personal hours through email alerts or team chat messages. Personal distractions, social media, streaming content, online games, intrude on your professional day as well. Resolving this tension means establishing strict boundaries. For instance, confine professional communications to a specific window and log out of your work apps once the day ends. If you can't fully exit them, at least silence non-urgent alerts. Reciprocally, limit personal browsing during working hours by designating short intervals to handle personal online tasks. This separation helps preserve mental clarity and prevents you from drifting in a digital haze all day.

Your approach to information intake also needs reassessment. With countless newsletters, online publications, and social feeds, you can waste hours sifting through trivial updates if you're not careful. Make your content consumption purposeful. Decide on the topics truly relevant to your career or personal growth, subscribe to a few high-quality sources, and skip the rest. Batch your reading, gather the articles you want to explore and tackle them in one block rather than dipping in and out perpetually. This practice stops you from continually checking for new items and directs your attention where it counts.

Another essential practice is refining your online communication. Virtual collaboration can be a blessing, but back-and-forth messages can devour your hours. Whenever possible, opt for direct, concise communication. Try picking up the phone or scheduling a quick video chat if issues can be resolved more swiftly that way. Reserve lengthy email threads for when they genuinely add value.

Being proactive with your online presence can help you guard your time further. If you notice that you're compulsively checking social media platforms or news apps, install productivity extensions that limit usage. Alternatively, block distracting websites during peak work periods. Your short-term gratification might suffer, but the long-term gains in focus and mental space are enormous.

Finally, remember that technology should serve your goals, not dictate them. Many productivity apps promise to organise your tasks and streamline your calendar, but rely on them only if they genuinely improve your process. If an app creates unnecessary complexities, ditch it. Your objective is to remain in control of how you spend time, not to chase the next trendy tool.

In a fast-paced digital world, the ability to differentiate meaningful engagement from trivial screen time is a superpower. By drawing firm boundaries, consuming information mindfully, communicating effectively, and wielding the right tools thoughtfully, you free yourself to concentrate on tasks that uphold your ambitions. You'll enjoy the best of technology's benefits while protecting your mental energy from the perpetual buzz of online distractions.

9. The Impact of Time Mastery on Your Success

Time mastery sets high achievers apart from those who never quite reach their potential. Once you grasp that skilled time management underpins every other form of success, you see why so many accomplished individuals swear by disciplined schedules and the unwavering commitment to purposeful work. It's often that extra hour of focused effort or a carefully planned day that catapults someone to the next level in their field.

Professional success is one clear outcome of time mastery. By prioritising tasks that yield the greatest long-term value, you direct your efforts where they matter. Rather than scattering your energy, you launch your career upward through targeted, consistent strides forward. This advantage isn't reserved for executives or entrepreneurs; it applies just as well to individuals in all roles who commit themselves to excellence in their domain. When you maximise your hours, your expertise grows faster, and your contributions become more noticeable.

Beyond the work sphere, managing time effectively enriches your personal life. You free yourself to take on activities that fuel personal growth or bring you joy, new hobbies, creative endeavours, or volunteering. Rather than lamenting the lack of time, you create it through careful planning. This sense of control extends to how you handle relationships as well. When your days aren't consumed by chaotic, last-minute rushes, you can devote genuine attention to the people who matter. This fosters deeper connections and a stronger sense of support.

Health is another area shaped by your approach to time. Quality rest, exercise, and nutritious meals all demand consistent pockets of time. If you're perpetually in a hurry, you're more likely to sacrifice sleep, skip workouts, or grab unbalanced meals. Each of those compromises chips away at your vitality. Conversely, a structured schedule makes room for a healthy lifestyle, letting you sustain the energy and focus needed to excel in all facets of your life.

As you see the positive outcomes of time mastery accumulate, your confidence grows. You understand that you're not at the mercy of events. You realise you can shape your day-to-day reality to produce the life you envision. That shift in mindset propels you forward, enabling you to set even more ambitious targets. Instead of feeling anxious about new challenges, you tackle them with a calm resolve, knowing you have the systems and habits in place to succeed.

Crucially, time mastery doesn't involve a rigid existence. True mastery lets you navigate spontaneous events without derailing your overall plan. You learn to pivot gracefully when surprises arise, returning to your structured approach once the crisis is handled. This balance between flexibility and discipline grants you a sense of self-assured calm rather than suffocating regimentation.

Mastering your hours is a hidden powerhouse that supports growth in your career, personal passions, relationships, and well-being. By continuing to refine how you allocate your most precious resource, you solidify a foundation upon which all your aspirations can flourish. You'll look back and see that many of your proudest achievements emerged from the determination to use your time effectively.

10. Charting Your Path Forward with Intentional Time Management

As you reach the close of this chapter, you can see that time management is much more than a checklist or a batch of tips. It's a guiding principle that lets you deliberately craft the life you desire. Instead of fumbling through random tasks or losing valuable hours to distractions, you'll own your schedule and direct it toward whatever fires up your ambitions. This clarity gives you a sense of control and empowerment, ensuring your hard work brings genuine progress rather than fleeting satisfaction.

Bringing every strategy together, prioritisation, planning, procrastination-busting, focus, technology use, and balance, sets you on a path marked by intentionality. You'll know precisely why you choose certain tasks and reject others. You'll see tangible results day after day, with your confidence expanding as you prove to yourself that real growth happens when you manage your time. This sense of achievement often motivates you to reach higher, whether that means launching a new venture, signing up for a creative project, or devoting energy to personal wellness.

However, time management isn't something you master and ignore. It's a continuous practice that evolves alongside your changing goals. You might transition from a period of intense, detail-oriented focus on a major work assignment to a phase where you emphasise rest and reflection. Stay attentive to your current circumstances, adjusting your approach to match your new priorities. This fluidity keeps you from falling into stagnant routines that no longer serve your progress.

Remember to celebrate milestones. Each time you finish a task ahead of schedule or see a project flourish under your leadership, pause to recognise that your structured use of time played a crucial role. This acknowledgement keeps you motivated and reinforces the habits you're developing. Equally, remain patient with yourself if you slip occasionally. Old habits can pop back up, and unexpected events can throw off your routines. A short recovery period is normal, and each stumble teaches you to refine your system further.

Lastly, turn your focus outward from time to time. Encourage those around you to adopt better time management, whether they're colleagues, team members, or loved ones. When everyone embraces clear priorities, efficient schedules, and balanced living, it elevates not only individual achievements but the collective atmosphere as well. You'll see synergy in group efforts, with projects running smoothly and personal relationships benefiting from the mutual respect for one another's time.

This chapter has equipped you with the perspective and the tools to become the architect of your schedule. The aim now is to apply these principles daily. Take what resonates, discard what doesn't serve you, and create a personal framework that champions a disciplined but flexible approach to your hours. By committing to intentional time management, you set yourself on a trajectory marked by resilience, effectiveness, and sustained fulfilment. Let every hour reflect your deeper purpose, fuelling the future you envision, one carefully chosen moment at a time.

CHAPTER 15

Lifelong Learning: The Path to Self-Improvement

You live in a world that's always on the move, constantly evolving and bringing fresh challenges and opportunities your way. Learning doesn't stop the day you leave school or complete a course; it's something that continues through every chapter of your life. Lifelong learning is your secret weapon for personal growth and self-improvement, giving you the tools to adapt, succeed, and stay sharp in an ever-changing landscape. It's about cultivating a mindset where you're always hungry for new knowledge, skills, and experiences.

Think about some of the most successful people you admire; they didn't get there by settling for what they already knew. Leaders, innovators, and great achievers are perpetual learners, constantly seeking ways to expand their abilities and understanding. Lifelong learning isn't a chore; it's a mindset that keeps your brain agile, your confidence high, and your opportunities endless. In this chapter, you'll discover how nurturing curiosity and committing to continuous growth can transform not just your career but your whole life.

1. A Compelling Start: Why Lifelong Learning Matters

You live in a world that never stands still. Knowledge expands every day, new skills emerge, and fresh

Lifelong Learning: The Path to Self-Improvement

opportunities take shape. In this environment, deciding to learn across your entire life becomes a power move. Lifelong learning means you keep collecting knowledge and capabilities well beyond formal education. It reflects your adaptability, curiosity, and determination to remain sharp in a rapidly changing world. This chapter focuses on why that spirit of continuous growth is a direct route to self-improvement and ongoing success.

You may have experienced moments when you finished a course or landed a promotion and then felt your drive to learn fizzle out. Those periods often appear when you believe you have "arrived." Yet the best achievers, from pioneering entrepreneurs to trailblazers in science, share a perspective that learning never ends. Picture someone like Bill McDermott, who led major corporations with a mindset that staying relevant means constantly picking up new insights. By refusing to settle into comfort zones, individuals like him show the benefits of being ever-ready to acquire skills. If you treat learning as an ongoing mission, you open doors that remain shut to those who believe they have already learned everything worth knowing.

Lifelong learning puts you on a path of self-improvement because it trains you to embrace novelty rather than fear it. Every time you approach a skill you do not have or explore a concept you do not fully understand, you practise turning the unknown into something within reach. You strengthen your ability to adapt, and you reinforce a sense of personal agency. The thrill you feel when you master a new topic or see results from a fresh skill is not limited to the academic arena; it carries over into the rest of your life, building confidence in what you can accomplish.

You also sharpen your mental agility by committing to continuous learning. Research shows that the more you stretch your brain with new knowledge, the more resilient and flexible you become in your thinking. This resilience extends to your emotional life, where you find it easier to adapt to unexpected changes or challenges because you have trained yourself to handle the new and unfamiliar. In essence, you gain not only knowledge but a strengthened mind.

On top of all this, a lifelong learner holds a certain magnetism: employers recognise your adaptability, peers value your open-mindedness, and your circle often expands through shared learning pursuits. Socially and professionally, you become someone who sparks conversations and ideas. Opportunities gravitate toward you because you can engage with different subjects, and you show a willingness to learn from everyone around you.

So, think of lifelong learning as your personal evolution strategy. It is not confined to classrooms, nor does it end once you have a job title or certification. Whether you discover new career paths or adapt to unpredictable shifts in your field, your lifelong learning spirit fuels ongoing self-improvement. You become a person who always seeks more knowledge, more perspective, and more ways to grow, and that is exactly how you stay ahead and remain fulfilled in a world that never stops transforming.

2. Building an Unstoppable Curiosity: Cultivating a Passion for Knowledge

You have probably observed that some people seem inherently curious. They cannot help asking questions; they dig into how things work, and they find thrill in discovering new ideas. That zest for knowledge often propels them further than mere obligations or formal lessons ever could. While a few individuals might show curiosity from an early age, the truth is that you can cultivate this passion at any stage of life. By viewing your learning journey as an exciting exploration rather than a chore, you turn every day into a chance to unearth something fresh.

The first step is to embrace the mindset that curiosity is a choice. You can decide to look at life's challenges and opportunities through the lens of discovery. Instead of viewing an unfamiliar topic as intimidating, treat it as an open invitation to expand your horizon. Think of Tim Ferriss, known for experimenting with different skills, from cooking to languages. His secret was not an extraordinary innate ability; it was a decision to see every skill gap as an invitation to experiment and grow. That spirit transformed him into a model of unconventional learning.

Next, identify areas you genuinely find intriguing. Too often, individuals latch onto subjects because they believe those fields promise lucrative careers or social status. True curiosity flourishes when driven by genuine interest. If technology captivates you, immerse yourself in coding challenges or tech meetups. If you feel drawn to art, experiment with sketching or online creative workshops. By leaning into activities that spark your delight, you make learning a source of pleasure instead of a forced exercise.

Another powerful way to nurture curiosity is to keep a question journal. Write down anything that sparks a question during your day: "How does this process work?" "Why do we follow this tradition?" "Could this be improved?" Then, make time, even briefly, to investigate those questions. This practice trains your brain to seek answers proactively. Over time, your capacity to question grows into a habit, making curiosity an integral part of who you are.

You also want to connect with communities or individuals who radiate a love for learning. When you surround yourself with people who discuss ideas, share books, and talk enthusiastically about ongoing projects, your own curiosity naturally picks up momentum. You might join study groups, attend local seminars, or participate in online forums. In these spaces, you gain fresh insights and see how others feed their curiosity, an exchange of ideas that helps keep your passion alive.

Finally, approach failure with a different view: treat mistakes and missteps as signposts on your learning path, not reasons to give up. Curiosity thrives when you see each failure as new data about what to refine or explore next. This shift in perspective reduces the fear of getting things wrong, encouraging you to stretch beyond your comfort level.

Every day presents endless invitations to expand your mind. By shifting from a passive stance to an active, questioning one, you turn life into your classroom. The more curiosity you cultivate, the richer your journey becomes. You find not only new skills but also deeper insight into yourself, your environment, and your potential, forging a lifelong relationship with learning that keeps your mind energised.

3. Broadening Your Horizons: Lifelong Learning in Your Career

In your career, remaining the same is not an option. Industries evolve, job roles shift, and the technologies you depend upon may rapidly become outdated. If you adapt slowly or refuse to learn beyond the basics, you risk becoming stuck while others surge ahead. Lifelong learning in the professional world is not a luxury; it is the cornerstone of continued relevance and career growth. You boost your adaptability, expand your skill set, and open up new opportunities by refusing to stand still.

It helps to look at examples of individuals who have soared by embracing a learning mindset throughout their careers. Bill McDermott is a leader who has headed global tech enterprises and credits ongoing education for his resilience. Rather than clinging to prior achievements, he pursued insights into emerging trends, refined his leadership strategies, and stayed open to innovative concepts. This readiness to learn allowed him to transform entire organisations and guide them through market upheavals.

The practical side of lifelong learning in your job is straightforward: the more you know, the more resourceful you become. By seeking out workshops, professional courses, or even online tutorials relevant to your field, you enhance your value within a team and stand out when promotions arise. Beyond structured courses, you can also learn informally through conversations with mentors, reading authoritative books in your field, or exploring case studies. These efforts help you see patterns, notice gaps in your industry, and anticipate future developments.

A critical element of career-focused learning is developing what psychologist Carol Dweck calls a "growth mindset." That means believing your abilities can expand through effort rather than seeing them as fixed traits. If you treat each new challenge at work as a chance to sharpen a skill or gain fresh knowledge, you shift from feeling threatened by difficulties to feeling energised by them. This mindset protects you from stagnation and keeps you agile in uncertain times.

Networking also plays a role in your learning journey. When you participate in professional events, forums, or seminars, you get exposed to other people's experiences and insights. Through conversations with peers who face similar challenges, you discover new tools or angles you have never tried before. You may find mentors willing to guide you through professional hurdles or highlight knowledge areas you need to strengthen.

Above all, keep one principle in mind: your career is not static. Long gone are the days when you learned a trade once and spent decades refining it without significant changes. Today, you must continually retool and reskill. Such ongoing development helps you remain relevant and fuels your confidence. You walk into the office (or connect online) knowing you bring the most up-to-date perspective to your role.

In the end, a career anchored in learning will set you apart. It shows that you have the foresight to remain versatile and the willingness to adapt. Whether you aim for senior leadership, want to switch roles, or plan to launch your own venture, adopting lifelong learning is the ultimate insurance for your professional future.

4. Curious Minds Triumph: How Inquisitiveness Drives Your Learning

Curiosity is your secret weapon. It sparks questions, nudges you out of complacency, and invites you to examine the world from varied angles. While some people dismiss curiosity as childish or distracting, you can harness it as a

Lifelong Learning: The Path to Self-Improvement

force that propels you toward new insights and skill sets. By following your innate inquisitiveness, you end up tackling challenges with more creativity and spotting opportunities hidden in the unknown.

You have likely heard about the physicist Marie Curie, whose unquenchable curiosity led her to groundbreaking discoveries. Although her field was science, the trait that set her apart was the same quality you can nurture today: a willingness to pursue answers, even if they are not immediately apparent. Through that pursuit, she not only made pivotal discoveries but redefined how the world looked at radiation. In your context, curiosity pushes you to probe deeper into your tasks, shining a spotlight on areas you might improve or approaches you have never considered.

One effective method to harness curiosity is to cultivate the habit of asking "why?" repeatedly. When you face a procedure, strategy, or idea you do not fully grasp, query its rationale. The same applies to daily routines or widely accepted norms. This method of structured inquiry leads you to pinpoint inefficiencies or unexploited angles. For instance, if you see a business process that has run the same way for years, question each step. You may discover fresh ways to cut costs or raise efficiency. This willingness to dig deeper marks you as a problem-solver, not just an observer.

Another valuable tactic is to track your questions throughout the day. Keep a small notebook or a digital list and record any question that pops up, no matter how trivial it might seem. Perhaps you wonder about a new programming language mentioned by colleagues, or you see a pattern in customer feedback that puzzles you. By gathering these queries, you train your mind to remain alert. During your downtime, pick a question to explore. This consistent practice feeds a cycle:

the more you answer, the more new questions emerge, and the more you learn.

Your curiosity also thrives when you surround yourself with people and experiences that encourage exploration. When you spend time with inquisitive colleagues, mentors, or friends, you get exposed to their lines of questioning, which sparks your own. Additionally, novel settings, like seminars outside your usual domain, travel experiences, or cross-functional team projects, fuel curiosity by introducing perspectives you never encountered before. The spark of curiosity can transform routine tasks into interesting problems to solve.

Ultimately, inquisitiveness allows you to see the connection between unrelated concepts. It encourages you to experiment, test assumptions, and glean insights from unexpected sources. Each time you let your curiosity guide you, you develop a richer understanding of your environment and your capabilities. In effect, you become a perpetual student of life: never too complacent, never too certain, and always open to the spark of inspiration that propels you one step further on the path of self-improvement.

5. Expanding Your World: How Online Learning Transforms Growth

Gone are the days when learning was confined to classrooms or rigid timetables. Today, online learning platforms bring you face-to-face with experts worldwide, letting you dive into subjects at your own pace. This revolution means you are no longer limited by geography or schedules; you can tap into an endless source of knowledge, whether you are at home, in the office, or on the move. Embracing these digital tools can supercharge your journey as a lifelong learner.

Lifelong Learning: The Path to Self-Improvement

Imagine you are intrigued by data analysis, or you fancy developing a creative hobby like digital illustration. Online courses, whether from established universities or specialised learning portals, turn your curiosity into tangible skills. Tim Ferriss once detailed how he taught himself intricate subjects through online resources, turning theory into hands-on mastery. He discovered that you could refine your approach by taking advantage of expert-led tutorials, community forums, and immediate feedback. You, too, can take those steps, shaping your expertise without abandoning your everyday responsibilities.

Convenience is a major benefit: you can pause and revisit lessons, play them at double speed if you learn fast, or replay them for clarity. Online learning platforms usually host discussion boards where you interact with peers and instructors, posing questions that might not arise in a traditional classroom. This dynamic fosters collaborative learning as you and your virtual classmates help each other tackle sticking points. Such interactive methods keep your motivation high, especially if you juggle a career, family obligations, or other pursuits.

Additionally, online learning encourages you to explore multiple areas. If you want to sharpen your leadership skills while delving into basic coding, you can find separate modules to address both. This varied approach ensures you continue to broaden your horizons. You never know; dabbling in a new subject might lead to unexpected insights that enhance your main career path, or you might discover a fresh passion that becomes a side project or new profession.

Yet online learning demands self-discipline. Without a teacher checking attendance or a set classroom environment, you must take the initiative. Setting goals, whether to complete a single course module per week or to practise a newly learned skill daily, keeps you on track. Some learners form accountability groups: a few friends or colleagues agree on a schedule and then encourage one another to stay committed.

In a world where industries shift quickly, the capacity to learn on demand is invaluable. Online learning acts as your personal upgrade system, granting you the freedom to respond to emerging trends in real-time. Whether your aim is to earn certifications that boost your CV or to feed a personal interest, you hold the reins to shape the content and pace of your education. Adopting online learning as part of your routine turns you into a more versatile individual, prepared for the challenges of the future. Above all, it underlines the principle that no matter what stage of life you are in, the door to knowledge remains wide open.

6. Confronting Obstacles: Breaking Down Barriers to Lifelong Learning

When you decide to become a lifelong learner, obstacles show up in subtle and not-so-subtle ways. Perhaps your schedule is crammed with work and family commitments, or the costs of certain courses appear overwhelming. Maybe self-doubt nags at you, asking, "Am I too old to pick this up?" or "Do I have the aptitude?" Confronting these hurdles head-on is a vital step, revealing that most barriers are surmountable with the right approach and mindset.

Time is often the biggest culprit. You may feel your week is so full that introducing new lessons or reading might crowd out rest or leisure. But look closely, and you might discover pockets of time that slip by without much thought, scrolling through your phone or getting lost in aimless TV viewing. If you carve out even 30 minutes a day, it can accumulate into

Lifelong Learning: The Path to Self-Improvement

significant learning hours over a month. Creating a small daily or weekly routine, like studying during your commute or dedicating a portion of your lunch break to e-learning, makes a consistent learning habit more realistic.

Money can also be a sticking point. Some certificate programmes or degrees are undeniably expensive. However, the landscape of free or inexpensive resources is vast. Libraries offer free access to countless ebooks and online journals, while platforms like Khan Academy or various open educational resources provide no-cost lessons on a wide range of topics. If you dig a bit deeper, you will find professional bodies sometimes sponsor free webinars or discounted workshops for members. Employers might cover costs if the subject aligns with the company's goals. By exploring these possibilities, you discover that financial barriers are frequently more flexible than they appear.

Then there is the issue of self-doubt, the voice telling you that you lack the talent, intelligence, or youth to master a new skill. In truth, you are capable of learning at any stage if you stay persistent. Neuroscience supports the brain's ability to adapt at all ages, a trait known as neuroplasticity. Start small to build momentum. Each mini-success, like comprehending a tricky concept or finishing an introductory module, sends your mind the message that you can achieve the next challenge. Over time, your confidence grows alongside your knowledge.

It is also important to recognise that obstacles are not signs to quit but signposts directing you to refine your approach. Rather than giving up when the cost is too high, you look for alternative resources. If your schedule is packed, you reorganise or trim unproductive activities. If you encounter a stumbling block in your learning, you seek a different explanation or a tutor. This problem-solving approach not only keeps you on the path of lifelong learning but also trains you in resourcefulness.

Every learner faces hurdles. What counts is how you respond. By systematically dismantling the barriers of time, cost, and self-doubt, you demonstrate that no external factor can permanently block your growth. The more adept you become at overcoming these obstacles, the stronger your sense of personal control. You turn each challenge into proof that lifelong learning, although not always easy, remains entirely within your grasp.

7. Practical Strategies: Elevating Your Learning Habits

Maintaining the momentum of lifelong learning hinges on the habits you weave into your daily life. Without a clear plan, good intentions can dissolve into procrastination and scattered attempts at study. Constructing purposeful strategies ensures that your learning does not get pushed aside by immediate pressures or daily distractions.

Start by setting SMART targets: Specific, Measurable, Achievable, Relevant, and Time-bound. Instead of vaguely declaring, "I want to learn coding," decide: "I will complete an introductory programming module within three weeks, focusing on Python basics." That specificity keeps you motivated and provides a clear finish line to aim for. Tracking your progress along the way affirms that you are moving forward and prevents you from drifting.

Another core element is deliberate practice. Psychologist Anders Ericsson found that top performers in many fields did not magically become the best; they engaged in targeted exercises that challenge them beyond their comfort zone. Say you want to enhance your public speaking. Instead of reading about techniques alone, you might record yourself

Lifelong Learning: The Path to Self-Improvement

delivering a speech, observe the playback, note your weaknesses, and refine your delivery. This method ensures you continuously push your boundaries rather than passively absorbing theory.

Regular reflection also boosts your learning habit. Dedicate a small window each day or week to ponder what you have absorbed, what remains confusing, and what skills are taking shape. You could keep a learning journal to detail the breakthroughs or questions that arose. By articulating your insights, you sharpen your memory and identify areas requiring extra attention. Reflection might reveal patterns; for instance, you might notice you retain information better in the mornings or learn more effectively after a quick review of previous material.

Accountability can be another driving force. Some form small mastermind groups with colleagues or friends who share similar learning goals. If you are learning a language, for instance, you could commit to practising conversation sessions or exchanging updates about new vocabulary. When you have someone expecting you to show up and demonstrate progress, your motivation to stay consistent rises. You could also use apps that track your study time or prompt you with reminders.

Finally, make space for enjoyment. When you view learning as drudgery, it becomes a chore you avoid. Find ways to infuse fun, maybe you love narratives, so you approach new topics through documentaries or engaging books. If gamification appeals to you, some learning platforms offer rewards or levels that satisfy your sense of competition. The more you associate learning with enjoyment and meaning, the less willpower you need to maintain your routine.

Effective strategies do not have to be complicated. By focusing on clear goals, deliberate practice, reflection, accountability, and a dash of fun, you create a structured environment where learning thrives. The habits you build transform fleeting enthusiasm into ongoing progress, ensuring that your journey toward self-improvement continues steadily, no matter how busy or challenging life gets.

8. Looking After Your Mind: Mental Health Benefits of Learning

When you devote yourself to lifelong learning, you improve more than your intellect or career, your mental health benefits significantly too. Engaging the mind in fresh pursuits boosts confidence, fights monotony, and often counters feelings of loneliness or depression. In essence, every new skill or piece of knowledge lights up a spark in your mental landscape, pushing back against negativity and inactivity.

Medical studies point out that consistent mental engagement helps maintain cognitive function as you age. Puzzles, new languages, or complex subjects encourage the brain to forge new neural connections, potentially delaying cognitive decline. This means that by exploring areas that challenge you, such as advanced cooking techniques or unfamiliar software tools, you not only enhance your skill set but also fortify your brain's agility. With each step, you feel sharper and more present, which does wonders for your self-esteem and overall positivity.

Learning also promotes a sense of purpose. People often find their mental well-being dips when they lose direction. Launching into a new course or a personal research project reminds you that there is always something engaging to aim for. That sense of direction proves especially valuable in transitional moments, such as switching jobs or retiring. If you fill your days with discovery and new objectives, you cushion yourself against the aimlessness that sometimes emerges during big life changes.

Additionally, the social dimension of learning can greatly help your emotional resilience. Whether you take an in-person class or join an online study group, the connections you forge with fellow learners create a support network. You find people with shared interests, and these acquaintances can become friends or professional contacts. Exchanging ideas, sharing tips, and even commiserating over difficulties fosters a sense of belonging. Loneliness or isolation often diminishes when you see how many others walk a similar path.

Your emotional health benefits in another way: achieving learning milestones gives you a chance to celebrate progress. Perhaps you have completed a complicated certificate programme or mastered a new instrument piece. That wave of accomplishment releases feel-good chemicals in your brain, reinforcing the desire to keep striving. Setting and reaching learning milestones also trains you to handle smaller challenges with confidence, reducing stress in other parts of your life.

It is worth noting that learning does not erase serious mental health concerns by itself, but it can be an important pillar of a balanced lifestyle that includes professional help if necessary. Sometimes, the simple act of immersing yourself in a constructive project, like reading about philosophy or practising a new skill, can provide a mental break from persistent worries. That break, combined with the satisfaction of growth, eases strain and brightens your daily outlook.

So, when you pick up new knowledge, whether for career advancement or personal pleasure, remember it is more than an intellectual exercise. You are nurturing your mind's resilience, feeding your sense of purpose, and creating bonds with others on a similar journey. Lifelong learning proves to be a secret ingredient for improved mental well-being, empowering you to stay mentally agile, connected, and emotionally grounded.

9. Embracing the Modern Age: Lifelong Learning in the 21st Century

Your world stands on the brink of technological leaps that can reshape entire industries in a blink. The digital revolution, the advent of artificial intelligence, and the global connectivity we enjoy mean that your skill set must adapt faster than ever. Lifelong learning in the 21st century is not merely an option; it is your strategic advantage. When you embrace ongoing education, you keep pace with these changes and position yourself to thrive in evolving scenarios.

First, digital technology has made many skills quickly out of date. If you rely on knowledge you gained five or ten years ago, you risk lagging behind today's standards. By continuously seeking updated resources and tutorials, often available online, you ensure your competence remains fresh. Whether it is understanding data analytics, mastering digital marketing techniques, or becoming fluent in remote collaboration, each newly acquired skill keeps you relevant and able to pivot when needed.

Lifelong Learning: The Path to Self-Improvement

A second driver is the interconnected nature of modern work. You may collaborate with international partners, manage global teams, or serve customers halfway around the planet. In this context, being a lifelong learner involves cultural adaptability. Learning about different customs, communication styles, and worldviews can determine whether you succeed in forging partnerships or misunderstandings arise. By studying global trends and paying attention to international developments, you expand your perspective, preparing yourself for cross-cultural engagements.

A third element shaping 21st-century learning is the sheer volume of data. You can find more information about a niche subject than entire libraries held decades ago. Yet quantity does not always translate to clarity. Lifelong learners develop skills in critical thinking, evaluating which sources are credible, and discerning actionable insights from random noise. You sharpen your ability to sift through data, extract what truly matters, and apply it constructively. This skill becomes essential in a time when misinformation can hamper your decision-making.

Another dimension to consider is how artificial intelligence and automation shift job landscapes. Tasks once done by humans are increasingly handled by machines or AI-driven systems, creating new roles even as some positions fade away. In this environment, the capacity to learn new competencies, whether coding, data literacy, or creative problem-solving, marks you as someone who can transition rather than cling to obsolete roles.

You also encounter a reality where side projects, freelancing, and entrepreneurial ventures merge with traditional employment. Lifelong learning powers you to excel across these varied platforms. You might dabble in freelance graphic design while still working full-time or start a small e-commerce site that complements your office job. The knowledge you acquire in design, marketing, or business administration can help you flourish in that hybrid career approach.

Ultimately, the 21st century does not slow down for anyone. The pace of change accelerates each year. By actively engaging in continuous education, you future-proof your skill set. You also demonstrate adaptability, a trait highly valued by clients, employers, and collaborators. Rather than waiting for change to catch you off guard, you steer the course of your own development, harnessing new trends to remain a valuable contributor in any environment. Lifelong learning thus transforms from a mere ideal into a practical must-have in this whirlwind century.

10. True Inspirations: Stories of Lifelong Learners

To see the real impact of ongoing education, you need only look at the stories of individuals who have persisted in their pursuit of knowledge long after many would have stopped. These tales do more than impress; they prove that you can always reimagine your future, no matter where you begin.

Take, for instance, the writer Maya Angelou. She was not confined to literature alone; she wore many hats: poet, singer, and civil rights activist. Angelou approached life as one extended classroom. Each chapter in her journey, whether living abroad or engaging in activism, fed her writing, shaping her unique voice. Even when she achieved global fame, she continued to explore new perspectives, never content to remain static. Her work resonates because she wove fresh insights from every stage of her life into her art.

Or consider someone like Ray Kroc, who was past middle age when he transformed a small burger outlet into the worldwide chain known as McDonald's. He had dabbled in various fields, piano playing, real estate, paper cup sales, yet he kept learning, refining his business acumen along the way. By the time he encountered the McDonald brothers' system, he possessed both curiosity and an expanded set of commercial skills. That mixture empowered him to reshape fast food on a global scale. His case exemplifies that you can reinvent your career path at an age when many think it is time to slow down.

Another modern figure to note is Malala Yousafzai, who has championed girls' education despite facing extreme adversity. Her commitment to education extends well beyond personal ambition: it stands as a testament to how knowledge can liberate entire communities. Instead of pausing after winning the Nobel Peace Prize, she continued her own studies, underscoring the truth that learning remains ongoing regardless of external accolades.

These stories illustrate that your determination to learn can conquer age limitations, external hurdles, and even societal expectations. You do not need to become an international icon to appreciate the benefits. Perhaps you simply wish to pivot careers, discovering an untapped talent in graphic design after years in administration. Or maybe you want to combine an existing expertise in finance with a new fascination for data science. Lifelong learning paves the way for growth, allowing you to add unexpected layers to your skill set or pivot entirely if you so choose.

When you adopt the role of a lifelong learner, you approach each day with a readiness to absorb, adapt, and innovate. Rather than concluding that you have arrived or that time has run out, you remind yourself that every experience can sharpen your understanding. Look to those who have gone before you, individuals who defied assumptions and refused to let inertia claim them. Their journeys reveal the power of staying open to fresh insights. As you commit to learning across your entire life, your own narrative expands in ways you might never have predicted, proving that transformation is always within reach.

Chapter 16

Creativity: Unleashing Your Inner Genius

Creativity isn't just a special gift that only a select few possess; it's an inner genius waiting to be tapped into right within you. Each of us is born with the natural ability to imagine, to innovate, and to create something fresh out of the ordinary. You might think creativity belongs exclusively to artists, musicians, or inventors, but it's much broader than that; it's the key to solving everyday problems, sparking new ideas, and adding excitement to routine tasks. Creativity is your hidden superpower, ready to help you approach life in ways you've never considered before.

In this chapter, you'll learn to unlock this powerful tool and harness it for your personal and professional success. From overcoming those pesky mental blocks to discovering practical ways to boost your creative potential, you'll find out how simple shifts in mindset can transform the ordinary into something remarkable. So get ready; your creative genius is about to make its grand entrance.

1. The Creative Spark: Why Creativity Matters

Your life thrives on fresh ideas and novel approaches. Creativity is not reserved for the few who paint or compose symphonies; it is the ability to find unique solutions, innovate in unexpected ways, and see possibilities where others spot dead ends. Your inner genius does not depend on formal training in the arts; it emerges from your willingness to step outside the ordinary and approach challenges from new angles. Tapping into creativity enriches your personal and professional life, fuelling your capacity to adapt and excel.

You may doubt your creative side, thinking you lack an "artistic flair." Yet creativity extends well beyond paintbrushes and poetry. Entrepreneurs innovate products, educators devise engaging lessons, and scientists imagine bold experiments. Even in everyday life, arranging your living space, planning events, or cooking, you have opportunities to express creativity. Apple's late co-founder, Steve Jobs, famously bridged technology and artistry, believing that creative expression in design and user experience set his company apart. Jobs's success illustrates that creativity is not an optional extra; it is a driving force that can elevate entire industries.

At its heart, creativity involves looking at your environment with a playful or questioning mindset. It means asking, "How else might this be done?" rather than accepting things as they are. That shift in perspective often leads to solutions you would never see if you relied solely on established approaches. For instance, the story of the Dyson vacuum's invention began with a question: "Why accept vacuum cleaners that lose suction?" That question sparked a journey that reimagined how vacuum technology could function.

Developing creativity also combats stagnation. When faced with routine tasks, you might start to feel bored or unmotivated. But if you challenge yourself to refine the process, introduce new methods, or set a novel goal, you bring fresh energy to the mundane. Creativity transforms repetitive tasks into platforms for experimentation and growth. This reinvention keeps you mentally engaged, boosting satisfaction and productivity.

Furthermore, creativity encourages risk-taking. When you push boundaries, you inevitably face the possibility of failure. Yet by treating those outcomes as lessons, you cultivate resilience. Filmmakers, for example, often endure multiple script rewrites, receiving feedback that might be disheartening. The final product emerges only after they have bravely tested different story angles, discarding what does not work and polishing what does. Through each revision, they learn about their craft, refining their vision until they achieve a result that resonates deeply.

When you unlock your creative spark, you begin to see that challenges are not threats but invitations to innovate. You discover the thrill of solving problems your own way. Even better, your creative mindset often inspires those around you to join in the excitement, fostering an environment of innovation. Whether you are designing a marketing campaign, planning a birthday celebration, or exploring a career shift, your inner genius stands ready to guide you. Seize that spark, and you discover that creativity is not about lofty dreams; it is about applying your unique perspective to ignite something extraordinary in every corner of your life.

2. A Problem-Solving Superpower: Creativity in Everyday Challenges

Creativity is often associated with art studios or recording booths, but in reality, it delivers immense value in day-to-day problem-solving. Picture a recurring challenge in your workplace; maybe team communication stalls, or a budget shrinks unexpectedly. In these scenarios, harnessing creativity can open doors you did not know existed, revealing hidden routes out of the difficulties. You can turn chaos into clarity by thinking beyond standard routines and daring to attempt untested methods.

For instance, you might recall the inventor Thomas Edison, who famously tested countless filament materials before producing a functioning light bulb. Many saw repeated failure, but he viewed each attempt as a step closer to the correct solution. This approach encapsulates creative problem-solving: staying flexible, looking for alternatives, and persisting through trial and error. Though you may not be on the verge of a major invention, the principle applies whenever you face a stumbling block. Each time you attempt a different angle, you multiply your chances of success.

One effective technique is reframing the problem. Instead of dwelling on constraints, "We lack funds", or "This deadline is impossible", shift your focus to what resources you do have or to the ultimate goal you want to achieve. If your department lacks a budget for a big campaign, maybe you can leverage social media to create buzz at virtually no cost. If time is tight, see how you could redefine tasks or delegate them differently. This creative pivot transforms "We cannot do it" into "How might we do it differently?" Even small reframes can produce major breakthroughs.

Another strategy is collaborating with people outside your usual circle. If your team keeps hitting the same wall, perhaps you can invite someone from a completely different department to offer a fresh perspective. This cross-pollination of ideas often yields creative solutions that more homogenous groups might overlook. By bringing new voices into the conversation, you tap into diverse thought processes, and those novel inputs may be precisely the spark you need to progress.

Adopting a playful mindset further strengthens your creative problem-solving. In your free moments, brainstorm outrageous ideas without judging feasibility. Encourage colleagues or friends to pitch the wildest concepts they can imagine. While most of these suggestions may not be practical, they loosen mental barriers and often lead to a workable adaptation. This method resembles how some tech companies host hackathons, where employees brainstorm overnight on crazy concepts, sometimes birthing next-generation features.

Ultimately, creativity in problem-solving is about viewing challenges as puzzles rather than barriers. When you stop seeing obstacles as reasons to abandon a project and start viewing them as intellectual riddles, you free your mind to roam. That mental shift can change not only your success rate but also your attitude at work or in personal projects. Problem-solving evolves into a dynamic quest, fuelling your motivation. With each challenge you tackle through creative methods, you refine your approach, making you more agile and resourceful in whatever crisis or opportunity appears next.

3. Boosting Your Creative Edge: Techniques and Strategies

You might look at prolific creators, artists, entrepreneurs, innovators, and wonder, "How do they keep generating fresh ideas?" While innate talent plays a part, creativity can be nurtured through practical strategies and consistent habits. You do not have to rely on sudden flashes of inspiration; you can structure your environment and mindset to boost imaginative thinking whenever you need it.

One approach is deliberate idea generation. Set aside short sessions where you brainstorm solutions or concepts without filtering them. Write down every possibility, no matter how bizarre. The point is to let your mind roam freely before fine-tuning. For instance, if you want to design a new marketing campaign, spend fifteen minutes jotting down anything that comes to mind: slogans, visuals, even outlandish stunts. Later, sift through these notions to find hidden gems or adapt an out-there concept into a practical plan. This approach mirrors how Leonardo da Vinci filled notebooks with sketches and thoughts that, at first glance, seemed scattered, yet later fuelled great inventions and artworks.

Stepping away from a task can also sharpen your creative mind. Research suggests that incubating a problem, taking a walk, sleeping on it, or doing a non-related activity often results in a fresh perspective. By allowing your subconscious to process ideas, you return with renewed clarity and occasionally an "aha" solution. Think about those moments when you stumble on an answer during a shower or while jogging. That is your brain tapping into background processing. Embrace these breaks as a valuable part of idea generation, not wasted time.

Experimenting with different mediums or skills can further revitalise your creativity. If you spend hours on spreadsheets or analytics, try learning a musical instrument or painting in your off-hours. This switch from left-brain to right-brain tasks (though the brain division is more myth than science) helps you approach problems from multiple angles. Musicians, for instance, often excel at pattern recognition, which can benefit fields ranging from mathematics to marketing. Similarly, delving into new experiences trains your mind to forge connections between seemingly unrelated domains.

It is also wise to cultivate an accepting attitude toward failure. Creativity thrives when you are not paralysed by the fear of getting it wrong. Many famous creators experienced countless missteps before achieving breakthroughs. J. K. Rowling faced multiple rejections of her manuscript before finding a publisher for Harry Potter. The difference lay in her perseverance and willingness to keep refining and presenting her material. Each rejection served as feedback, not an indication that she should quit.

Finally, consider seeking out creative role models or mentors. Observing how inventive thinkers approach their work, from their morning routines to their methods of collaboration, can offer you a framework to adapt. Whether you read biographies or watch interviews, note the behaviours or mindsets that resonate with you and test them out in your own process.

Nurturing creativity is not about chasing rare bursts of inspiration; it is about developing techniques that help you tap into your creative reserves consistently. By engaging in purposeful brainstorming, strategic downtime, cross-disciplinary exploration, a failure-friendly attitude, and gleaning insights from role models, you build a reliable system for imaginative thinking. Over time, your mind grows more flexible and open, ready to craft solutions that stand out in any setting you choose to explore.

4. Unlocking Blocks: Overcoming Creative Obstacles

No matter how inventive you are, you will encounter creative slumps. You sit in front of a blank screen or a project that will not budge, your mind as still as a stagnant pond. These blocks can be disheartening, but they are neither permanent nor insurmountable. With the right adjustments, you can clear the mental clutter that stifles your ideas and reignite your creative spark.

One frequent culprit behind creative blocks is excessive self-criticism. You might reject an idea before it has time to develop because you believe it is not original or is doomed to fail. It helps to separate the generation phase from the critique phase. During the initial brainstorming, aim to produce as many ideas as possible, good or bad. Judgement can come later when you refine or discard them. This separation frees your mind to roam without fear of scrutiny, often unearthing creative nuggets you would otherwise shut down.

Another common cause is burnout. If you have been pushing yourself relentlessly or juggling multiple commitments, your mental resources wear thin. Sometimes, the best remedy is rest. Even short breaks, walks, naps, or mindless reading can recharge your creative reserves. By granting yourself permission to pause, you return with fresh energy. It sounds simple, but the willingness to step away can mean the difference between churning out stale ideas and conjuring up something new and engaging.

You might also feel trapped by routines that have gone stale. While structure can promote productivity, rigid schedules or the same work environment day after day might starve your creative impulses. Shake things up: rearrange your workspace, explore a park you have never visited, or work from a café if you usually stay at home. These small shifts in scenery and habit can jolt you out of autopilot, giving your brain new stimuli to process. This novelty often triggers fresh connections or perspectives.

At times, you might need an external boost, such as feedback or collaboration. If you are stuck on a particular design or concept, consult a friend or colleague. They might offer a viewpoint that dissolves your block instantly. Alternatively, examine creative work from fields beyond your own, music, architecture, or entrepreneurship. Observing how innovators approach challenges in a different domain can spark ideas for your current roadblock. Inspiration can arrive from the most unexpected sources if you remain open.

Finally, keep your sense of play alive. Creativity often emerges when you treat the process like a game, free from the weight of results. Children are a perfect example: they experiment endlessly with crayons, building blocks, or imaginary scenarios, not because they need to create something perfect, but because the process itself is enjoyable. Recapturing that spirit in your work means letting go of the pressure to be brilliant on command. When the process stops feeling like a high-stakes endeavour, your mind relaxes enough to explore new possibilities.

Creative blocks are not a sign of failure; they are temporary hurdles. By reducing self-criticism, allowing rest, introducing variation, seeking input, and approaching tasks with a playful attitude, you can break through those walls. Each time you do, you strengthen your creative muscle, becoming more confident in your ability to produce fresh ideas whenever you need them.

5. Mind-Body Connection: How Creativity Fuels Emotional Well-being

You might view creativity as a skill for making art or improving work projects, but it also deeply affects how you feel emotionally. Engaging in creative activities can lift your mood, reduce stress, and give you a sense of purpose. In this way, creativity becomes a tool not just for practical problem-solving but also for emotional resilience, helping you confront life's ups and downs with greater equilibrium.

Think about how you feel after devoting an hour to a favourite hobby, perhaps painting, writing in a journal, or playing a musical instrument. You often emerge calmer and more focused. Studies in psychology highlight that such creative engagements release dopamine, a chemical tied to pleasure and motivation. This natural reward system encourages you to return to the activity, building a positive cycle: the more you create, the better you feel, and the more you wish to continue creating.

During stressful or overwhelming times, creativity can act as an emotional anchor. It allows you to channel anxieties, joys, and frustrations into something tangible. For instance, many successful authors have transformed personal challenges into writing that resonates with readers worldwide. The process of writing or creating serves as catharsis, turning intangible feelings into a concrete output that you can observe, reflect on, or share. Even if you never show your creative work to anyone, it becomes a private space to process emotions and regain balance.

When you collaborate creatively, whether through a craft group, a band, or a design project, social bonds flourish. Working alongside people who share your interests provides support and camaraderie. This connection plays a protective role in mental health, as feeling part of a creative community diminishes loneliness and fosters belonging. You see it in quilting circles, open mic nights, or online communities where amateurs and professionals alike share their work and cheer each other on.

Creativity also supports your sense of self-efficacy. Each time you solve a creative puzzle or produce something you find meaningful, you reaffirm your ability to influence the world around you. That sense of competence nurtures confidence, reminding you that challenges can be overcome with enough resourcefulness. This positive reinforcement seeps into other parts of your life, reducing feelings of helplessness or anxiety when problems arise.

If you want to deepen creativity's benefits for your well-being, incorporate small creative breaks into your daily routine, ten minutes sketching, half an hour piecing together a digital music loop, or a quick photography stroll. These short sessions offer mental rest from the day's demands, replenishing your emotional reserves. Over time, you learn to rely on creativity not just for producing results but for maintaining your emotional harmony.

So, view creativity as your ally in emotional strength. Whether you are exploring a new art form, penning heartfelt journal entries, or brainstorming your next personal project, you are effectively caring for your mental state. Creativity transforms intangible thoughts and feelings into something you can handle, examine, and sometimes even celebrate, making the burdens of life feel a bit lighter and the joys more fulfilling.

6. Creative Cultures: Fostering Innovation in Workplaces

Picture a workplace where every team member feels inspired to pitch bold concepts and experiment with out-of-the-box ideas. That environment can transform an ordinary organisation into a hub of innovation. Cultivating such a culture of creativity calls for deliberate effort, but the payoff includes breakthroughs in products, processes, and overall morale. If you play a leadership role or hope to influence your environment, encouraging creative thinking can propel both your team and your career forward.

Consider how 3M nurtured a culture that led to inventions like the Post-it Note. The company allowed employees to devote a slice of their time to side projects unrelated to their formal tasks. That freedom encouraged curiosity-driven exploration, often sparking innovative products that might never have emerged under rigid directives. As you think about your own team or workplace, you can mirror this principle by granting autonomy for people to explore novel angles, setting aside time or resources for that purpose.

Communication stands at the heart of a creative culture. Leaders who openly invite suggestions, listen attentively, and reward risk-taking model the behaviours that make creativity possible. You might adopt a practice where, rather than shooting down unusual proposals with "That will not work," you respond with "Tell me more about how we can refine this." This approach transforms potential rejections into gateways for discussion, helping your team feel safe enough to share half-formed ideas. That sense of psychological safety often differentiates an innovative group from one stuck in safe, predictable patterns.

Another key is diversity of thought. When team members come from various backgrounds or areas of expertise, you cover more ground in your brainstorming. You challenge assumptions and adopt multiple viewpoints. If you notice a lack of diversity, you might invite external consultants for a workshop or encourage collaboration with other departments. This infusion of fresh perspectives can remove blind spots and lead to surprising insights.

Additionally, recognising and celebrating creativity cements it within the workplace culture. Praise employees who experiment, even if the outcome falls short. Knowing that the organisation values attempts at innovation can embolden them to keep trying. Hewlett-Packard once famously used the slogan "Invent," showcasing an ethos that welcomed risk and occasional failures as a natural cost of progress. While not every creative gamble pays off, the ones that do often usher in leaps forward.

Finally, streamline administrative hurdles. If employees drown in bureaucracy or fear blame for mistakes, they will not feel free to think creatively. Evaluate whether your approval processes or performance metrics stifle new thinking. Sometimes, adjusting these frameworks can remove invisible barriers that hold back creative energy. Remember that creativity flourishes not through pure luck but through consistent support, constructive feedback, and an environment that encourages challenges to the status quo.

By championing a creative culture, you help your workplace become more adaptable, competitive, and satisfying for everyone involved. It is not about gimmicks or forced fun but about embedding curiosity and trust into daily routines. In this environment, your team members evolve into creative powerhouses, and the organisation can reinvent itself repeatedly, staying one step ahead of an ever-shifting market.

7. The Tech Dimension: Navigating Creativity in a Digital World

Your devices are both blessings and potential distractions. On one hand, digital tools can open infinite avenues for creativity, enabling you to produce music on your tablet, design logos with user-friendly software, or collaborate globally in real time. On the other hand, constant notifications, social media feeds, and digital noise threaten to scatter your focus. Steering technology toward creativity requires balance and self-awareness, ensuring that devices become enablers of innovation rather than obstacles.

Firstly, technology lets you share ideas instantly with a worldwide audience. Platforms like YouTube or creative networks allow you to display your work, be it a short film, a coded project, or a new culinary invention, and gain feedback from people across continents. This exposure can spur faster development. If you are toying with a concept for a mobile app, posting early prototypes online might attract feedback that refines your design. That crowd-sourced input helps you iterate more effectively and see angles you missed.

Additionally, many apps and software now exist to stimulate creative thinking, from brainstorming platforms to digital whiteboards. These tools help you structure mind-maps, organise tasks, and visually outline your concepts. They are particularly handy for group ideation, bridging geographical gaps through shared virtual spaces. Yet you must guard against falling into the trap of relying on the tool itself as the creative solution. The software can guide or capture your ideas, but your mind remains the true source of innovation.

Still, it is easy to drown in tech-driven distractions. You can open an app intending to research something, then find yourself scrolling aimlessly. To manage this, set boundaries for your digital use. Allocate time blocks for unplugged brainstorming, free from pings or pop-ups. Perhaps you designate morning hours for deep creative work, leaving your phone in another room or switching off notifications. This disciplined approach fosters an environment where your brain can wander without interruption, often leading to breakthrough ideas.

Emerging technologies also invite brand-new forms of creative expression. Virtual reality, for example, allows artists to paint in three-dimensional space. Artificial intelligence can act as a collaborator, providing suggestions for image generation or writing. These developments may feel daunting, but by experimenting with them, you expand your creative toolkit. You do not need to be an expert to dabble; curiosity and willingness to learn suffice. By merging your imagination with cutting-edge tech, you could conceive solutions or artworks impossible just a decade ago.

In short, technology can be a powerful ally in the creative process, granting you tools and connectivity that previous generations lacked. Yet it demands intentional handling to prevent mental clutter or a shallow approach. By setting digital boundaries, exploring innovative platforms, and remembering that your intellect and emotions form the creative core, you harness the best of both worlds. The digital realm becomes a space where imagination flourishes, bridging your ideas to global audiences and forging unexpected collaborations, all while boosting the creative spark you hold within.

8. Nurturing Young Minds: Supporting Children's Creativity

When you help a child express creativity, you give them more than entertainment, you empower them to develop resilience, problem-solving skills, and self-confidence. Young minds are naturally exploratory, hungry to experiment and imagine. By providing the right environment and encouragement, you cultivate a generation that embraces original thinking and dares to dream beyond established norms.

Children often start with unfiltered creativity; they do not fret about whether a painting is "good" or if an idea is feasible. They just jump in. Yet as they grow older, fear of making mistakes or peer judgement can dampen that spontaneous spark. You can counteract these inhibitions by normalising experimentation. Let them see that unpolished attempts are stepping stones, not failures. Suppose a child writes a short story full of plot holes. Instead of pointing out every flaw, celebrate the initiative and engage them in thinking about how to refine their narrative. This supportive approach teaches them that creativity is an evolving process, not a one-shot event.

You can also broaden their perspective by exposing them to varied experiences. Museum trips, theatre performances, or nature hikes show them different forms of creativity at work, in art, in performance, and in the natural world. Such experiences feed their curiosity, granting them a broader palette of ideas to draw upon. Telling stories or reading books from multiple cultures expands their sense of possibility, letting them see that other communities express creativity in unique ways. This fosters open-mindedness, an essential ingredient for imaginative thinking.

Moreover, providing a specific space or resources for creative play can make a difference. A corner filled with simple art supplies, pencils, craft paper, or building materials, offers a tangible invitation to create. If they show interest in music, a modest keyboard or basic drum kit can channel their impulses into practice. Remember that creativity thrives in play, so do not turn these resources into strict tasks. Let them discover the joy of creation at their own pace.

Interaction with technology can be both a barrier and a boon. While many digital tools exist for drawing, coding, or composing, too much screen time can curb a child's inclination to explore physical mediums. Striking a balance is key: offer them digital platforms to develop new skills but also encourage hands-on projects, where they manipulate paint, paper, or clay. Engaging different senses cements creativity more deeply than a purely digital environment can.

Finally, model creativity yourself. Children learn by observing. If they see you experimenting, whether in cooking, crafting, or brainstorming, they internalise the message that creativity is not limited to a special few. If you encounter a stumble, let them witness how you adapt and try again. This real-life demonstration of perseverance teaches them that being imaginative includes dealing with hiccups along the way.

By providing supportive spaces, exposing them to diversity, and showing them that mistakes are part of learning, you keep their creative spark alive. In time, these children grow into adults who do not fear new ideas and who see innovation as second nature. Encouraging creativity in the young ensures that future generations inherit the tools they need to shape a world driven by originality and ingenuity.

9. The Drive for Innovation: Connecting Creativity and Progress

It is no coincidence that every significant leap forward, be it technological, cultural, or social, has creativity at its core. From the steam engine revolution to the space programmes, from smartphone breakthroughs to artistic movements, progress often begins when individuals refuse to accept old solutions as the final word. By connecting creativity to innovation, you open doors to transformative ideas that shape entire industries and societies.

When you think about innovation, you might picture large research labs or billionaire inventors. Yet the spark of groundbreaking ideas can happen anywhere, provided you cultivate a problem-solving mindset. It may occur in a small startup where a handful of determined individuals disrupt an entire sector with a novel app or in a workshop where a craftsperson refines a centuries-old process. Such feats arise when people view existing situations not as fixed but as prompts to be reimagined.

Collaboration accelerates this process. Imagine a team of diverse talents, a coder, a designer, a marketing strategist, pooling their unique perspectives to tackle a user problem. The synergy of varied views sparks creative friction. When team members respectfully challenge each other, they refine raw ideas into robust prototypes. This environment mimics the success stories of places like Silicon Valley, which thrived by clustering bright minds who cross-pollinated insights, leading to waves of global innovations.

Sometimes, an unconventional combination of technologies or concepts produces the biggest breakthroughs. Think about the fusion of GPS and mobile internet that gave birth to ridesharing apps. Or the blend of social media and e-commerce that enabled direct-to-consumer brands to flourish. These outcomes did not materialise by chance.

Creativity: Unleashing Your Inner Genius

They emerged from people who dared to merge fields and test synergy. You too can practise this approach by exposing yourself to fields different from your own and pondering how their principles might apply to the challenges you face.

Risk-taking is another pillar connecting creativity and innovation. Implementing an untested idea always involves the possibility of failure. Many groundbreaking ideas met doubt initially. Yet if you treat failures as part of the process, gleaning lessons each time, you can refine your attempts until you hit that sweet spot. This cycle of experimentation, reflection, and improvement is the bedrock of innovation. Each iteration sharpens your concept, propelling it closer to something that can change your community or industry.

Creativity also propels you to anticipate future needs rather than merely react to present conditions. When you engage in imaginative thinking, you ask, "What if technology advanced here?" or "How might future consumers behave?" This forward-looking stance sets you apart from those who remain satisfied with the current picture. By planning for tomorrow's world, you stay relevant as trends shift, giving you the agility to pivot or capitalise on emerging opportunities.

Therefore, linking creativity to innovation means embracing the unknown, welcoming collaboration, blending separate concepts, and turning failures into stepping stones. This attitude fosters not only personal achievements but also broader progress that resonates beyond your immediate circle. Each idea you refine and push forward has the potential to spark ripples in society, proving that creativity underpins the grand tapestry of advancement. When you nurture that link in your life or organisation, you stand on the front lines of progress, ready to mould tomorrow through the power of original thinking.

10. Great Creators: Lessons from Inspiring Journeys

When you look at the landscape of human achievements, you find visionaries who shaped entire eras through bold, inventive thinking. Their journeys offer guidance that can illuminate your own path, no matter your field. By examining how they persevered, adapted, and brought their ideas to life, you gather insights to strengthen your own creative endeavours.

One individual who exemplifies this is Anna Wintour, a powerful figure in the fashion world. As the editor-in-chief of Vogue and a major influencer in the industry, her success stems not from following trends but from defining them. Her eye for style, combined with a willingness to take creative risks, featuring distinctive fashion narratives, set her magazine apart. While she is associated with high style, the principle that stands out is her readiness to champion newness. She consistently searches for fresh voices in photography and design, proving that staying open to the untried can sustain influence for decades.

Another story worth mentioning is that of Frank Gehry, the architect behind bold, unconventional buildings like the Guggenheim Museum Bilbao. His approach often merges sculpture with function, creating works that challenge people's ideas of what architecture should look like. Gehry's path was not free of critics who dismissed his fluid forms as impractical. Yet he kept pushing boundaries, trusting that genuine creativity sometimes provokes discomfort before winning admiration. His resilience in the face of scepticism underscores a key lesson: breakthrough ideas rarely fit neatly into established norms.

Consider Melinda Gates as well. Though widely recognised for philanthropic efforts, she embodies creativity in how she addresses global challenges. Her campaigns to reshape healthcare and education rely on rethinking solutions, mixing data-driven strategies with empathy for local cultures. Her approach shows that creativity flourishes when it responds to real people's needs, fusing imagination with a grounded, human touch. The results often transform entire communities, indicating that creative thinking does not belong solely to the arts but can guide humanitarian work or social progress.

These figures reveal common themes: a willingness to challenge the status quo, the ability to absorb criticism without losing focus, and a hunger for constant renewal. They did not wait for permission to experiment; they claimed the right to reimagine what was possible. You can apply this same mindset. Even if your sphere seems small compared to a global stage, your creative endeavours can shift your environment. A fresh take on a business model, a bold reorganisation of a community event, or an inventive approach to teaching children can reverberate far beyond your immediate circle.

When you face doubt about your creative abilities, recall these lessons. Original thinking sometimes ruffles feathers, but it also propels the world to novel heights. Balancing visionary leaps with practical steps ensures that your bold concepts do not remain fantasies but materialise into tangible outcomes. In your quest to unleash your inner genius, look to trailblazers, not to imitate them exactly but to gain confidence from their stories. By daring to act on your ideas and staying resilient through setbacks, you follow the same pattern that led these creative powerhouses to leave an indelible mark.

Chapter 17

Mindfulness: The Power of Now

Imagine waking up each day feeling calm, focused, and ready to handle whatever life throws at you. Imagine facing your challenges without anxiety, living your moments without distractions, and savouring life instead of merely racing through it. This isn't some distant dream or elusive promise; it's precisely what mindfulness offers: a powerful way to truly live in the present, right here, right now.

Mindfulness isn't about escaping your thoughts or finding instant tranquillity at the push of a button; it's about paying close attention to what's happening within you and around you without getting tangled up in past regrets or future worries. It's the practice of gently bringing your focus back to the present moment, again and again, until that moment becomes a source of strength, clarity, and empowerment. In this chapter, you'll discover practical techniques to anchor yourself firmly in the present, understand how mindfulness can alleviate stress, boost your productivity, and strengthen emotional resilience. It's about taking the reins of your mind, learning to respond rather than react, and paving the way towards a balanced, purposeful, and deeply fulfilling life.

1. Beginning Your Journey: Laying the Groundwork for Mindful Living

You stand at the brink of a powerful practice that has the potential to transform how you navigate each day. Mindfulness is not about shutting down your thoughts or forcing yourself into an unnatural calm; it is a process of anchoring your awareness in the present moment so you can experience more clarity, steadiness, and purpose. Many people drift through life on autopilot, pulled in countless directions by endless distractions. You can break that cycle by developing a deliberate approach to being present in all aspects of your daily life.

When you fully engage with the here and now, you place yourself in a position of true authority over your responses rather than feeling trapped by them. This shift does not happen overnight; it involves methodical effort and a willingness to allow your mind and body to settle into a more focused state. There is no secret magic trick. Instead, mindfulness emerges from your decision to pause, inhale, and notice what is unfolding within and around you. That choice alone grants you the ability to respond instead of react, whether you are dealing with work demands, personal relationships, or unexpected obstacles.

For centuries, various cultures and disciplines have embraced mindfulness as a tool to develop mental clarity and emotional strength. Contemporary research supports what ancient practitioners have long known: when you fix your attention on the present, you decrease your stress levels, sharpen your attention, and enhance your emotional well-being. Many workplaces now encourage mindfulness sessions to help employees handle pressure and produce more thoughtful work. Athletes train their minds to stay rooted in the moment, discovering that the mental discipline of mindfulness improves their physical performance. Ordinary individuals find that carrying out simple household tasks with deliberate attention turns an otherwise dull chore into a moment of steady calm.

The first step in this journey is simply to observe, without self-criticism, how your mind bounces from one thought to another. Recognise that your mind does this to protect you and keep you alert, so approaching it with kindness is key. Each time you notice your thoughts wandering, guide them back to the present moment. At first, you might feel restless. You might question whether you are doing this "correctly." Over time, you will see that this process of bringing your mind back is exactly where growth happens. It is akin to exercising a muscle. Each repetition strengthens your capacity to stay grounded, even when life grows hectic.

Cultivating a mindful lifestyle is not about striving to become someone else; it is about revealing the clear-thinking, self-possessed individual you already can be. As you move forward, know that mindfulness is accessible to everyone. No matter how chaotic your life has felt, you can develop greater composure by learning to be present. You are taking a decisive step toward steering your life rather than being pushed off course by external forces. By committing to mindfulness, you chart a path to more empowered living, beginning right here and now.

2. The Inner Mechanics: How Mindfulness Tackles Stress

You already know that stress can manifest in many forms: tight shoulders, stomach knots, a racing mind at night. What you may not realise is how effectively mindfulness can dismantle those patterns, preventing your body and mind from spinning out of control. Stress often begins when you project yourself into future worries or dwell excessively on past regrets, diverting your attention from the tasks that matter right now. By retraining your mind to remain aware of what is happening in this moment, you can relieve mental strain and help your body unwind.

Physiologically, stress triggers an ancient survival mechanism, flooding your system with hormones such as cortisol and adrenaline. This response was once vital for escaping immediate dangers, but modern life can leave you stuck in prolonged states of tension, even when genuine threats are absent. Mindfulness provides a crucial counterbalance, prompting the parasympathetic nervous system to restore a sense of calm. Breathing techniques, for example, directly tap into the rhythm of your body, slowing your heart rate and lowering stress hormone levels. In those moments, you shift from a perpetual state of alarm to a mode of rest and recovery.

Being mindful does not imply denying your challenges. Instead, it allows you to face them with a greater degree of composure. Imagine you are rushing to meet a deadline, and your mind floods with panic about possible negative outcomes. A mindful approach invites you to pause, inhale slowly, exhale fully, and refocus your attention on what needs doing in that instant. By doing so, you stop feeding the panic with further anxiety and funnel your mental energy into constructive action.

Consider how everyday tasks become triggers for stress when you are not fully present. A mundane drive to work might morph into a harried commute if your mind is fixated on looming responsibilities. While you might reach your destination physically, your mental state is fragmented and unsettled. In contrast, if you remain in the present as you drive, focusing on the road, noticing your surroundings, maintaining awareness of your posture behind the wheel, you are less likely to arrive frazzled. You reclaim a sense of control over your inner state.

The beauty of mindfulness-based stress reduction lies in its simplicity. You do not need elaborate tools to begin calming yourself down in stressful moments. Whether you are caught in a tense conversation or dealing with personal deadlines, you have your breath, your physical senses, and your power to observe and respond thoughtfully. Each time you catch your mind drifting into a storm of anxious thoughts, that very moment of awareness is your anchor back to calm.

When you become consistently mindful, you reach a point where stress no longer dominates you. Challenges continue to arise; that is inevitable. However, the difference is in your ability to face them from a stable, balanced perspective. You cease to be at the mercy of external circumstances or internal doubts. By devoting yourself to mindful awareness, you fortify your resilience and find that stress, while persistent, loses its grip on your life.

3. Building Emotional Resilience Through Present Awareness

Your emotions can either propel you forward or trip you up. They can connect you to others in powerful ways or lead you into unnecessary disputes. The question is not whether you have emotions; everyone does, but how you handle them. Mindfulness teaches you to observe your emotional landscape without being dominated by every passing feeling. Instead of repressing or indulging your emotions, you learn to engage them with a balanced view.

When an emotion like anger appears, for instance, the mindful approach is to notice its arrival. You observe the physical signs: maybe your stomach tightens, your jaw clenches, and your breathing becomes shallow. You recognize that anger is taking shape in your body and mind. Rather than launching into an impulsive reaction, you pause, breathe, and give yourself a moment to acknowledge what is happening internally. In that space of awareness, you can choose a measured response. You might speak firmly but calmly, or you might opt to step away for a moment to gather yourself.

Studies from psychological research show that individuals who regularly practise mindfulness display greater emotional intelligence. They can name and understand their feelings, recognise them in others, and handle emotional triggers more gracefully. This skill set not only serves you during times of conflict but also strengthens relationships, both personal and professional. People are drawn to those who remain level-headed under pressure, and mindful emotional regulation is at the root of that composure.

Emotional resilience goes beyond regulating negative feelings. It also involves amplifying positive emotions such as gratitude, compassion, and joy. When you are fully present, you absorb the pleasant aspects of your experience more thoroughly. Whether it is a friendly exchange with a colleague or a quiet walk through a local park, you learn to savour uplifting moments. This heightened appreciation can act as a buffer against stress and negativity, giving you an emotional reserve that you can draw upon when times get tough.

The practice of self-compassion is another crucial dimension. It is one thing to extend kindness toward others; it is another to direct that kindness inward. Mindfulness encourages a gentle attitude toward your own shortcomings and mistakes, allowing you to confront them without self-condemnation. It is a powerful step toward personal growth. When you do not waste time berating yourself, you move faster toward solutions and learn lessons more effectively.

Some people worry that observing their emotions might dull their intensity or spontaneity. The reality is that mindfulness does not numb you; it refines your perception. You still experience the full spectrum of feelings, but you become the one who guides them instead of being pulled in every direction. The result is a life with deeper, richer emotional engagement. You feel more connected to the people around you because your reactions are more authentic and considered. By grounding yourself in present awareness, you cultivate an emotional sturdiness that serves you in all corners of your life, from major upheavals to everyday tensions.

4. Meditative Practice: Your Portal to Steady Focus

Meditation often appears mysterious or reserved for monks on remote mountaintops. In truth, it is an accessible method that grounds you in the present, creating space for calm reflection. Meditative practice serves as one of the most straightforward gateways to mindfulness. You do not need fancy cushions or lengthy sessions in silence. You need only the willingness to dedicate a few minutes to grounding your attention.

When you begin meditating, you might settle into a chair, close your eyes, and follow the rhythm of your breath. That initial moment can feel odd if you are accustomed to perpetual busyness. Persist through that discomfort; with each breath, your mind learns how to reset. Thoughts will arise, perhaps about tasks to complete or past regrets. Instead of fighting them, note their presence and gently steer your focus back to your breathing. This cycle of drifting away and returning to your chosen point of focus is the very essence of meditative training.

Meditation changes the brain. Research using brain imaging has shown that regular meditation enhances the prefrontal cortex, the region responsible for decision-making, emotional control, and self-awareness. By dedicating consistent time to this practice, you develop the neurological pathways that reinforce calm and attentiveness. Over time, you become less susceptible to the impulsive flurry of thoughts that often sabotage your productivity or escalate your stress.

Famous figures from many fields acknowledge the power of meditation. High-level athletes speak of their improved mental clarity, which helps them withstand pressure in critical moments. Executives turn to meditation to navigate the complexities of corporate life, reducing burnout and sharpening strategic thinking. Students discover it can enhance concentration, boosting their ability to learn and recall information.

Contrary to popular belief, meditation does not aim to empty your mind entirely. Rather, it teaches you to watch your thoughts without blindly following them. By stepping back, you gain clarity on which thoughts warrant attention and which serve only as distractions. This skill is invaluable in everyday life. Whether you are tackling a new project, preparing for a challenging conversation, or planning a busy week, your heightened ability to remain centred can save you from wasted energy and misdirected focus.

If you feel hesitant about starting, remember that even a few minutes each day can create tangible benefits. Set a timer for five minutes, find a quiet spot, and sit upright yet relaxed.

Focus on the inflow and outflow of your breath. When a thought intrudes, acknowledge it, then release it. As you build consistency, you might gradually increase the duration. Some people find early mornings peaceful for meditation; others discover that a short midday session resets their mood. Choose whatever fits your schedule best. Step by step, you will notice a shift in how you react to daily challenges, forging a calmer, more-centred way of being.

5. Infusing Mindfulness into Everyday Tasks

You do not need to break away to distant retreats in search of mindfulness; you can integrate it into the fabric of your daily routine. When you apply mindful awareness to mundane tasks, you uncover opportunities to train your mind and nurture a calmer disposition. Everyday activities such as walking, cleaning, or making a meal can serve as valuable training grounds for staying present.

Begin by examining how you walk. If you are typically lost in thought, thinking about plans and problems while your feet move on autopilot, you are missing a chance to cultivate awareness. Instead, the next time you stroll, slow down for a moment and notice the sensation of each step. Feel the ground beneath your shoes, observe the motion of your arms, and sense the air moving across your skin. This intentional focus transforms a routine walk into an exercise in grounding yourself. You no longer walk aimlessly; you walk alert and connected.

Consider your household tasks. Whether it is washing dishes, tidying a room, or organising paperwork, these chores can easily become tedious when your mind is elsewhere. Turn them into mindfulness practice instead. Pay attention to the water temperature, the sound of dishes clinking, and your breathing as you work. Each swipe of a cloth or each rinse under the tap becomes a reminder that you can direct your attention wherever you choose. This approach not only improves your mental clarity but also increases the quality of the task itself.

This philosophy carries over to any daily habit. Even brushing your teeth can become a mindful activity. Feel the bristles against your gums, the flavour of the toothpaste, the motion of your arm. When your mind starts drifting to your upcoming schedule, recognise the wandering thought, then refocus on the task. In these small, seemingly trivial exercises, you train yourself to remain rooted in the present moment, a skill that proves invaluable when life grows intense.

Some individuals worry that focusing on a simple task might slow them down, yet the opposite is often true. When you fully engage with what you are doing, you work more efficiently and effectively. You cut down on careless errors, reduce mental fatigue, and finish each step with a sense of completion. By clearing away mental clutter, you might even spark creativity. Your mind can generate fresh ideas precisely because it is no longer overloaded with random thoughts competing for attention.

Applying mindfulness to everyday activities also helps you bring a sense of gratitude into your life. You appreciate the running water when washing dishes or the nourishment your meal provides. These small acknowledgements can shift your mindset from one of perpetual dissatisfaction to one that recognises the abundance of simple joys. By turning ordinary tasks into mindful moments, you build a habit of presence that enriches your entire day, grounding you in the reality of now and boosting your capacity to face bigger challenges with a clear head.

6. Embracing Mindful Eating: Nurturing Body and Mind

Eating can become hasty and thoughtless, especially when you are juggling responsibilities or scrolling through your phone at mealtimes. Mindful eating brings this act of nourishment back into clear focus, transforming meals into moments of attentive awareness. You shift from consuming on autopilot to honouring each bite, noticing the taste, texture, and satisfaction that real nutrition offers.

When you slow down to eat, you experience more than flavours. You begin to recognise bodily cues of hunger and fullness. You know the difference between genuine hunger and mindless munching out of habit, boredom, or stress. This awareness protects you from overindulging or denying your body the nutrients it needs. Instead of rushing through a meal, you start to appreciate the subtleties of how your body reacts to food. This can improve digestion, elevate energy levels, and lead to better overall health.

Mindful eating also fosters a deeper connection to the sources of your food. You might reflect on the effort involved in growing fresh produce or in preparing a well-crafted dish. Such thoughtfulness has a grounding effect, instilling a sense of gratitude and shifting your perspective from treating food as mere fuel to recognising it as an integral part of your well-being. When you take time to acknowledge the entire process, from farm to plate, you create a more respectful relationship with the nourishment you receive.

In practical terms, adopting mindful eating habits can be straightforward. Set aside your devices or any distractions during meals. Before taking the first bite, pause. Observe the colours and smells. Then, take a mouthful slowly, savouring the flavours. Chew thoroughly, letting your taste buds register each nuance. Pay attention to how your stomach feels as you proceed. This approach requires a slight reordering of your priorities. Rather than wolfing down a meal while thinking about tasks or screens, you grant yourself permission to be present for the simple act of eating.

This shift in focus can illuminate emotional triggers around food. Maybe you notice that you crave sugary snacks when feeling anxious, or you skip meals when tense. Instead of ignoring these patterns, you acknowledge them. Through mindful eating, you become aware of the feelings intertwined with your eating habits, giving you the power to reshape those habits if they no longer serve you.

By practising mindful eating consistently, you may find that your relationship with food transforms. Meals become more satisfying. You gain greater control over impulsive eating and reduce the guilt or discomfort often associated with rushed consumption. This approach also supports healthier lifestyle choices by encouraging you to select ingredients that truly nourish you rather than grab whatever is handy or artificially enticing. Ultimately, mindful eating is not about imposing rigid rules but about learning to listen to your body and honour its signals. Your body thanks you by functioning at a higher level of vitality, and your mind reaps the calm that comes from paying genuine attention.

7. Overcoming Roadblocks: Sustaining Mindfulness in a Demanding World

Sticking to mindfulness might feel straightforward in a quiet setting, but as you re-enter the busyness of modern life, roadblocks appear. Work deadlines, family obligations, and digital distractions can quickly derail your best intentions.

Mindfulness: The Power of Now

The key is not to avoid life's demands but to adapt your mindfulness practice, so it weaves seamlessly into your daily routine.

First, accept that your mind will stray; it is part of the human condition. If you catch yourself losing concentration, congratulate yourself for noticing, then shift back to the present. This process of returning is where the real mastery lies. Far from indicating failure, these moments of refocusing are the building blocks of a sharper, more alert mind. Over time, you learn to redirect your attention swiftly, even when chaos surrounds you.

Next, create intervals for mindfulness throughout your day. You do not have to isolate yourself in a silent room for extended periods. Instead, take purposeful pauses when you arrive at your desk, when you turn on your computer, or even when stepping away from a meeting. These micro-moments of awareness help you reset, preventing overwhelm from stacking up. Reminding yourself periodically to pause and check in with your breath and physical sensations keeps you tethered to the present.

Technology is a major hurdle for many. The digital age floods you with notifications and messages, snatching your attention at every turn. Combat this by assigning strict time slots for checking emails or social media. Turn off non-essential alerts to minimise disruptions. Each time you resist the impulse to browse your phone mindlessly, you reinforce your capacity to remain focused. Even if your profession requires high connectivity, structured guidelines can prevent digital overload.

Stressful environments also test your commitment to mindfulness. Perhaps you manage a large team or have a complex family life. Tensions inevitably arise, but mindful strategies allow you to respond more calmly. When disputes flare up, rely on the grounding techniques you have practised. Breathe, identify your physical cues of tension, and remind yourself to approach the situation from a place of clarity rather than reactivity. This approach not only benefits you but also helps defuse conflict before it escalates.

Lastly, you might face internal resistance if you view mindfulness as optional or see it as a chore. Reframing your mindset helps. Think of it as an essential pillar of mental fitness, akin to how you maintain your physical health through exercise. When you recognise that mindfulness underpins your resilience and well-being, skipping it becomes less tempting. You see the difference in your concentration and emotional balance on days when you engage deeply versus days when you do not.

These challenges are not insurmountable. They are part of living in a demanding world. By acknowledging obstacles and preparing for them, you build a consistent mindfulness practice that withstands real-life pressures. Each time you navigate a hectic day without losing your mindful footing, you prove that you can remain grounded, alert, and composed, no matter what life flings your way.

8. Boosting Efficiency: How Mindfulness Fuels Productivity

In a culture that equates busyness with accomplishment, you might think that cramming more tasks into your day is the route to success. But real productivity emerges from steady focus, strategic action, and mental clarity, qualities that mindfulness cultivates. By honing your ability to remain present, you refine your output and avoid spinning your wheels on needless tasks.

Mindfulness: The Power of Now

Imagine you have a challenging project at work with multiple moving parts. Unchecked, your brain might scramble under the weight of details, propelling you into multitasking or frantic bursts of effort. Mindfulness encourages a different approach: sit calmly, outline the key objectives, and tackle them one at a time with unwavering attention. Each segment of the project receives the best of your mental capacity because your focus is not diluted. As a result, you produce work of higher quality, and your stress levels remain manageable.

Research indicates that mindful practices can drastically improve your problem-solving abilities. When you are overwhelmed, you might default to rushed decisions or rely on familiar but outdated methods. By staying present, you allow your mind to spot fresh angles and innovative solutions. The problem you face may be complex, but clarity comes when you quiet the mental static. In these moments, your mind has the space to connect dots and generate creative insights that would otherwise remain hidden under stress-induced haste.

Effective time management also intertwines with mindfulness. When you plan your day in a grounded state, you differentiate between tasks that truly matter and those that can be minimised or postponed. Rather than juggling tasks continuously, you allocate focused blocks of attention. This not only prevents errors but also preserves energy. You finish your obligations feeling accomplished instead of drained. The day does not slip away in frantic busyness; it moves with intention.

Additionally, being fully present at meetings or when exchanging ideas with colleagues produces more fruitful collaboration. You pick up on nuances in conversation, notice cues in others' tone or body language, and respond with precision. Communicating with clarity and composure elevates your professional relationships, contributing to a productive atmosphere where mutual respect flourishes.

You may encounter resistance if you believe you thrive under pressure. Some claim they produce their best work in a frenzy of last-minute chaos. However, real excellence often arises when you blend discipline with a calm focus. Tight deadlines might still exist, but mindful approaches allow you to harness pressure as a motivator rather than a trigger for panic. You discover that completing tasks ahead of schedule with composure yields more consistent and refined outcomes.

When mindfulness becomes a habit, productivity stops feeling like a sprint that leaves you winded. Instead, it evolves into a marathon you can sustain day after day. Your mind, no longer cluttered by irrelevant thoughts or nagging anxieties, becomes a precision tool. You gain the ability to do more in less time without compromising quality, which frees you to engage in other meaningful aspects of life. Ultimately, mindfulness is not a pause from being productive; it is the bedrock that propels you forward with clear eyes and a steady grip on your goals.

9. Remarkable Transformations: Lessons from Real-Life Mindful Practice

Nothing cements the power of mindfulness like witnessing its effect on real lives. Around the world, people from every walk of life have redefined their experiences through consistent mindful awareness. Consider the story of a high-performing executive who spent years at the brink of burnout. Deadlines, back-to-back meetings, and unrelenting pressure had chipped away at this individual's well-being. After integrating short daily meditation sessions, this executive reported clearer thinking, more controlled responses to stress, and stronger professional relationships. By pausing to recalibrate, the executive minimised the emotional toll and improved decision-making.

On the other side of the spectrum, individuals dealing with chronic health conditions have found relief through mindful practices. People facing long-term pain or ongoing medical treatments often wrestle with anxiety and the mental burden of uncertainty. Mindfulness does not wipe out physical hardship, but it shifts how it is perceived and handled. Through present-moment awareness, patients learn to observe discomfort without compounding it with catastrophic thoughts. They build emotional endurance, maintaining a sense of personal agency despite ongoing challenges.

Athletes, too, demonstrate how mindfulness can spark breakthroughs. High-intensity sports demand more than physical prowess; they require sharp mental acuity. Take the example of a professional basketball player who struggled with performance anxiety. After adopting mindful breathing exercises and visualisation strategies, the player reported feeling less weighed down by negative self-talk and more alert during games. Those small mental shifts translated to improvements on the court. Fans might see better free-throw percentages or sharper defensive moves, but the deeper transformation lies in the athlete's calmer inner state.

Even among students, mindful study routines can produce notable gains. Instead of cramming information with the television blaring or a smartphone in hand, some learners choose to dedicate focused, distraction-free time to revision. By treating each study session as an exercise in presence, these students often find their comprehension and retention rise. They approach exams with reduced test anxiety and clearer recall, reaping benefits that extend beyond the classroom and into their future careers.

In personal relationships, mindfulness has helped many people stay grounded when conflicts or disagreements arise. Rather than reacting with frustration, mindful individuals pause, notice their physical tension, and choose a response aligned with respect. Couples who adopt mindful communication often report fewer heated arguments and a deeper sense of mutual understanding. Friendships grow more authentic because each person truly listens instead of waiting for a chance to interject.

All these stories underscore a shared principle: true change begins inside. Mindfulness shapes how you interpret the events of your life, turning potential chaos into moments of clarity. As you hear about these transformations, reflect on how mindfulness might uplift your own circumstances. Do you grapple with pressure at work, health concerns, or tension in personal relationships? Mindful practice can shift your perspective so you can respond more thoughtfully. The result might appear outwardly as professional success, emotional healing, athletic excellence, or harmonious relationships. At its core, it is a testament to the fact that when you reclaim command of your attention, you empower yourself in every dimension of life.

10. Moving Ahead: A Mindful Future of Confidence and Clarity

You now possess a foundation for living each day with greater awareness, steadiness, and self-command. Mindfulness is not a fleeting cure-all but a sustainable practice that can reshape your approach to work, relationships, and your inner dialogue. By learning to anchor yourself in the present, you begin to notice the old triggers that used to rattle you, the automatic habits that complicated your life, and the unproductive patterns that held you back. Armed with this awareness, you can select more beneficial ways forward.

The beauty of mindfulness is its adaptability to every stage of life. If you are navigating a fast-paced career, mindful techniques can transform how you cope with deadlines, engage with colleagues, and deliver on ambitious objectives. If you are managing family responsibilities, mindfulness helps you face tantrums or conflicts with a calmer presence, reducing stress for everyone involved. If you are seeking personal growth or spiritual development, mindfulness acts as a stepping stone toward deeper insights. No matter your path, anchoring your mind to the present moment fuels genuine progress.

Looking ahead, your challenge is to maintain this practice consistently. Fresh distractions and challenges will continue to surface. Each day is an invitation to apply the methods you have discovered: mindful breathing, the art of returning to the moment when your focus scatters, integrating awareness into simple daily tasks and stepping away from autopilot when eating or interacting with loved ones. These actions, small yet powerful, accumulate into a more composed and purposeful life.

Remain patient with yourself. The mind does not transform overnight, and mindfulness is a gradual, evolving skill. There may be days when you feel scattered and believe you have slipped back into reactive habits. In truth, noticing this regression is evidence that your awareness is intact. Rather than criticise yourself, take a breath and choose to begin anew. This ongoing cycle of drifting and returning is precisely how you develop mental fortitude.

Celebrate the victories along the way. Perhaps you handled a volatile work situation with less tension or engaged in a difficult conversation without harsh words. Each instance of mindful presence is a win, confirming that your practice is bearing fruit. Acknowledge those moments, for they bolster your motivation to continue refining your skills.

Eventually, mindfulness becomes part of who you are. You will feel less turmoil when adversity strikes, remain calmer under pressure, and recover from setbacks with greater ease. This newfound sense of self-assurance does not rely on external affirmations. Rather, it grows from within, arising from the certainty that you can direct your attention and respond with clarity. Challenges become stepping stones, not insurmountable walls.

Stepping forward, hold tight to your mindful awareness. Carry it into your ambitions and personal endeavours, trusting that each intentional breath, each moment of calm focus, compounds into a life of resilience, effectiveness, and meaningful connections. You stand on the threshold of a future shaped by your presence in the here and now. Seize it, live it, and watch as your confidence and clarity blossom with each passing day.

Chapter 18

Resilience: Bouncing Back from Adversity

Life rarely unfolds exactly how you expect it to. At some point, everyone faces setbacks, disappointments, or outright failures. What sets you apart isn't whether adversity finds you but how you respond when it inevitably does. Resilience isn't about being untouched by hardships; it's about bouncing back stronger, wiser, and more prepared to handle whatever life throws at you next.

In this chapter, you'll discover that resilience is not an exclusive gift given only to a chosen few; it's a skill you can cultivate and nurture within yourself every single day. It's your personal toolkit for navigating tough times, providing you with the strength to adapt and push through challenges without becoming overwhelmed. By learning the principles outlined in this chapter, you'll not only cope better in difficult situations but also thrive in them, turning life's toughest moments into opportunities for meaningful growth.

1. The Driving Force Behind Your Power to Adapt

You are wired to endure even the toughest experiences, and your ability to adapt through hardships is a defining trait of your character. This quality is called resilience. When you grow your resilience, you do more than survive under stress. You thrive in uncertain conditions, recovering faster and stepping forward with renewed strength. Many people mistakenly believe resilience is an inborn trait for a rare few. In truth, you can cultivate it through daily practice and purposeful thinking. You begin by grasping why resilience matters, acknowledging the inner power it holds, and realising how it empowers you to adapt to any challenge.

Resilience benefits every domain of your life, from personal relationships to professional ambitions. In a family setting, resilience helps you solve misunderstandings instead of feeling defeated. In your working world, resilience keeps you focused when plans fall apart or deadlines loom. Every setback you encounter can become a stepping stone to something greater when you harness this inner toughness. What you need to understand is that resilience is not the same as blindly tolerating hardship. It is the conscious choice to face what you fear, manage your emotions, and emerge from the trial as a stronger version of yourself. It gives you the edge over those who give in to despair or apathy.

Think about the profound impact of believing in your ability to rebound. When your mind accepts that you have the resources to endure, it changes the way you process challenges. Instead of viewing obstacles as unmovable roadblocks, you approach them as surmountable puzzles. Take, for example, a sudden job loss. Rather than allowing self-doubt to paralyse you, resilience helps you see possible opportunities and a plan for moving forward. This mindset enables you to adapt, opening doors you might have missed if you felt powerless. Resilience is the core of turning dramatic events into turning points that shift your perspective on what you can accomplish.

One effective way to unlock resilience is to remind yourself of your past achievements. Recall moments when you felt cornered yet found a way through. This reflection is not about dwelling on difficulties but appreciating the strength that carried you through them. By concentrating on previous triumphs, you reinforce the belief that you can do it again. You realise that resilience is not an accidental occurrence; it is a skill you have already demonstrated. When new problems arise, you lean on this memory bank of victories to refuel your determination.

You must also recognise that resilience is not about appearing emotionless. Feeling upset, afraid, or even uncertain is human. Resilience is the conscious act of letting those emotions come while deciding not to remain in despair. You learn to direct your energy toward solutions and progress. When you adopt resilience as a daily practice, you no longer view obstacles as permanent failures. Instead, you turn them into chances for growth, renewal, and a deeper understanding of your true potential. In the following subheadings, you will see how resilience forms a solid base for mental well-being, purposeful thinking, and meaningful achievements that transform your life.

2. Mental Foundations: How Your Mind Strengthens Your Resolve

You might believe external circumstances dictate how you respond to stress, but in reality, much of your resilience comes from how your mind interprets events. Your mind is your stronghold, a place where thoughts, beliefs, and emotions shape the decisions you make. When you treat resilience as a mental discipline, you take control of your mindset and, by extension, your reactions. This is vital to grasp because it highlights that resilience originates within you, not from luck or random chance. By honing your mental framework, you prepare yourself to face challenges with unwavering fortitude.

A key part of nurturing this mental strength involves regulating your emotions. A person who has mastered resilience allows themselves to experience discomfort and distress, but they refuse to let these feelings take over their actions. Instead, they methodically observe and address the emotional strain without succumbing to panic or gloom. One approach involves pausing when tension escalates. You step back, acknowledge the situation, and examine the emotions swirling inside you. By naming and understanding them, you rob them of their overwhelming power. Rather than trying to shut off anger or anxiety, you learn to channel them into thoughtful behaviour and reflective problem-solving.

Another crucial aspect of your mental foundation is developing an optimistic perspective. This does not involve denying difficulties or refusing to see problems. Rather, it means viewing misfortunes as moments in time rather than permanent failures. Psychologists studying resilience have often concluded that people who maintain a forward-looking mindset endure difficulties better and remain enthusiastic in the face of repeated hurdles. Optimism triggers creative thinking. Instead of giving up, your mind starts searching for any glimmer of possibility, amplifying your ability to adapt.

Yet confidence in yourself is equally significant. If you deeply believe you can manage life's adversities, that conviction elevates your sense of agency. Self-belief acts like an invisible safety net that cushions you from hitting rock bottom. It is essential to develop this belief by tackling smaller issues first. By conquering minor battles, like sticking to a daily exercise routine or learning a new skill, you build confidence in your capacity to handle bigger challenges. Each small victory proves you have the talent and determination to prevail.

Of course, you cannot overlook adaptability. A resilient mindset thrives on flexibility. When you are rigid or attached to a single outcome, you become more vulnerable to disappointment. However, when you remain open-minded and flexible, you not only weather storms but sometimes even find better directions than you initially planned. Resilience involves a willingness to pivot or modify your goals as your circumstances change. This mental readiness makes you stronger against sudden disruptions, ensuring you remain balanced and resourceful.

The mental groundwork for resilience is not about pretending everything is perfect. It is about perceiving the world realistically and then deciding to respond in a way that keeps you moving forward. Emotional regulation, optimism, self-belief, and adaptability fortify your mind, giving you the confidence to overcome any storm. As you will see next, these mental building blocks naturally extend to practical methods that enable you to carry resilience into all areas of your life.

3. Practical Steps: Strengthening Your Resilience Day by Day

It is one thing to believe in resilience as a concept, yet another to apply it to everyday life. You grow this vital quality through deliberate habits and persistent efforts that reinforce a resilient state of mind. Rather than depending on good fortune, you can build specific routines and coping strategies designed to enhance your mental and emotional strength. In doing so, you create a lifestyle that sustains you, no matter how hectic or unexpected life becomes.

One of the simplest ways to begin is by reframing adversity. Instead of viewing a setback as a sign that you have no hope, you treat it as an invitation to learn. For instance, if your project at work fails, your first reaction might be to question your competence. A resilient frame of mind prompts you to identify errors in planning, communication, or time management and then use that information to refine your next project. This does not mean you dismiss the disappointment of failing. Instead, you turn disappointment into the energy needed to adapt and push forward. A small tweak in perspective changes the quality of your response and sets the stage for personal growth.

Another foundational step involves solving problems in a methodical way. Large, intimidating issues often become more manageable when broken down into smaller goals. Resilient individuals excel at simplifying a massive dilemma into bite-sized tasks. For instance, if you face a health crisis, you do not try to fix everything at once. You might start with consulting a trusted professional, then proceed with a clear treatment plan, adjusting as you learn more. By taking problems on gradually, you reduce anxiety and gain momentum, preserving your strength instead of wasting it all at once in panic.

In addition, your resilience grows stronger when you stay socially connected. Studies consistently confirm that a supportive network can make a considerable difference in how you handle difficulties. Family members, close friends, and mentors offer emotional backing and alternative perspectives you may miss on your own. Knowing you have people willing to help or even listen eases the mental toll of confronting hard times alone. If you feel hesitant to lean on others, remind yourself that true support is reciprocal: when they need you, you will do the same for them.

Mindfulness or mental presence in the current moment also plays a key role. Activities like quiet reflection, deep breathing, or moments of mental stillness help reduce the chaos of swirling thoughts. By observing your thoughts without judgment, you build self-awareness. This awareness gives you extra control over your responses and helps you recover from stress more rapidly. You can perform these activities in as little as five minutes a day, whether at your desk, on a walk, or before going to sleep.

All these methods emphasise a core truth: resilience is not an unattainable ideal, nor is it limited to extreme crises. It is the outcome of steady, devoted practice in the small details of life. By reframing adversity, tackling problems systematically, drawing strength from meaningful relationships, and staying mindful, you lay a firm foundation that holds up when major challenges hit. Next, you will delve into how resilience plays a vital role in safeguarding your overall mental well-being.

4. Emotional Well-being: Protecting Your Mind Through Resilience

Your emotional health is intimately tied to how resilient you are. When you enhance resilience, you do more than cope with tough circumstances; you also form a barrier against chronic stress, anxiety, and depression. Think of resilience as your protective layer, helping you navigate the full spectrum of life's emotional ups and downs. This protective quality ensures you remain robust in the face of strain and better equipped to find light in gloomy times.

A chief benefit of resilience is emotional agility. Emotional agility signifies your capacity to experience emotions like fear, sadness, or frustration without surrendering to them. While you still feel each emotion, you do not let it govern your choices or future outlook. This distinction is powerful.

Rather than burying sadness or running from anxiety, you engage with these emotions as signals from your mind and body. With resilience, you process your feelings more purposefully instead of drowning in them.

Another aspect of emotional well-being relates to hope. This might sound abstract, but hope has a tangible impact on how you react to adversity. Resilience and hope often work hand in hand. When you are resilient, it is easier to find a reason to push forward during low points. Rather than dismissing a challenge as a dead end, you view it as temporary or solvable. This hopeful stance reduces the risk of getting trapped in despair and energises you to keep searching for improvements or better paths. It is not about pretending problems vanish; instead, it is trusting that your efforts will eventually lead to tangible results.

Also critical is the practice of self-compassion. Overly critical self-talk magnifies stress and undermines your emotional health, especially during tough periods. When you scold yourself for errors or label yourself as a failure, you weaken your capacity to cope. In contrast, self-compassion acts like emotional oxygen, allowing you to recover more quickly. You grant yourself the same kindness you would extend to a close friend. This approach reduces guilt, shame, and the downward spirals that come with them, keeping your mind clearer and more stable.

Resilience further nurtures mental health by providing a sense of purpose. When you hold onto purpose, whether it is being an anchor for loved ones or working towards a cherished ambition, you find motivation to continue despite hardships. Purpose directs your emotional response away from hopelessness and towards constructive action. In moments of doubt, the knowledge that you have something meaningful to fight for keeps you committed to forging a path through trouble.

When you cultivate this mental fortress, you do more than shrug off occasional setbacks; you reinforce an underlying approach to life. By embracing emotional agility, nurturing hope, and practising self-compassion, you transform struggles into stepping stones for improved emotional well-being. In the next subheading, you will examine how to harness these strengths to tackle the unavoidable obstacles that arise throughout life's unpredictable journey.

5. Overcoming Life's Highs and Lows: How Resilience Guides You

Life never proceeds in a neat, straightforward fashion. You might see your plans collapse under unforeseen disruptions or watch your personal goals get postponed by events outside your control. During such times, resilience acts as a lifeline that steadies you through the turbulence. It is not about denying your struggles or minimising your pain. Rather, it is the difference between feeling stuck in despair and moving forward with the conviction that you can overcome. Resilience gives you something truly valuable: the realisation that adversity, though uncomfortable, need not be the end of your aspirations.

At times, difficulties strike like sudden storms, a loved one passes away, an economic slump leads to job loss, or a health problem emerges from nowhere. In those moments, it is perfectly natural to feel shock, sorrow, or fear. Yet resilience encourages you to claim that first moment of choice. Will you let this event define your life, or will you interpret it as a call to realign your perspective and priorities?

Resilience does not promise an easy path, but it clears a path, however narrow, through the darkness.

Adaptability plays a defining role here. Because life's challenges rarely match your ideal plans, resilience prompts you to rethink, recalibrate, and act differently. When a business proposal fails, a resilient outlook tells you to pivot strategies, seek fresh input, or adjust your offerings. If a personal relationship hits a snag, this adaptive mindset guides you to listen more deeply, communicate openly, and make meaningful changes. In each instance, resilience underpins your ability to pivot from one approach to another while preserving your core intentions.

It is also essential to acknowledge the value of incremental steps. Sweeping changes often overwhelm you, especially when already under emotional strain. By breaking down big hurdles into smaller tasks, you lessen your sense of being overwhelmed and build small victories that spark your confidence. Each success story, no matter how small, serves as concrete evidence that you can face further complications. When you experience repeated wins, the accumulative effect reinforces your self-belief in your capacity to handle unexpected turns.

Most importantly, resilience draws upon your support system. You might lean on friends, family, or a mentor who has navigated similar situations. Reaching out for help is not a sign of weakness but evidence of your determination to keep going. Others can point out options you never considered, share past lessons, or simply offer a sense of comfort that eases the emotional toll. In this way, resilience is also about humility and a willingness to benefit from other people's wisdom.

These principles show that resilience is practical and tangible; it keeps your spirit from breaking when you encounter life's rougher patches. By choosing to adapt, seeking support, and celebrating small achievements, you transform obstacles into catalysts for growth. As you progress, you will see how resilience is not restricted to adult concerns; children benefit greatly from it, too. Developing resilience early can prepare youngsters to handle life's inevitable twists and turns with confidence.

6. Raising Resilient Children: Building a Strong Future

Children face their own range of ups and downs. From shaky friendships and classroom challenges to the stress of performing in sports, they are no strangers to difficult emotions. Resilience, when introduced early in life, forms a shield that helps them handle these pains in a healthier way. By teaching children to recognise failure as a growth opportunity and mistakes as lessons, you equip them with invaluable skills that set the tone for their future approach to adversity.

One foundation of nurturing resilience in children is fostering a mindset of development. By encouraging them to see ability as something that can increase through effort and curiosity, you shield them from the belief that a bad outcome makes them incapable. Suppose a child struggles in mathematics. Rather than letting them say, "I am no good at numbers," encourage them to practise more, learn different techniques, or ask for help from a teacher or sibling. Such an approach teaches them that hurdles can be defeated with determination and the right strategies.

You can also support children by giving them space to solve smaller problems independently. While your instinct might be to step in and provide immediate solutions, allowing them to figure out small challenges by themselves builds their self-confidence. A child who has resolved playground disputes or come up with an idea for a school project on their own feels proud of that accomplishment. This sense of triumph fosters a belief in their capacity to manage bigger difficulties down the line.

Emotional literacy is another key component. Many children experience intense feelings but lack the words to identify them. Encouraging them to talk about what they feel helps them develop an emotional vocabulary. For instance, when a child feels nervous about a school play, helping them name the feeling as "nervous" or "anxious" takes away some of its mystery. They learn that an emotion is not an indication that something is permanently wrong; it is a signal they can address. With guidance, they figure out ways to cope, like practising a script more often or learning calming exercises.

A stable support system is equally vital. Children who feel loved and safe at home learn they have a fallback when external events rattle them. They absorb the lesson that leaning on trusted people is a natural part of coping with setbacks. This does not mean granting them a life free of struggle, rather, it is making sure they never feel isolated or helpless. Together, love and appropriate discipline convey the message that they are valued and capable.

Through these measures, you give children a crucial gift: the confidence that life's tests can be overcome rather than dreaded. They realise resilience is not the absence of fear or mistakes but the willingness to adapt and endure. Consequently, they carry this perspective into adolescence and adulthood, better prepared to remain unshaken when confronted with the inevitable curveballs of life. As you will see, these lessons extend beyond individual experiences, resonating in professional environments where resilience can distinguish you from the crowd.

7. Thriving Professionally: Resilience on the Job

Your workplace, often filled with demands and rapid changes, can rapidly deplete your mental and emotional energy if you are not prepared. When you bring resilience into your professional environment, you give yourself a decisive advantage. You adapt to new realities more smoothly, maintain composure during crises, and find innovative ways to contribute even when resources are stretched thin. In short, resilience allows you to transform workplace pressure into opportunities for growth and leadership.

Adaptability becomes your primary ally at work. Rather than complaining when organisational structures shift, or new policies roll out, you spot openings for improvement and find ways to excel within the new framework. This mindset stands out, showing your leaders and team members that you are dependable under shifting circumstances. In industries that evolve quickly, like technology, finance, or healthcare, a resilient employee is often the one who remains steady while everyone else is panicking.

Stress, of course, is hard to avoid at work. Resilience helps you regulate your response to that stress, turning it into a driving force instead of a debilitating obstacle. By retaining your composure, you think clearly under tight deadlines, solve problems effectively, and maintain your confidence even if you take on heavier workloads. This approach also reduces burnout since resilient people pace themselves and understand the significance of rest and recovery. They know an exhausted mind is less creative and more error-prone, so stepping back is not laziness but a strategic measure to keep performance high.

Beyond your own tasks, resilience amplifies your leadership potential. Colleagues often gravitate toward individuals who radiate calm and decisiveness in the midst of chaos. When you consistently display resilience, you become the person co-workers trust for advice or reassurance. Over time, this sets the stage for career advancements; someone who can handle crisis situations effectively is an asset to any organisation. Resilient leaders also promote a culture of open communication, ensuring that setbacks are addressed and used as lessons to refine strategies.

Another facet of professional resilience is the willingness to update your skills. As industries evolve, employees who resist new learning will inevitably lag behind. In contrast, a resilient employee is open to continuous education, whether through workshops, online courses, or mentorship. This willingness to expand skills keeps you competitive and shows your organisation that you are invested in long-term growth. You do not see unfamiliar technology or processes as threats but as further territory to conquer.

When resilience becomes part of your professional identity, your career takes on a new dimension. Challenges no longer appear as reasons to shrink back but as chances to gain experience, test your mettle, and refine your craft. You grow from each test, evolving into a more resourceful version of yourself. Next, you will discover how resilience is linked to various forms of achievement, showing that your capacity to bounce back can open doors you never anticipated.

8. Resilience and the Path to Personal Triumph

Resilience: Bouncing Back from Adversity

Resilience is more than a defensive shield that deflects adversity. It also plays a pivotal part in achieving personal victory in any arena you choose. Whether your aim is professional acclaim, academic milestones, or personal improvement, your perseverance in the face of hurdles can make all the difference. Resilience does not magically eliminate life's obstacles, but it strengthens your resolve to keep going until you accomplish your objectives.

One of the strongest connections between resilience and success lies in tenacity. Even highly skilled individuals fail at times, not because they lack talent but because they give up when confronted with difficulties. In contrast, a resilient person acknowledges setbacks as temporary. They pause, adapt, and then press forward. This persistent mindset is often what differentiates those who reach their goals from those who abandon them halfway. Critically, tenacity is not blind stubbornness. It is an informed decision to persist, fuelled by your belief that growth and learning will eventually bring the outcomes you desire.

In addition, resilience keeps you flexible. When you are set on a significant endeavour, obstacles are almost certain to appear. Perhaps the job market changes, new technologies disrupt your field, or personal circumstances demand a shift in priority. Individuals lacking resilience tend to see these shifts as insurmountable barriers. By contrast, resilient people pivot. They refine their strategies, tweak their methods, or even alter their final targets if the landscape requires it. This dynamism ensures you remain competitive and relevant, enhancing your chance of succeeding long-term.

Another way resilience supports triumph is by helping you maintain your motivation. Sustaining effort in large projects can be draining, especially if results do not come as quickly as anticipated. If you easily grow discouraged, you may quit just before your breakthrough. Resilience nudges you to stay consistent, to endure repeated trials, and to keep faith in your abilities. Over time, this unwavering commitment often leads to surprising achievements. You have the staying power to outlast those who opt for quick wins and immediate comfort.

Consider people who have overcome tremendous odds to reach unprecedented heights. Their stories frequently share the same threads: unforeseen hardship, periods of self-doubt, yet an unrelenting determination to persevere. Resilience fortifies their core and makes them unstoppable, even when everyone else sees failure. While it is easy to envy those who stand on the podium, their behind-the-scenes journey is typically marked by numerous knocks and comebacks.

Ultimately, success tends to favour those who show up repeatedly, driven by a mindset that weaves hope with realism. They neither ignore risks nor magnify them beyond reason; rather, they calibrate, recalibrate, and continue striving. You will see next how resilience is vital in rebounding from setbacks that appear to threaten your progress. Every triumph, after all, is built on the foundation of bouncing back when defeat seems likely.

9. Bouncing Back from Defeat: Resilience as Your Safety Net

Failure is inevitable for anyone aiming to do something worthwhile. No matter how cautious or talented you are, at times, your plans will unravel, your goals will stall, or your ideal outcomes simply will not materialise. In those moments, resilience emerges as your most dependable ally, transforming defeat into a learning experience rather than a final verdict on your abilities. You stop viewing a single disappointment as the last chapter and instead treat it as one step in a longer story of growth and progress.

The first stage of recovering from a setback is to be honest about what went wrong. Did you underestimate the effort required, or did you rely on incomplete information? Were there external factors beyond your control, such as a sudden economic slump or unexpected competition? A resilient approach avoids letting these questions turn into self-blame or denial. Instead, you use them to collect information about how to improve. By inspecting the causes behind the defeat, you remove the element of mystery, realising that setbacks are rarely random punishments but consequences of variables you can influence or navigate differently next time.

Another beneficial habit is self-forgiveness. After a failure, it is very easy to start criticising yourself. However, unrestrained self-blame drains your emotional energy and clouds your ability to plan your next move. Acknowledging that failure does not make you unworthy or incompetent is an important part of bouncing back. This step frees your mind from destructive thinking and helps you renew your determination to move on. Self-forgiveness paves the way for growth and stops you from locking yourself into a negative identity centred around failure.

Resilience also involves swiftly reorienting your focus towards actionable steps. Once you have gleaned lessons from what went wrong, turning those lessons into practical goals is the next logical phase. Picture someone who loses out on a promotion. A resilient response might be to ask for feedback from managers, adopt a new set of leadership courses, or even adjust their career path if the role no longer aligns with their aspirations. By focusing on what can be done rather than what is lost, you feed momentum and reclaim a sense of control.

You must also keep in mind that resilience frequently draws strength from unity. Sharing your disappointment with trusted friends, mentors, or a supportive community can alleviate feelings of isolation. Sometimes, fresh insights come from someone outside the situation, offering angles you had not even considered. Plus, the emotional relief of talking through your experiences breaks down the belief that you must carry failure alone.

Defeats and errors can indeed feel demoralising in the moment. Yet, through resilience, you harness these moments for personal development. Each setback serves as a signpost guiding you away from previous pitfalls and toward a sharper sense of judgement or skill. In the final subheading, you will discover how the experiences of highly resilient individuals can illuminate the road to a more empowered, flexible life, no matter your current circumstances.

10. Stories of Strength: Learning from Resilient Trailblazers

Throughout history, many notable individuals have risen above adversity by wielding resilience as their guiding star. These stories serve as living proof that the human spirit, when fortified by an unbreakable will, can transform setbacks into stepping stones. Taking inspiration from them does more than spark hope; it equips you with real-life lessons on how to develop a courageous, unwavering approach to life's toughest blows.

Resilience: Bouncing Back from Adversity

Look at the story of the writer whose first manuscript was rejected by numerous publishers, leaving her on the brink of giving up. Rather than surrendering, she refined her work, held to her vision, and finally found someone willing to see its merit. The world has now celebrated that series for decades, and her journey from poverty to literary acclaim continues to inspire those who doubt their own worth. It was resilience that propelled her from countless rejections to unprecedented success.

Another example is the athlete who lost almost every competition early in their career. Instead of seeing these losses as proof of inability, they dug deeper into training, identified flaws in their technique, and refined their mental game. Little by little, those small improvements accumulated until the athlete began to dominate events. The power of resilience lies in this refusal to accept repeated defeats as a final outcome. When others would have quit, resilience urged them to face another day of training and another chance to excel.

Then there is the innovator who poured time and funds into products that flopped spectacularly. While observers mocked these failed attempts, the innovator dissected each outcome for insights. They investigated the root causes, pivoted strategies, and refined the next project. Eventually, one creation took off, changing how the world did business. Without resilience, that final breakthrough would never have been reached because the journey required enduring wave after wave of disappointment and persistent revision of original ideas.

These examples highlight a shared pattern: an unwavering commitment to keep striving, learning, and adapting. Resilience does not imply you will never feel deflated or uncertain; rather, it gives you a solid footing when the ground beneath you seems to quake. It offers you the chance to see meaning in your difficulties, to extract lessons that strengthen and sharpen your sense of purpose. Your resilience is not measured by how many times you fall but by how decisively you rise, armed with the knowledge gained from each fall.

As you follow the path of these trailblazers, you see that resilience is not the exclusive realm of extraordinary talents. It is available to you through consistent practice of mental discipline, emotional regulation, and belief in your capacity to come out stronger than before. By examining these real-life success stories, you recognise that no trial is final and no setback absolute. Resilience becomes the engine driving your transformation from a passive bystander in your own life to an active participant shaping your destiny. With resilience at your side, you discover that the unpredictable nature of life is an invitation to become bolder, more purposeful, and more resolved than you ever imagined.

Chapter 19

Self-Esteem: Embracing Your Worth

Your self-esteem is like an internal compass; it shapes the way you navigate life's opportunities and setbacks. You might have spent years believing your worth is something that must be earned through achievements or validated by others, but true self-esteem lies deeper. It's about embracing an unwavering truth: your inherent worth remains constant, unaffected by external opinions or life's inevitable ups and downs. Recognising and accepting this fact can transform your relationship with yourself and, consequently, your life.

When you understand your intrinsic value, you start to view successes and failures with balanced clarity, knowing they neither enhance nor diminish your true worth. Self-esteem isn't about perfection or constant praise; it's about respect, kindness, and patience towards yourself. It provides a solid foundation that empowers you to approach life's challenges without the constant need for external validation. In the pages ahead, you'll uncover insights to help you recognise and break free from the invisible chains of low self-esteem and discover practical strategies for cultivating genuine, resilient confidence.

Let's explore together how embracing your authentic worth can open doors to a fulfilling and empowered life.

1. Your Value and the Essence of Self-Esteem

You have a core worth that remains constant, no matter where you live or what external achievements you pursue. This knowledge might not always feel obvious, especially if you have spent years seeking approval from bosses, relatives, or acquaintances. However, understanding that your value is not earned but inherent is the cornerstone of healthy self-esteem. Self-esteem reflects how much you appreciate your fundamental nature and see yourself as worthy of respect and care. When you recognise that your value is unquestionable, you begin to view challenges and triumphs with the same calm acceptance rather than letting outcomes define your sense of self.

This inherent worth never vanishes; it is not reduced by mistakes or magnified by plaques on your wall. Some individuals discover this truth during a difficult turning point, perhaps when they realise they cannot rely on applause or external praise indefinitely. Others sense it during quiet reflection, noticing that their sense of dignity persists regardless of how others treat them. You can begin this awareness by intentionally reminding yourself that you are more than a salary figure, more than your reflection in the mirror, and more than any accomplishment or shortcoming on your résumé. Even if you have regrets from the past, you retain the power to accept your unconditional significance.

When you embrace the essence of self-esteem, you shift from hungry pursuit of validation to a peaceful knowledge of your intrinsic value. This calmness then influences every area of your life. If you decide to embark on a new business venture, for instance, you will not tie your worth to the outcome. Whether the endeavour thrives or encounters roadblocks, your self-esteem remains unshaken, meaning you will rise again if the first try fails. In personal relationships, this grounded confidence allows you to be genuine instead of bending to others' preferences for fear of appearing unimportant. It also lets you draw boundaries, ensuring that you are neither dominating others nor erasing your own needs.

As you reflect on your daily encounters, remind yourself that your value precedes any action or triumph. You might feel more driven to chase your aspirations or focus on health, but this motivation comes from a sense of possibility, not desperation. Confident people do not rely on constant reassurance. They appreciate compliments but do not crave them. They learn from mistakes but do not treat slip-ups as verdicts on their essence. They pursue ambitions but do not attach their identity to a title.

To begin aligning with this perspective, pause whenever doubt creeps in and ask yourself whether you are giving external opinions too much power. Have you ever felt your spirit deflate from a single piece of criticism? Releasing that hold starts with reminding yourself of your worth daily. This is not a shallow mantra. Instead, it is an ongoing shift in how you treat yourself. Your core value is immovable, and when you truly honour that, you lay the foundation for resilient self-esteem, setting the stage for deeper growth in every facet of your life.

Transitioning into the next subheading, you will gain insights into how self-esteem can waver when external pressures and thought patterns begin to shape how you see yourself, sometimes creating invisible chains that hold you back.

2. Invisible Chains of Low Self-Esteem

Low self-esteem can settle in so quietly that you barely notice its presence. It acts like a silent weight, nudging you to question your capabilities and your worthiness. These invisible chains often originate from childhood experiences, environments where criticism overshadowed encouragement or comparisons that left you feeling second-best. Sometimes, it grows out of societal standards telling you how you should look or what you should achieve, placing tremendous pressure on you to conform. Over time, these factors can merge into a persistent belief that you are somehow lacking.

Rather than confronting you head-on, low self-esteem seeps into your daily life through subtle thoughts, choices, and patterns. You might habitually avoid speaking up in meetings, convinced your ideas are inadequate. You could stay in draining relationships because you secretly feel you do not deserve better. It could even affect your body language, slumped shoulders, minimal eye contact, and an apologetic manner. These small tendencies might appear inconsequential, but they gradually shape your identity in your own mind and the minds of those around you.

Moreover, low self-esteem can trigger a chain reaction in your mental and emotional landscape. If you constantly berate yourself for not meeting unrealistic expectations, you can slip into a cycle of self-sabotage. This might reveal itself in procrastination, hesitancy to apply for more challenging roles, or anxiety that flares up whenever you face something unknown. Even if you have mastered new skills or surpassed certain goals, the shadow of self-doubt can linger, making you think it was merely luck or a fluke. You may downplay your achievements or refuse to celebrate them, believing you are undeserving of praise.

Another profound impact of low self-esteem is on how you let others treat you. When your inner voice keeps whispering that you are not valuable enough, you might turn a blind eye to disrespect. You accept demands without question or let colleagues take credit for your efforts. You might remain silent in conflict situations, hesitant to assert your perspective. Over time, this can mould your surroundings into places where your voice remains unheard, reinforcing the faulty conclusion that your thoughts do not matter. In relationships, this dynamic can create unhealthy imbalances, with your needs continuously sidelined.

Recognising these invisible chains is the first crucial step to breaking free. You must become aware of patterns and moments when you downplay your merits, shy away from opportunities, or accept behaviour that is detrimental to your well-being. You can then begin to challenge these internal narratives. Ask yourself whether these limiting beliefs reflect reality or whether they have been carried over from past experiences that do not define you any longer. Low self-esteem thrives in unchallenged assumptions. The day you decide to question them is the day you begin dismantling that weight.

In moving forward, it is vital to realise that these invisible chains can be dismantled with deliberate action and reflection. The next subheading explores how you can construct a healthy, confident self-perception using practical strategies and a renewed understanding that you are far stronger than any negative scripts swirling in your mind.

3. Cultivating Unshakable Confidence

Building a powerful sense of self-esteem requires more than upbeat talk. You need a combination of intentional habits, consistent self-awareness, and a willingness to step outside familiar comfort zones. One of the most effective ways to begin is to remind yourself daily of your inherent worthiness, an idea that must go from your mind into your actions. Each time you choose a path that resonates with your true goals or turn away from one that disrespects your needs, you are reinforcing a healthier self-view.

A crucial habit for cultivating deep confidence is consistently challenging negative self-talk. It is easy to fall into the pattern of calling yourself names or blaming yourself when life becomes difficult. Monitor this self-critical voice. Does it exaggerate your flaws or label you incompetent after minor setbacks? Rather than allowing those automatic thoughts to run unchecked, respond with balance. You might say: "I made an error, but that does not define me long-term. I can learn from this and adapt." Replacing sweeping, judgemental statements with balanced reflections over time rewires your mindset toward growth.

Another key strategy involves setting goals that stretch you without triggering overwhelm. Choose objectives that align with your values, then commit to them with a structured plan. Each time you meet a new milestone, your brain receives the message that you are capable. In that sense, well-chosen goals act as stepping stones for your self-esteem, showing you concrete evidence of your ability to pursue worthwhile aims. This also discourages perfectionism, reminding you that progress is more significant than a flawless outcome.

Surrounding yourself with supportive influences is equally important. Seek friends or colleagues who uplift, not belittle, your aspirations. If your circle is full of sceptics or cynics, it may be time to expand your network or set firmer boundaries. Remember, the people around you can either fuel your confidence or drain it. Likewise, read uplifting books, engage with positive media, and find role models who inspire resilience. While external validation should never be your core source of worth, choosing a healthier social environment makes it easier to stay on track.

Physical self-care can also amplify self-esteem. Whether this is staying active, maintaining balanced nutrition, or getting adequate sleep, treating your body with respect can translate into greater self-respect. Your discipline in one realm often spills into others, showing you how capable you are of making beneficial choices. Over time, you will sense a congruence between your internal belief in your value and the external actions that reflect that.

As you adopt these habits, challenging negative thoughts, setting meaningful objectives, curating your environment, and caring for your physical self, you build a foundation that external opinions cannot easily shake. You start to experience confidence as a steady backdrop in your life rather than a momentary uptick when someone compliments you. This sense of assurance does not demand perfection; it allows for missteps while holding on to the knowledge that a misstep is merely a moment of learning, not a verdict on who you are.

Now that you have examined how to elevate your personal self-worth, the next subheading reveals the important link between self-esteem and the relationships in your life, showing how strong self-value enriches the bonds you cultivate with others.

4. Self-Esteem and Healthy Bonds with Others

Every connection in your life, whether it is with a partner, friend, or colleague, is influenced by how you perceive yourself. When your self-esteem is intact, you approach interactions from a position of stability rather than neediness. You share opinions without fear that disagreements will threaten your sense of worth. You also become more receptive to others' viewpoints since you are not constantly defending yourself against imagined threats to your identity.

In contrast, if you doubt your value, your relationships can become a constant hunt for affirmation or a vehicle for proof that you matter. This often leads to unhealthy dynamics. For instance, you might dread voicing your boundaries, worrying that any sign of assertiveness will drive people away. Alternatively, you might cling to relationships even when they turn detrimental, convinced you will not find better. Low self-esteem can even manifest as excessive jealousy or suspicion, fuelled by the fear that you are not enough to keep someone's interest or loyalty.

On the other hand, healthy self-esteem encourages mutual respect. You can offer empathy and support without sacrificing your own well-being. This sense of balance fosters a climate where both individuals can be honest. You are not scared to say, "I need some time to myself," nor are you threatened when the other person does the same. By asserting your needs calmly, you also grant them space to express theirs. Conflict, when it arises, is approached with the perspective that a disagreement about an issue does not equal a rejection of your core self.

The type of relationships you attract can also shift when your self-esteem is solid. If you have been settling for those who criticise or manipulate you, developing robust self-worth can prompt you to step away and seek connections rooted in mutual understanding. Respect, compassion, and genuine interest in each other's growth become your guiding criteria. This change might feel unfamiliar at first, but it paves the way for more fulfilling bonds. It shows in your interactions, from how you ask questions about the other person's experiences to the calmness you display when resolving disagreements.

Improving self-esteem in a relationship context often involves honest dialogues, both with yourself and those close to you. Be transparent about how you prefer to handle conflicts or how you expect to be treated. While it might feel risky, especially if you have been accommodating or silent in the past, this forthrightness underscores the value you place on your own perspective. In a healthy bond, the other individual will respond with openness, willing to adapt for the relationship to thrive.

Ultimately, when you carry yourself with confidence, you contribute to relationships built on trust, respect, and shared empathy. That is the true power of self-esteem: it allows you to bring your authentic self to the table, free from the urge to perform or overcompensate. As you move forward, you will see how this self-assured approach can also help you conquer internal obstacles of self-doubt, clearing a path for greater emotional freedom.

5. Triumphing Over Self-Doubt

Many people believe self-doubt is an unchanging flaw in their personality. In reality, it is frequently a learned response shaped by experiences that made you question whether you measure up. You might have been overshadowed by peers or criticised by authority figures, creating a loop of uncertainty in your thoughts. While self-doubt can be persistent, it is not immovable. You can triumph over it by dismantling its sources, confronting its distortions, and practising new mental habits.

First, identify where your doubt originates. Reflect on your past, but avoid sinking into blame or regret. The aim is to observe patterns and see how certain experiences may have contributed to your current mindset. This awareness alone can bring a sense of relief because you recognise that self-doubt did not appear out of thin air, nor does it have to define your future decisions. Once you pinpoint its roots, you can approach each moment of insecurity as an echo from those old situations rather than treating every spark of doubt as cold fact.

Next, challenge the assumptions that feed your self-doubt. The mind can magnify minor failings into sweeping generalisations, such as "I always fail at new things." When this voice pipes up, counter it with evidence to the contrary. Maybe you learnt a new language last year or mastered an unfamiliar skill at work. Remind yourself of these accomplishments to undercut the notion of permanent inadequacy. By consistently offering a balanced, factual perspective to your inner critic, you begin to weaken its hold and promote a more flexible self-image.

It also helps to visualise success scenarios. Professional athletes frequently use mental rehearsal to see themselves conquering formidable opponents. You can adopt a similar practice in daily life. Whether you are preparing for an interview or an important presentation, spend a few moments picturing yourself delivering strong answers, receiving positive feedback, and staying calm under pressure. Although visualisation alone does not guarantee success, it primes your mind to remain focused and resilient rather than letting anxieties run wild.

Action is your ally in this process. Face tasks that trigger your self-doubt instead of avoiding them. Each time you do so and gather a small win, you reinforce the narrative that you are capable of growth. Remember, progress involves trial and error, not instantaneous excellence. By taking small, manageable steps and celebrating every improvement, you tilt the balance in your internal conversation away from self-doubt and towards self-assurance. Even if you slip up, you will gain insights you can use next time.

Triumphing over self-doubt is not about eradicating every hint of insecurity; it is about learning to push forward despite them. Sometimes, being courageous means taking the next step before feeling completely ready. When you conquer these hesitations, you discover that doubt has far less power than you once believed. With this realisation, you can advance to nurturing self-esteem in the next generation, seeing how early influences can shape a child's lifelong sense of worth.

6. Instilling a Sense of Worth in the Young

When children view themselves as worthy and capable, they set foundations for healthy relationships, resilience, and success. As a parent, educator, or mentor, you have the chance to model and encourage positive self-esteem in them. Rather than envelop them in constant praise, aim for constructive reinforcement that acknowledges both their efforts and their inherent dignity.

Begin by showing genuine attention. Put aside your phone and look them in the eye when they talk about their day.

Children notice whether your interest is real or distracted. By actively engaging, you send a powerful message: "Your thoughts count." This practice is more than courtesy; it teaches them that their voice matters, a key pillar of stable self-esteem. Over time, they learn to trust that their ideas deserve attention and to speak up in other contexts, such as classrooms or social groups.

Another crucial step involves guiding them to explore challenges instead of rescuing them from every difficulty. While you want to protect them, stepping in too soon can unintentionally communicate that they cannot handle adversity. Let them puzzle through situations like learning to ride a bike or solving a homework problem. You can stand ready to assist if genuine distress arises, but allow them the satisfaction of incremental achievements. Each time they conquer a small challenge independently, they discover a new level of confidence.

Also, be consistent in how you respond to both their successes and their missteps. Excessive compliments can lead them to rely on external validation. Similarly, severe scolding for minor slips can create fear of failure. Find balance by highlighting the learning value in mistakes, perhaps by saying, "That approach did not work; what can you try next?" This calm, instructive response shows them mistakes are a natural part of growth. They see that their worth remains intact regardless of whether they excel or stumble, which helps them become resilient.

In conversations about body image, talents, or academic performance, be mindful of the language you use. Refer to their achievements in a way that emphasises effort, not personal worth. For example, "Your spelling improved because you kept practising" guides them to appreciate perseverance. If they struggle with a particular subject, remind them that skills can develop with time. Encourage them to see self-improvement as ongoing rather than fixed. Children absorb these messages and internalise them as scripts for how they measure their abilities.

Finally, remember that children emulate you more than you might realise. If you demonstrate self-respect, treating yourself with kindness when mistakes happen or speaking about your goals with enthusiasm, they pick up on that. They learn that confidence is not arrogance; it is an assured view of oneself that coexists with humility. Small interactions, from praising them for tidying their room to teaching them to accept praise graciously, all add up. By fostering their self-belief early, you equip them to handle the inevitable complexities of life with dignity and optimism.

Building self-esteem in young people is an ongoing process. Next, you will see how this confident self-perception carries over into professional settings, giving individuals a clear edge in workplace success and leadership.

7. Self-Esteem as Your Edge in the Workplace

In any professional environment, a steady sense of self-worth can be your most valuable resource. You are likely to handle new tasks willingly, speak up in meetings, and pursue promotions more confidently when you trust in your capabilities. When your self-esteem is solid, rejection or setbacks do not crush your spirit. Instead, they become catalysts for learning and eventually returning stronger.

A robust sense of worth also influences how peers perceive you. If you often doubt yourself and shy away from opportunities, colleagues may misinterpret that as disinterest or believe you do not have the capacity to contribute at a higher level. On the other hand, an assured but respectful demeanour sets the tone for how others treat you. You are not afraid to volunteer for projects slightly outside your comfort zone because you trust you will grow into them. Managers often notice this proactive attitude and see it as a sign of leadership potential, leading to more challenging and rewarding roles.

Moreover, when you maintain healthy self-esteem, you are less likely to be derailed by office politics or gossip. You can keep your focus on doing quality work and nurturing positive professional relationships. Solid self-esteem discourages you from taking every remark personally or snapping at co-workers under stress. You understand your identity is not decided by fleeting remarks or minor misunderstandings. This level-headed approach fosters collaboration. People come to respect how you navigate tensions without letting them escalate into personal conflicts.

Of course, strong workplace confidence does not mean strutting around expecting constant praise. It is about knowing your worth and balancing that with genuine humility. You still acknowledge when others have the right ideas or when your suggestions could use refinement. Self-esteem drives you to keep learning rather than clinging to the belief that you have reached the peak of your ability. In a fast-moving world, the flexibility to adapt is crucial, and those who balance confidence with willingness to develop remain assets to any organisation.

To harness this edge, you might start by listing achievements or experiences that highlight your strengths. Keep it where you can glance at it on tough days, not to brag, but to remind yourself of your capability. Additionally, approach each task with the mindset that improvement is always possible, even if you have done something similar before. Ask for feedback from mentors or colleagues. Recognising areas for growth becomes simpler when you see them as part of a continuing journey, not as threats to your self-image.

Self-esteem can create momentum in your career, allowing you to seize chances and remain resilient when faced with temporary defeats. Ultimately, you stand out as someone who can manage responsibility, communicate effectively, and stay calm under pressure. As you see how these qualities elevate your performance at work, do not forget that self-esteem also holds profound importance in your mental and emotional realm, something we will delve into next.

8. Emotional Well-being and Self-Worth

Your emotional life is closely tied to your sense of worth. When you see yourself as valuable, you are more equipped to handle disappointments or conflicts without allowing them to unravel your mental state. If your identity does not hinge on external outcomes, you can weather personal storms with composure. Unexpected setbacks, such as losing a promotion or receiving criticism, hurt but do not shatter you. Instead, you process the feelings and then refocus, knowing that your core dignity remains intact.

On the flip side, when self-esteem is fragile, emotional highs and lows can be extreme. A minor success might lift you momentarily, but the impact fades quickly because you are waiting for the next validation. Meanwhile, a small criticism might feel catastrophic, as though it confirms your worst suspicions about yourself. This kind of emotional rollercoaster is exhausting. It can lead you to second-guess your choices, over-apologise, or become consumed by envy when peers achieve victories. You might find yourself unable to celebrate others' good fortune because it feels like a direct commentary on your own perceived inadequacies.

Building a strong emotional bedrock involves consistent internal dialogue. Whenever you face disappointments, talk yourself through them in a balanced, empowering way. Acknowledge the hurt, but also remind yourself of your enduring qualities. The same approach applies to triumphs: yes, appreciate the achievement, but do not treat it as the singular proof that you matter. This balanced response helps keep you from being swayed by each gust of external feedback.

Mindfulness also plays a role here. By practising mindfulness, you remain attuned to shifting moods without letting them dictate your entire day. If sadness arises, you let it run its course, recognising it as one emotion among many. If excitement arrives, you savour it but do not spiral into daydreams of how everything must remain perfect. Through this balanced perspective, you see yourself as constant while emotions ebb and flow around you.

Cultivating healthy outlets is another valuable step. This could be journalling, speaking to a trusted confidant, or participating in activities that let you process emotions in a constructive manner. By venting frustration or sorrow in a healthy way, you prevent pent-up feelings from chipping away at your sense of worth. Sometimes, it helps to repeat a calm reminder, such as, "I am allowed to experience emotions without judging myself for having them." This stance recognises that you are a multifaceted being, capable of weathering emotional waves while remaining grounded in your unshakeable value.

Ultimately, your emotional health benefits enormously when you anchor yourself in self-esteem. You become less fearful of life's ups and downs, trusting that no temporary incident can define you. As you learn to navigate these internal tides, you also become better equipped to resist external pressures, like comparisons in the modern world, which we will address next.

9. Staying Grounded in a Competitive World

In an age of social media and continuous comparisons, it is easy to let the success of others influence your own self-esteem. You might see acquaintances celebrating promotions, new homes, or seemingly perfect relationships and question why your life does not measure up. This unending feed of highlight reels can evoke envy and self-criticism. Yet, the reality is that nobody's life is faultless, no matter how sparkling it appears online.

Building a healthy buffer against these comparisons starts by controlling your digital intake. Limit time spent scrolling through platforms that leave you feeling more negative than inspired. Curate your feeds so they feature content that uplifts or educates you rather than drowning you in others' achievements. By being intentional with your online environment, you create space for genuine growth instead of self-deprecation.

Equally important is celebrating your personal journey. Document your own milestones, whether you have solved a tough project at work or learned a new skill for the first time in years. Focusing on your progress helps counteract the temptation to judge yourself by someone else's story. Each time you reflect on how far you have come, you gather evidence of your strengths. This perspective realignment reminds you that life is not a race but an individual path shaped by your values, resources, and pace.

A supportive network plays a similar role. Stay connected with individuals who view competition in a healthy manner rather than encouraging constant rivalry. True allies want you to thrive, and they will champion your successes instead of belittling them. If your circle is dominated by people who fixate on comparing salaries, possessions, or social status, you may need firmer personal boundaries or a deliberate effort to add more encouraging influences to your life. This choice is not disloyal; it is an act of self-care and respect for your mental well-being.

Another powerful strategy is to set personal goals that revolve around growth. Instead of aiming to outshine a colleague or keep pace with a friend's lifestyle, define objectives that align with your genuine aspirations. Perhaps you want to refine a professional skill or gain deeper insights into your creative side. Your motivation then comes from within, not from a perceived race against someone else's accomplishments. This internal focus fosters a calm sense of purpose, insulating you from envy or undue disappointment.

By staying rooted in your own path, you release the need to measure your worth against external benchmarks. You realise that what you bring to the table is distinct; your achievements do not lose their merit because someone else gained success in a different arena. Embracing this view allows you to stand firm in your self-esteem, even amidst external chatter or curated social media snapshots. In the final subheading, we will explore stories of individuals who redefined their worth and how they stayed dedicated to fostering lasting, solid self-esteem.

10. Stories of Renewed Confidence and Final Inspiration

Throughout history, countless individuals have risen above self-doubt and discovered untapped reserves of inner strength. Their experiences underscore the notion that self-esteem is not reserved for those with charmed lives; it is a journey open to anyone prepared to reshape their mindset. You can find stories of people who emerged from challenging backgrounds, shedding old labels and forging self-belief through grit and clarity. You can also find everyday examples, from someone who decided to go back to education later in life to someone who overcame stage fright, turning an apparent weakness into a confidence-building victory.

Picture a young person who struggled with reading during primary school, frequently teased by peers. Feeling embarrassed, they withdrew from group discussions, convinced that they did not fit in academically. Over the years, they discovered reading strategies and gained unstoppable momentum. By university, they were not only reading fluently but also debating literature with passion. What changed was not just technique; it was a paradigm shift in self-image, from incompetent to driven learner.

Likewise, imagine an entrepreneur who faced multiple failed ventures in their early twenties. They carried a heavy burden of guilt, convinced they lacked the talent or insight to succeed. However, through connecting with supportive mentors and re-evaluating the lessons gleaned from those failures, they forged a renewed sense of self-assurance. Instead of defining themselves by what went wrong, they saw each collapse as a rung on the ladder. By their mid-thirties, they founded a successful enterprise rooted in the very lessons gleaned from earlier missteps. Their self-esteem soared, grounded in the truth that tenacity often outweighs initial fortune.

The lesson from such narratives is that your sense of worth can be reshaped at any stage. Mistakes do not have to become your identity, and old criticisms do not have to haunt you forever. By welcoming growth, embracing the possibility of reinvention, and handling each stumble as a step in the process, you align with the reality that you hold deep value. This newfound perspective allows you to be kinder to yourself, to recognise achievements, even small ones, and to build on them in any field, whether personal or professional.

As you integrate the strategies outlined across these subheadings, remember that your self-esteem is like a constantly evolving relationship with yourself. Each action, each promise kept, and each boundary defended fortifies that relationship. The shift is usually gradual, but it becomes more natural over time. A sturdy self-esteem radiates into all corners of your existence, influencing how you engage with loved ones, colleagues, and even with your own past regrets and future hopes.

You have now seen how to view your worth as intrinsic and how to dismantle harmful beliefs. You have learned how a healthy self-view nurtures emotional stability and more balanced bonds with others. You have discovered methods to navigate modern pressures and gleaned ideas on helping children grow up with a sense of their own dignity. Step forward with the conviction that self-esteem is not a fixed

Self-Esteem: Embracing Your Worth

trait but a quality you shape by your daily choices. Through resilience, honesty, and compassion towards yourself, you can continue to nurture and protect this invaluable sense of worth for a lifetime.

Chapter 20

Emotional Intelligence: Key to Personal and Professional Success

Life isn't only about how smart you are or how many degrees you hold; it's fundamentally about connecting with people and understanding yourself deeply enough to manage life's ups and downs gracefully. Emotional Intelligence, often called EI, might sound fancy, but it's really about having the ability to recognise and handle your own feelings, and also grasp and respond thoughtfully to what others are experiencing. Imagine navigating your personal relationships or professional interactions with ease, clarity, and genuine empathy; this is exactly what EI offers. When you master Emotional Intelligence, you equip yourself with a powerful tool that boosts your chances of success in every area of life, whether at home, at work, or in social settings.

This chapter will guide you through practical steps to sharpen your emotional skills, starting from understanding your own emotions to managing them effectively, empathising deeply with others, and navigating social situations with confidence. You'll see how simple adjustments in your self-awareness, attitude, and interactions can create profound changes, enabling stronger bonds, clearer communication, and greater personal fulfilment. Ready to unlock the full potential of your emotional life and transform the way you connect with the world around you? Let's dive in.

1. Emotional Intelligence: Your Foundational Advantage

Emotional Intelligence, or EI, is your anchor for forging meaningful connections with others. It transcends your academic achievements or cognitive intelligence by emphasising a critical yet often overlooked dimension of human interaction: the mastery of your own emotions, coupled with the capacity to discern and respond effectively to the emotions of the people around you. When you operate from a place of emotional awareness, you command a crucial advantage in every domain of life. Workplaces become smoother, personal relationships more fulfilling, and your capacity for growth expands as you learn to interpret subtle emotional cues and navigate daily challenges with poise.

At its core, Emotional Intelligence centres on how well you understand yourself. If you neglect to grasp why your emotions take shape and how they affect you, you risk being swayed by impulses, frustration, or fleeting moods. Conversely, a robust sense of self-awareness empowers you to detect those moments when your temper flares or your spirits sink. It grants you the chance to pause, reflect on what drives these inner surges, and decide on your response with discipline rather than rashness. This discipline forms the bedrock of all emotionally intelligent action because, unless you learn to recognise and manage your own emotional tendencies, you cannot realistically guide others or build deeper interpersonal bonds.

Crucially, Emotional Intelligence is far more than a personal tool; it is a catalyst for creating synergy in professional and social settings. Within a team environment, EI propels you to read the room effectively, spot unspoken concerns, and champion an atmosphere of mutual trust. Individuals with high EI encourage open communication and empathy, fostering confidence that is indispensable for motivation and collaborative success. Such qualities are especially prized among leaders, whose influence radiates through large groups. When you incorporate Emotional Intelligence into your leadership approach, you transcend micromanagement and mere authority, guiding people through sincerity and emotional resonance.

Moreover, EI is not limited to grand leadership roles or public arenas; it is equally pivotal in everyday life. Households, friendships, and any social circle benefit from clear communication, regulated emotions, and a strong sense of empathy. Families flourish when members speak openly about frustrations or anxieties and do so in a respectful tone. Friendships deepen when partners can sense each other's distress, joys, or hidden worries. This awareness leads to genuine support, erasing any pretence or indifference. In short, EI encourages authentic connections that elevate the quality of day-to-day interactions.

Recognise that this capability is no static trait. You can train your emotional awareness in the same way that you train your muscles in a gym. It involves focus, reflection, and the intention to engage with others at a deeper level. By honing your self-awareness, refining how you handle emotional triggers, and cultivating empathy, you secure a lifelong asset that guides you toward satisfying relationships and remarkable achievements in all spheres. Emotional Intelligence underpins your personal influence and helps you carve a meaningful path through life's varied trials. As you start to refine your EI, prepare to witness a transformative ripple effect, both within yourself and in all the communities you belong to.

2. Self-Awareness and Emotional Mastery

The path to meaningful Emotional Intelligence begins with self-awareness, a principle as profound as it is straightforward. When you fail to detect your own emotional currents, you leave yourself at the mercy of fleeting moods and automatic responses, which can wreak havoc on both personal and professional endeavours. Conversely, self-awareness allows you to identify the subtle signs of changing emotions within, along with the reasons behind those shifts. This clarity lays the groundwork for emotional mastery, an ability to influence your own reactions rather than be governed by them.

Elevating your self-awareness starts with a willingness to notice the feelings swirling inside you, whether it's irritation simmering when your schedule changes at the last minute or a surge of excitement that appears out of nowhere. By pausing and labelling these feelings without judgment, you build a more balanced perspective on your own tendencies. The purpose is not to eliminate emotional responses altogether but to recognise them in their raw form. From there, you can choose how best to channel them. Such internal observation leads to better choices under pressure because you can see the difference between a genuine threat and a mere inconvenience.

Crucially, self-awareness equips you with data about who you are, how you function, and what you stand for. Suppose you realise you feel uneasy whenever you lack control over a project. Armed with that knowledge, you can plan ways to adapt or manage your boundaries more effectively. Rather than lashing out in frustration or retreating into passive inaction, you can address your need for clarity by asking questions or requesting resources. In other words, understanding your emotional triggers transforms them from burdens into potential areas for growth.

In a broader sense, self-awareness underpins the entire spectrum of EI. If you cannot grasp why you lash out during family disagreements or freeze up when faced with a high-stakes presentation, you will struggle to improve. Reflecting on these patterns through journaling, meditation, or introspective self-questioning serves as a potent springboard for emotional development. By consistently monitoring which stimuli evoke powerful reactions, you become better positioned to predict and steer your emotional states. You also become more adept at explaining your needs to others, paving the way for deeper mutual respect.

Additionally, self-awareness fosters humility. Recognising that you have blind spots or emotional sore points creates a more balanced perspective, helping you remain open to feedback. True humility is not about shrinking yourself; it's about honestly evaluating your strengths, gaps, and vulnerabilities. Armed with that knowledge, you can adjust, learn from errors, and refine how you carry yourself in challenging situations. In turn, others see you as genuine rather than arrogant or self-absorbed.

Ultimately, self-awareness is your entry point into the wider landscape of Emotional Intelligence. It teaches you to understand the origins of your feelings, to decode your motives with candour, and to recalibrate your behaviour when it no longer aligns with your deeper values. In cultivating this foundation, you set the stage for the other facets of EI, self-regulation, empathy, motivation, and social aptitude, to flourish. Once you commit to truly knowing yourself, you gain the power to direct your emotional world rather than remain a passive bystander in your own life.

3. Self-Regulation: Shaping Your Emotional Reactions

Building on self-awareness, self-regulation is the art of responding rather than reacting to life's inevitable emotional waves. Where self-awareness teaches you to spot and label your emotions, self-regulation pushes you to transform these raw feelings into constructive outcomes. It is the difference between firing off an angry email on a bad day and calmly gathering your thoughts to address the matter productively. By honing self-regulation, you stand poised to handle stress and frustration and even triumph with dignity, staying true to your core principles.

Self-regulation does not mean repressing emotions or pretending that negativity never arises. Instead, you learn to channel your emotional energy in a way that aligns with your larger goals and personal ethics. Emotions serve as signals, telling you if something has gone wrong or right. It's your choice in how you respond to these signals that shapes your relationships and sense of self. Suppose you feel your temper rising during a meeting at work. Pausing to note this sensation, acknowledging you're under stress, and taking a measured breath before speaking can shift a volatile outburst into a thoughtful, solution-focused conversation. That conscious moment of redirection may be brief, but it's enough to elevate the tone of the entire interaction.

In many cases, self-regulation requires healthy coping strategies to deal with tension or adversity. Physical exercise, structured breathing, or mindful breaks can help diffuse pent-up frustration and restore equilibrium to your emotional state. Equally important is adopting a reflective approach after challenging episodes. Asking yourself how you might improve your response next time or what triggered your strong reaction transforms each emotional hurdle into a valuable lesson. Over time, you build resilience and reduce the likelihood of impulsive outbursts.

A key advantage of self-regulation is the credibility you establish in the eyes of others. Friends, colleagues, and family members quickly recognise when you can maintain composure under strain. This reputation for calm steadiness can make you an anchor during turbulent times, drawing people to seek your counsel or partnership when challenges arise. Leaders who consistently demonstrate emotional poise often gain deeper trust and loyalty from their teams. They model an environment where issues are tackled head-on but with respect and understanding, and that sets the tone for healthier communication at every level.

The consistency inherent in self-regulation also nurtures personal well-being. Instead of reeling through emotional highs and lows, you learn to course-correct and keep yourself in a state conducive to clear judgment. When unexpected setbacks occur, like losing a job opportunity or receiving negative feedback, you have the emotional fortitude to evaluate the situation calmly, identifying what can be fixed and what must be accepted. This balanced stance doesn't eliminate pain or disappointment, but it cushions the blow, lessening the sting and allowing you to regroup faster.

Ultimately, self-regulation is about choice. In a world full of unpredictability, you cannot always control external events, but you can dictate how you respond. From small irritations to major upheavals, your capacity to self-regulate steers you away from hasty decisions and emotional outbursts, guiding you toward measured actions that serve your principles. With mastery of self-regulation, you transform emotional volatility into grounded resilience, forging a more stable path in both your personal and professional life.

4. Empathy: Forging Deeper Bonds

Empathy stands as the bridge linking your inner emotional realm to that of others, enabling you to perceive and understand perspectives outside your immediate experiences. Where self-awareness and self-regulation focus on mastering your internal environment, empathy propels you outward, urging you to connect with individuals in ways that transcend the superficial. In an era awash with impersonal digital contact, genuine empathy can be the glue that cements truly profound relationships.

At the heart of empathy is the readiness to momentarily step out of your frame of reference and see situations through another's eyes. You don't need to sacrifice your viewpoints, but you suspend them long enough to absorb how a colleague, friend, or family member experiences a situation. This mental shift fosters compassion. When a coworker seems aloof or exasperated, empathy helps you realise they may be burdened by personal troubles rather than harbouring ill will. This insight can soften friction, paving the way for tactful communication and sincere support.

Empathy in professional settings is a major force for collaboration. Teams that function on an empathetic basis develop stronger bonds, handle disagreements more productively, and foster a culture of open dialogue. By truly absorbing a teammate's concerns, you widen the scope of possible solutions, often uncovering more innovative or inclusive answers. Leaders who demonstrate empathy discover that staff morale improves, as individuals feel valued not merely for their output but for who they are as people. This sense of validation often translates to heightened loyalty and motivation, elevating overall performance.

In private life, empathy nurtures connections that extend beyond polite banter. Friendships thrive when both parties sense a willingness to listen and grasp each other's emotional landscape. Family ties deepen when members feel safe sharing thoughts and vulnerabilities. Even casual acquaintances can develop into meaningful relationships when empathy opens the door to genuine dialogue. Trust blossoms when someone feels heard, unjudged, and respected for their viewpoints or emotions.

Putting empathy into practice can be as straightforward as asking open-ended questions and allowing space for detailed answers. Rather than hastily offering solutions or re-centring the spotlight on your own experiences, you focus on the speaker's needs. This act of generous listening, often called "listening to understand", lays the groundwork for true empathetic engagement. Another effective approach is to reflect their sentiments back in your own words, showing them that you have absorbed both the explicit content and the emotional undercurrent of their message.

However, empathy need not lead to personal overwhelm. Boundaries remain vital. While you open your heart to others' emotions, it is healthy to preserve your sense of self. Empathy does not mean wearing the burdens of the entire world; it simply means respecting those burdens and offering what help you can, within reason. This balance ensures that you remain a constructive ally for others while safeguarding your own emotional resources.

Ultimately, empathy transforms the texture of your interactions, intensifying understanding and dissolving unnecessary rifts. By tuning in to the emotional undercurrents that flow beneath surface conversations, you create a space where authenticity can flourish. Whether it's comforting a friend, guiding a team member, or supporting a relative through a crisis, empathy empowers you to make a positive, enduring difference. Embracing empathy is not about ceding your individuality but about extending a bridge that allows two emotional worlds to meet, often to the benefit of both.

5. Motivation: Unleashing Drive from Within

While self-awareness, self-regulation, and empathy provide essential pillars of Emotional Intelligence, motivation adds the dynamic spark that propels you forward. True motivation is not forced upon you from the outside; it ignites from within, shaped by a sense of purpose and the belief that your efforts lead toward meaningful growth. In the context of EI, motivation extends beyond collecting achievements or impressing onlookers; it's rooted in intrinsic passion and a willingness to pursue improvement for its own sake.

When motivation springs from your core values, you develop resilience that no external reward alone can match. Monetary gains or public accolades may feel good momentarily, yet that feeling can fade if unaccompanied by an internal sense of purpose. On the other hand, if you truly resonate with the goals you set, perhaps aiming to refine your communication style or guide your team to new accomplishments, you are far more likely to persevere despite stumbling blocks. This self-driven approach fosters consistency, a precious commodity in both personal development and professional success.

A significant aspect of nurturing motivation is the ability to visualise your aims while staying aware of the work required to get there. Instead of daydreaming about a perfect outcome, EI-focused motivation balances aspiration with an honest grasp of the challenges ahead. For example, if you long to become more patient in heated conversations, your motivation arises from valuing calmer relationships and a sense of self-respect rather than from an obligation to tick a behavioural box. Each moment you practise measured responses is guided by that core desire, reinforcing your dedication and helping you endure the discomfort of stepping beyond habitual reactions.

Moreover, motivation in EI underscores the role of optimism. This form of optimism does not disguise or deny the existence of hurdles, but it insists that progress is possible with sustained effort. When you hold onto that positive view, you not only embolden yourself but also spark enthusiasm in those around you. Leaders who embody optimism, tied to clear goals, often cultivate workplace cultures where setbacks are treated as valuable lessons. Likewise, within families and friendships, a hopeful approach can keep morale intact when life's curveballs arrive.

Yet motivation does not mean relentless hustle without rest. Incorporating balanced breaks, celebrating small gains, and tracking gradual improvements are all part of sustaining high drive. These habits preserve energy and enthusiasm across demanding tasks. In essence, healthy motivation balances the push to achieve with the patience to let growth unfold at a natural pace. By doing so, it avoids the burnout often linked with chasing external validations or abiding by rigid standards of perfection.

Ultimately, motivation within the EI framework enriches your life with purpose and focus. It propels you through trials and emerges from your authentic convictions, making your accomplishments more meaningful. Whether you're striving to master a challenging skill or aiming to guide a family member through a stressful transition, your genuine internal drive keeps you going when others might falter. When shaped by Emotional Intelligence, motivation becomes more than raw ambition; it is the fuel that allows you to persevere, innovate, and emerge stronger at every stage of your personal and professional journey.

6. Social Skills: Influencing and Collaborating with Confidence

No matter how deep your self-awareness runs or how adept you are at regulating emotions, the true test of Emotional Intelligence emerges in how you interact with others. Social skills, in essence, define your ability to navigate group dynamics, communicate ideas effectively, and build networks that serve a collective benefit. Whether you're influencing team members in the workplace, rallying friends for a community event, or simply cooperating with a partner on household responsibilities, strong social skills help ensure that mutual respect and understanding take centre stage.

A crucial element of social skills is the capacity to convey your points with clarity, warmth, and conviction. People often talk about the importance of "reading the room." This intuitive sense means you pick up on conversational rhythms, body language, and unspoken tensions. You then adjust your approach in real-time, knowing when to interject with an idea or when to listen attentively. By staying tuned to these subtle social cues, you build rapport faster and avoid pushing your perspective prematurely.

Social skills also involve making space for others to contribute their views. Individuals with advanced Emotional Intelligence recognise the value of inclusive dialogues. They pose questions that invite thoughtful responses, encourage quieter voices to speak up and summarise or clarify statements to ensure everyone's ideas are heard accurately. That inclusive environment fosters a deeper sense of camaraderie and trust, driving better outcomes whether the setting is a brainstorming session at work or a casual gathering among friends.

Conflict resolution is another facet of social skills. Disagreements are bound to arise in any group. The measure of your social aptitude is how you handle those frictions. Rather than resorting to personal attacks or sidelining tensions, you approach the matter openly, seeking an outcome that respects each participant's standpoint. This approach often involves listening for hidden motivations behind the conflict, acknowledging feelings, and guiding the conversation toward problem-solving. By treating each party's concerns with seriousness, you defuse tension and preserve the relationship, an essential trait in leadership, friendship, or family bonds.

Networking, a term that sometimes carries transactional overtones, can be reimagined through the lens of social skills rooted in Emotional Intelligence. Rather than gathering superficial contacts, you develop authentic, long-term connections based on shared interests and mutual benefit. This might mean offering support or knowledge when needed, remembering personal details that matter, and demonstrating genuine appreciation for the other person's perspective. Such relationships usually outlast short-lived, self-serving "networking" because they're anchored in trust and respect.

Arguably, the most meaningful outcome of strong social skills is the unifying influence it generates. Groups guided by a socially adept individual often experience greater harmony, with members inclined to collaborate more willingly. This environment encourages creative thinking and risk-taking because people feel safe sharing ideas or pointing out potential pitfalls. Over time, social skills become the invisible bond that knits teams, families, and communities together, enabling smoother communication and shared achievement.

In your journey to strengthen Emotional Intelligence, giving attention to your social skills pays rich dividends. Through small, consistent changes, like practising active listening, perfecting your approach to feedback, and learning to handle disputes with fairness, you lay the groundwork for effective collaboration. You become someone people trust, not because you demand authority, but because your actions radiate understanding and respect. That is the essence of wielding strong social skills, turning everyday interactions into opportunities for genuine connection.

7. Leadership Gains from Emotional Acuity

Emotional Intelligence has become a prized currency in leadership circles for good reason. In contrast to an older idea of leadership that leans heavily on top-down authority, leaders today must earn respect through genuine influence, adaptability, and empathy. Emotional acuity, your sharpened sense of both your own emotional climate and that of others, lies at the core of this modern leadership approach.

When you lead with high Emotional Intelligence, your team feels heard and valued. This sense of value is not merely a matter of courtesy; it is critical for sustaining morale and loyalty. Employees or collaborators who believe their viewpoints matter are more likely to trust leadership decisions, even when such decisions carry risks. They also tend to show initiative, share innovative suggestions, and support each other, strengthening the group's collective performance. This spirit of cooperation cannot be coerced; it flourishes naturally in an environment where emotional resonance is respected.

Leaders armed with Emotional Intelligence consistently guide their teams through challenges with calm determination. Instead of reacting from a place of panic or frustration when a project hits a snag, emotionally intelligent leaders pause to assess the situation, consider the emotional underpinnings of team members, and communicate possible solutions in a measured tone. This approach not only diffuses tension but also fosters a problem-solving mindset among everyone involved. Consequently, crises are tackled methodically, with less drama, leading to more efficient resolutions.

One distinguishing factor of an EI-driven leader is the capacity to provide feedback in a manner that empowers rather than alienates. Criticism, when delivered harshly or without sensitivity, can trigger defensiveness or shame, hampering morale and progress. On the other hand, leaders who blend honesty with empathy stand a better chance of motivating real change. They highlight areas needing growth while recognising accomplishments or effort. Recipients of such feedback often emerge with renewed motivation instead of feeling disheartened.

Emotional acuity also bolsters a leader's credibility across diverse cultural or organisational environments. As teams become increasingly global or multifunctional, leaders who can interpret emotional cues and subtle cultural nuances tend to excel. They adjust their tone, approach, or pace to match the environment, ensuring that no group feels neglected or misunderstood. This flexibility can make a significant difference in whether a merged team comes together seamlessly or remains fractured by invisible barriers.

Moreover, when leaders showcase self-regulation, an important aspect of EI, they set a vital precedent for the entire group. Observing a leader who maintains composure and fairness when under strain teaches team members that similar conduct is not only possible but expected. This collective pursuit of emotional balance can elevate an entire workplace culture, minimising backbiting or passive-aggressive conflicts. Over time, a calm, collaborative environment emerges, marked by fewer internal disruptions and higher achievements.

Ultimately, leadership anchored in Emotional Intelligence is not about perfect harmony or an absence of tension. Rather, it's about harnessing the natural ebb and flow of emotions as catalysts for growth, resilience, and innovation. By attuning yourself to both your own emotions and those of the people you lead, you create a foundation for trust, loyalty, and high performance. Leadership gains from emotional acuity are far-reaching, shaping not only project outcomes but also the deeper sense of unity and shared purpose among those striving toward a common goal.

8. Conflict Resolution: Applying Emotional Intelligence

Conflict can rattle any environment, from bustling offices to quiet family living rooms. Yet a disagreement or emotional standoff need not derail relationships or cause lasting damage if navigated with Emotional Intelligence. When conflict arises, it typically signals deeper issues, unmet needs, miscommunications, or clashing priorities. Armed with EI, you can discern these underlying drivers and approach the situation from a place of respect, composure, and empathy.

An effective first step in conflict resolution is to create an atmosphere of calm exchange, free from accusations or raised voices. That might mean stepping away briefly if tempers are flaring and letting everyone regroup before tackling the issue. Once cooler heads prevail, you can begin by stating your perception of the conflict, making it clear you recognise the other person's viewpoint matters. Validating the emotions on the other side does not concede defeat or compromise your stance; it demonstrates your willingness to understand rather than dominate.

Active listening remains as critical here as in any EI-related scenario. By asking clarifying questions, reflecting the other person's feelings, and paraphrasing their statements, you uncover what truly lies beneath the surface. Maybe a coworker's "laziness" is, in reality, a by-product of their confusion about assigned roles. Or perhaps a partner's irritable moods arise from anxiety around finances. Once the actual source of friction becomes visible, crafting a resolution that respects all parties' concerns gets easier.

Additionally, self-regulation helps prevent you from piling on personal attacks or letting anger run wild. If you sense you're about to lose composure, pausing to breathe and remind yourself of the overarching goal, a peaceful resolution, can keep things on track. Rather than criticising the person, focus on the issue. Expressing yourself with "I" phrases, like "I feel overlooked when my input isn't acknowledged," is more constructive than pointing fingers with statements like "You never listen." Such measured communication preserves dignity and fosters reciprocal respect.

Once all viewpoints are aired, the conversation can transition towards solutions. This stage thrives when each person feels they have contributed to shaping the outcome. Instead of imposing a unilateral remedy, invite ideas and collaboratively refine them. The resulting agreement, be it a shift in responsibilities, a clarified boundary, or a schedule adjustment, will likely command greater commitment because both sides had a hand in formulating it.

Finally, conflict resolution aided by Emotional Intelligence ensures you learn from each dispute. If the same misunderstanding recurs repeatedly, it suggests a pattern needing deeper attention. Perhaps people need more consistent feedback or certain roles require clearer definition. Viewing conflicts as learning opportunities transforms them from nuisances into catalysts for improvement. Over time, this approach can significantly reduce friction in any group setting because everyone becomes more attuned to preventing minor issues from snowballing into full-scale feuds.

In sum, conflicts will surface wherever human relationships exist, but EI-guided resolution can turn each potential blow-up into a stepping stone for stronger bonds. By valuing empathy, measured responses, and collaborative problem-solving, you ensure that disagreements lead to growth rather than resentment. This mindset shift requires patience and practice, but the payoff, a more harmonious and productive environment, makes the effort fully worthwhile.

9. Overcoming Challenges: Strengthening Emotional Intelligence

Though the benefits of Emotional Intelligence are immense, developing EI is not without its stumbling blocks. Many discover that old habits, such as reacting defensively, clinging to assumptions, or brushing aside difficult feelings, die hard. To strengthen EI, you must recognise these pitfalls and commit to steady self-improvement, even when progress feels slow.

One significant hurdle is the reluctance to confront vulnerabilities. Admitting you struggle with anger management or that you feel anxious in social settings can be uncomfortable. Nonetheless, acknowledging these areas serves as a pivotal starting point. Rather than evading them, you can formulate a plan to tackle them directly. Some individuals turn to personal coaching, therapy, or structured reading to better understand their emotional make-up and unearth the triggers that perpetuate negative patterns.

Another obstacle emerges when social or cultural environments do not support open emotional expression. Certain workplaces or family backgrounds may regard displays of vulnerability or empathy as signs of weakness. If you find yourself in such an environment, you may fear ridicule or disapproval if you share your emotional side. Overcoming this challenge often involves forging alliances with like-minded peers or mentors, quietly modelling EI-based behaviours, or choosing to distance yourself from consistently toxic spaces if necessary. While not always simple, maintaining your emotional health can, in some instances, require standing your ground against unsupportive norms.

Consistency is another factor that can trip people up. It's one thing to resolve to remain calm and measured in tough situations; it's another to do so repeatedly, week in and week out. Building new neural pathways demands repetition. Like physical exercise, you do not become emotionally agile after one or two attempts. You have to put in the work daily, resisting the temptation to revert to old habits. Reflective routines, like journalling in the evening or reviewing your interactions at day's end, reinforce your awareness and help you track incremental progress.

Emotional fatigue can also stall your growth. If you're juggling stressful demands at work, home, or school, carving out the mental space to practise new emotional habits may feel daunting. In such scenarios, it's essential to re-evaluate your priorities. Sometimes, you need an external break, perhaps a weekend away or a holiday, to recharge and rediscover your motivation to improve. Having a solid support system also lightens the load. Friends, family, or mentors who cheer you on and remind you of your goals can reignite your resolve when you feel your dedication waning.

Finally, don't overlook the role of patience. You cannot rush the process of rewiring your emotional patterns. There will be slip-ups. Perhaps you raise your voice at a friend or find yourself shutting down in a conflict at work. Rather than berating yourself, practise self-compassion, recognise the slip for what it is, a momentary lapse, and recommit to the path. By focusing on the broader trajectory of growth rather than isolated stumbles, you'll find that each challenge eventually becomes a stepping stone. Overcoming these obstacles gives your EI the resilience it needs to endure across new roles, relationships, and life chapters, ensuring you continue evolving in emotional depth and skill.

10. Emotional Intelligence: Your Lasting Pathway to Success

Emotional Intelligence is far more than an abstract concept, it stands as a long-term strategy for personal satisfaction, professional triumph, and stronger human connections. Mastering it is not an overnight endeavour; it unfolds steadily through self-reflection, mindful effort, and an unshakeable commitment to growth. When you refine your ability to be self-aware, self-regulating, empathetic, and motivated, you unlock reserves of resilience that guide you gracefully through setbacks and allow you to seize opportunities.

In practical terms, EI helps you refine your career prospects and your personal life. On the professional front, those with high EI often stand out as leaders, mentors, or collaborators who unify teams rather than divide them. By understanding the unique drives and stressors each person brings to the table, you empower problem-solving and creative thinking. This unique blend of empathy and leadership fosters loyalty, minimises interpersonal friction, and makes any environment you lead more dynamic. In interviews or promotions, it's not uncommon for hiring managers to gravitate towards those who exhibit emotional maturity because they foresee harmonious interactions and consistent performance under pressure.

In the realm of personal relationships, EI is no less influential. Friendships become stronger when you recognise subtle cries for help or celebrate others' joys wholeheartedly. Marriages and family ties gain depth when members communicate openly about emotions, turning disagreements into stepping stones for better understanding. This grounded approach fosters trust. People know they can speak their truth without fear of belittlement, and they trust you to approach discussions with insight rather than impulse. Such trust forms the backbone of lasting love and companionship.

Moreover, the true power of EI shines in your relationship with yourself. By continuously observing your emotional triggers and reining in counterproductive urges, you become adept at guiding your life with clear intent. Life's curveballs, whether it's an unexpected loss, a career disruption, or health struggles, still hurt, but they lose their capacity to derail you entirely. You respond with clarity, glean lessons from adversity, and navigate forward with a sense of dignity. This emotional agility frees you from self-sabotaging patterns, paving the way for a more purposeful life that aligns with what you genuinely value.

Crucially, EI is not the preserve of a chosen few. Anyone willing to invest time and honest effort can improve emotional competencies. Starting small, like pausing before you speak in tense circumstances, reflecting on your day to spot emotional highs and lows, or offering measured empathy when you detect another's distress, lays a solid foundation. Over weeks, months, and years, these modest actions accumulate, weaving emotional intelligence into the fabric of your character, giving you a steady compass even in the stormiest conditions.

Chapter 21

Leaving a Legacy That Resonates

Your legacy is more than just an inheritance left behind; it's a living reflection of your values, choices, and the influence you've imparted to those around you. As you move through life, each decision you make contributes to a larger picture, shaping how you'll be remembered. Leaving a legacy that resonates means being intentional about the impact you're having now and recognising that your actions echo long after you're gone.

In this chapter, you'll discover how your daily habits, the relationships you nurture, and the wisdom you share weave together to form a lasting imprint. It's about understanding that the true measure of a legacy lies not just in tangible assets but in the meaningful difference you've made in the lives of others. Here, you'll explore practical ways to ensure your legacy continues to inspire, guide, and empower future generations, resonating far beyond your own lifetime.

1. Legacy: The Ultimate Reflection of Purpose

Your legacy stands as the ultimate reflection of who you are. When you picture what you leave behind, it is tempting to think of physical assets, property, investments, or treasured heirlooms. Yet the greater part of your legacy extends far beyond material possessions. It encompasses the principles, wisdom, and positive impressions you embed in the world long after your time has passed. When you recognise that your legacy is not confined to wealth, you begin to see it as a testament to the fulfilment you found in life, as well as the influence you had on the future.

You cultivate your legacy day by day through your actions, beliefs, and interactions. Every encouraging word you speak, every bit of advice you share, and every problem you help solve sets the tone for what you pass down. Imagine how your daily choices shape a narrative that lives on in your family, colleagues, and community. Your example can guide them in embracing resilience, diligence, and honesty. These intangible markers are no less powerful than a piece of property or an inheritance fund; they can outlast you, rippling through generations.

Even individuals without vast financial resources can create a legacy of lasting significance. Some of the most influential legacies in history were built by those who had more conviction than cash. Your sincerity, empathy, and determination make an immense difference in how future generations remember you. The beauty of this is the equality of opportunity: you can leave behind hope, guidance, or an example that others follow. In that sense, your legacy is a greater measure of your true wealth than any bank account balance.

Defining your purpose is a pivotal step in shaping the legacy you want to leave. This means reflecting on what you value most, identifying the changes you want to see in the world, and living each day in alignment with those ideals. Individuals who know their purpose often find they are more intentional with their time. When you set your eyes on a specific goal or principle, you begin to see how each decision, large or small, contributes to the greater picture. This clarity focuses your energy on contributions that last rather than momentary pursuits that fade with time.

In essence, your legacy represents the story of your life's purpose, etched in the hearts and minds of those who come after you. It is the imprint you make, whether through uplifting others, advancing a cause, or offering people the tools to forge their own futures. Viewing legacy as a reflection of your core values illuminates why it matters. You are building a personal monument not carved from stone but shaped by memories of your character and the example you set.

When you acknowledge how deeply your purpose can influence those around you, you see that legacy is far more powerful than a simple handover of money or property. It is your enduring message to the world, revealing what truly mattered to you.

2. The Power of Paying It Forward

Paying it forward is the act of extending kindness or support in anticipation that the recipient will do the same for another. This approach magnifies the impact of a single generous act into a chain of goodwill. When you look at legacy through this lens, you realise that every positive gesture has the potential to inspire others, creating a culture of benevolence that can endure for years or even generations.

Your life is shaped by the people who helped you along the way. Perhaps a mentor guided you during a difficult career transition, a friend loaned you a small sum when you were in need, or someone offered you wisdom that changed your perspective for the better. Reflect on how such acts made a difference. Those moments shaped your ambitions and fortified your resilience. Paying it forward allows you to replicate that cycle of generosity. Even small, ongoing efforts, like offering free advice, helping neighbours with tasks, or championing someone's goals, carry a resonance that extends beyond the immediate moment.

This practice emphasises the communal nature of legacy. When you offer your time, skills, or resources, you invite others to do the same. The energy and possibilities expand exponentially; one kind act prompts another. Before you know it, a wide network of individuals are encouraging each other, creating a ripple effect that strengthens communities. If you have a family, think about the example you set for your children or relatives. They watch how you treat others, and that example can become a powerful lesson they adopt as their own, thus perpetuating your influence.

Paying it forward isn't exclusively about charity. It can also manifest in mentorship, where you invest in someone else's development. By guiding a colleague or a younger person, you pass on the expertise that shaped your own achievements. You allow them to learn from your mistakes and capitalise on your insights. This form of support doesn't always require significant resources; it might involve devoting an hour a week to someone's growth or using your network to connect them to valuable opportunities. The immediate benefit they receive can carry on, multiplying as they progress and eventually help another in turn.

When you pay it forward consistently, you cultivate a lifestyle grounded in empathy rather than obligation. The reward is not simply in seeing good outcomes for others; it is also in experiencing the uplifting sense of purpose that follows. You realise that you have the power to guide, heal, and propel people toward their dreams. More importantly, you do so in a spirit of generosity rather than duty, forging personal contentment alongside community betterment.

In building your legacy, paying it forward is a potent ingredient. You transcend the focus on personal accomplishments and actively contribute to a continuum of kindness. Your daily acts, however small, can initiate monumental change as they spread from person to person. When you fully embrace this approach, you elevate your legacy from a private undertaking to a shared journey of uplifting humanity.

3. Mentoring the Next Generation

Mentorship stands at the crossroads of personal legacy and future progress. When you guide someone else's path, you are effectively passing on a part of your own journey, helping them overcome obstacles and broaden their perspective. By devoting time and understanding to another person's growth, you breathe life into your values and experiences, transforming them into actionable wisdom for the next generation.

The power of mentorship extends well beyond the mentor-mentee relationship. It can spark long-term change in an entire community or industry. A gifted engineer might mentor a group of promising students, who then use those lessons to pioneer ground-breaking solutions. A skilled chef could teach a young protégé the deeper layers of culinary craft, inspiring that protégé to establish their own restaurant that revitalises local cuisine. By sharing insights, you become the catalyst for another person's breakthrough and, in turn, magnify the reach of your knowledge.

The first step is to identify who might benefit most from your guidance. This could be a junior colleague at work, a family member, or an eager learner who admires your expertise. Mentoring doesn't necessarily require formal programmes. It can emerge organically in day-to-day interactions as long as you keep your eyes open for individuals eager to learn. Once you see their potential, you can provide not only practical advice but also moral support, holding them accountable and championing their progress.

Effective mentorship involves being honest about your own triumphs and missteps. You can share anecdotes that reveal how you navigated certain challenges, what worked, what failed, and how you rebounded from setbacks. By offering these honest reflections, you humanise your achievements; you show that success is attainable but also shaped by perseverance and the courage to adapt. Rather than presenting yourself as an untouchable authority, highlight the real process that led you to mastery.

Mentoring also challenges you to refine your own understanding. Explaining a concept or technique forces you to distil your knowledge into its essential components. This exercise can sharpen your skills and renew your passion for your craft or profession. In essence, you learn by teaching. Each question posed by your mentee compels you to revisit your fundamentals, ensuring you remain engaged and current in your field.

As a mentor, your impact often continues after your formal role has ended. A mentee carries your lessons into their future, eventually reaching a new level of expertise. They might then mentor another aspiring individual, and the cycle continues, forming a generational chain of shared wisdom. In this way, your insight transcends your own career and extends to people you might never meet.

To incorporate mentorship into your legacy, you need not be an established master of your domain. Sometimes, you are merely a few steps ahead on the path, but that is enough to steer someone else in the right direction. By dedicating energy to mentorship, you expand your reach, safeguard your hard-won insights, and give the next generation a head start you may not have enjoyed yourself.

4. Financial Pass Down: More Than Money

Financial assets can be instrumental in leaving your loved ones a tangible foundation, yet focusing purely on material wealth overlooks a key dimension of your legacy. A well-structured financial pass down includes teaching the mindset and habits needed to sustain and grow that wealth responsibly. When you place education and sound values at the heart of your financial legacy, you help safeguard it from mismanagement and uphold the spirit in which it was bestowed.

A strong starting point is modelling discipline and stewardship. Often, heirs who receive considerable resources without guidance can misuse or squander them. On the other hand, an heir who has observed healthy financial practices, like prudent budgeting, strategic investing, and a balanced attitude toward spending, will likely replicate these habits. This approach stands as a far more enduring gift than a simple lump sum because it arms recipients with the principles to create their own prosperity.

Establishing trusts or drafting wills can be a constructive way to ensure your assets are preserved and allocated according to your wishes. However, be mindful that legal documents alone do not impart wisdom. Communication is key. Engage in discussions about the purpose behind your estate plan or trusts. If you have adult children or relatives who will benefit, ensure they know why certain decisions were made, how to manage the resources responsibly, and the values they are expected to uphold. This transparency gives them a sense of ownership and responsibility, encouraging them to honour your legacy as you intended.

Another valuable method involves philanthropic giving within the family context. By encouraging charitable contributions or establishing a family foundation, you highlight the significance of using financial assets to serve a larger good. This not only benefits society but also instils in your beneficiaries the notion that wealth carries obligations. The act of philanthropy becomes a living lesson that money is not merely for personal gratification but also a tool for improving the world around us. Such engagement can foster unity within a family as members come together to determine the causes they want to support.

Incorporating family meetings or annual reviews of investments and expenditures can help ensure that your legacy remains intact. These gatherings can serve as opportunities for heirs to learn about financial management in a hands-on manner, ask questions, and refine their strategies. When done consistently, such dialogues reduce confusion, mitigate conflicts, and keep every stakeholder accountable.

Ultimately, a meaningful financial pass down combines careful planning with continuous education. You aim not only to transfer funds but also to pass on the ideals that shaped your financial journey. Rather than handing over resources without any framework, you establish the conditions under which those resources can be most beneficial. This layered approach helps your legacy endure for decades and cements your values in the lives of those who inherit your estate. By uniting wealth with wisdom, you transform your financial pass down into a potent tool for positive impact across generations.

5. Creating Opportunities for the Future

Legacy deepens when you open doors for others, making the path a little smoother or more accessible. This goes beyond the direct monetary support we often imagine. You might set up a scholarship fund to help future scientists or entrepreneurs, sponsor an initiative that nurtures budding artists, or utilise your position to connect someone to a valuable network. These gestures can be the difference between a vision that fizzles out and a breakthrough that changes someone's life.

You can begin by looking around your immediate sphere. Can you introduce an ambitious co-worker to your professional circle? Can you fund a modest educational grant for a promising neighbour who lacks resources? Even a single introduction or a small scholarship can redirect someone's entire trajectory. When you find promising individuals and give them a pivotal opportunity, you effectively multiply your influence, allowing your legacy to take root in their subsequent achievements.

Consider how you might use your resources, skills, or platform to act as a bridge. Perhaps you own a property that can host community workshops, enabling young leaders to gain insights and form alliances. Alternatively, if you excel at a certain craft, whether it's software development, architecture, or marketing, you could provide internships or training sessions that equip novices with practical experience. These are not once-off gestures; they form a pipeline through which people can advance, building on the foundation you have offered.

Infrastructure for opportunity isn't limited to the professional domain. Think about personal growth as well. Community programmes that address mental resilience, leadership, or civic responsibility can transform how individuals approach life and handle adversity. Investing in these programmes, or even volunteering your time there, sets in motion a legacy of knowledge-sharing and inspiration. The aim is to cultivate a mindset in others that can help them thrive on their own terms.

Meanwhile, organisations often seek sponsors or advisors. By committing your resources or expertise, you shape the next wave of leaders in your chosen field. Whether you assist a non-profit dedicated to environmental conservation or a tech start-up accelerator, your involvement can accelerate the growth of ideas that benefit the broader community. This direct investment of time and guidance is a more personal expression of legacy as you form relationships with those who are driving the innovations of tomorrow.

There is also the intangible benefit to consider. When you are known as someone who opens doors, you encourage a culture of mutual support. Others see your willingness to uplift emerging talents, and they are inspired to replicate that approach. Over time, you nurture an ecosystem where each person's success fosters new opportunities for others. Rather than hoarding resources or insights, you encourage a cycle of development that can outlast you by generations.

In essence, crafting opportunities is about actively deciding who and what you want to support and then taking steps to make that support real. It goes well past writing a cheque. It calls for involvement, foresight, and a belief that you have the power to shape lives for the better. By doing so, you link your future impact to countless endeavours yet to unfold.

6. Designing a Legacy That Outlives You

Designing a legacy that stands the test of time requires a strategic mindset, a plan that extends well beyond any individual lifetime. While it is tempting to assume that the ripple effects of your good deeds will continue on their own, the reality is that frameworks and foresight are vital. Think of your legacy as a structure that needs robust planning and clear direction if it is to hold strong over the decades.

Begin by deciding which core values you want woven into the fabric of your legacy. These values act as guiding principles that shape every decision related to your estates, bequests, and philanthropic efforts. If you value entrepreneurship, you might fund small businesses or facilitate incubator programmes. If you are passionate about education, you might dedicate resources to scholarships or libraries. The clearer and more specific your values are, the simpler it becomes to design lasting systems that reflect them.

Next, consider establishing an entity, such as a trust, foundation, or endowed scholarship, that can function independently. These structures safeguard your resources and ensure that the beneficiaries or trustees cannot divert the assets away from your originally intended purpose. By setting clear guidelines and choosing responsible stewards, you make certain that the funds or properties remain dedicated to the causes you championed. Moreover, you can outline conditions for receiving grants or awards, thus ensuring that the recipients embody your ethos.

Building a legacy that endures often involves involving like-minded individuals who can carry the torch. Look for people in your circle who share your vision. They may be family members, close friends, or emerging leaders you have mentored. These individuals can serve as guardians of your mission, infusing fresh energy and perspective as time moves forward. Regular gatherings, virtual or physical, where these stewards discuss progress, challenges, and innovative ways to adapt your legacy to changing conditions can keep your vision alive and dynamic.

In addition, modern technology can play a pivotal role in preserving and promoting your legacy. Digital records, websites, or platforms dedicated to your philanthropic projects allow for transparency and community engagement. They also offer a means for future generations to learn from your experiences, keep track of milestones, and discover how your legacy has evolved. This permanent record ensures your guiding principles are never forgotten, even as the world transforms in ways you cannot predict.

Above all, remember that a lasting legacy is not a one-time decision but a continuous process. Regularly review the entities, funds, or initiatives you have set in motion. Adapt them when necessary, refining objectives to meet new challenges. This flexibility ensures your foundational vision remains anchored yet responsive to a world that rarely stands still. By planning for both structure and adaptability, you ensure that your influence echoes through time, never stagnating or losing relevance.

When all is said and done, designing a legacy that outlives you is an act of faith in tomorrow. You trust that your efforts today will be carried on by people with the resolve and moral clarity to uphold what you started. With forethought, organisation, and strategic partnerships, your impact can outlast your physical presence, leaving a mark that future generations recognise and appreciate.

7. Real-World Figures Who Illustrate Lasting Legacy

Examples of enduring legacies can be found throughout history, showcasing how an individual's passion and vision can keep shaping society long after they are gone. Rather than repeating case studies from earlier parts of this project, we will consider fresh instances that underline the power of a well-crafted legacy.

One such figure is a pioneering educator who established comprehensive learning centres in underserved communities. Although she is not a global household name, her influence resonates across multiple generations. She meticulously planned these centres to provide reading programmes, vocational training, and enrichment courses tailored to local needs. Long after she passed away, a board of trustees continued to operate these sites according to her guidelines, preserving both her mission and her unique ethos of compassion and self-improvement. Students who benefited from the programmes later returned as volunteer teachers, adding to the ripple effect of her impact.

Similarly, an inventor who revolutionised renewable energy technology stands as a beacon of forward-thinking. He spent years refining a particular solar-powered device that could be manufactured inexpensively, aiming to bring eco-friendly energy solutions to remote areas. Before his retirement, he arranged for open-source licensing, ensuring that budding entrepreneurs worldwide could produce and adapt this technology. This open framework granted millions access to green power, diminishing the reliance on fossil fuels. Through that single invention and the structural model he created, his environmental legacy remains ongoing, continuing to solve real-world problems and encourage local innovation.

We can also see a lasting legacy in someone who dedicated her life to fostering cross-cultural dialogue. She created an online platform that allowed students from different continents to exchange stories, discuss shared concerns, and practise language skills in a safe environment. She understood that misunderstandings often spark conflict and believed that genuine communication would foster greater harmony. By orchestrating student exchange programmes and virtual meetups, she bridged cultural divides. Now, under the stewardship of an international team, her platform continues to develop new features and expand its global reach. Her heritage lives on not only in the established system but also in the thousands of friendships and collaborative ventures formed worldwide.

These examples underscore that lasting legacies don't hinge purely on celebrity status or extraordinary wealth. Instead, they depend on commitment, clarity, and the willingness to put structures in place that enable ongoing growth. Each individual introduced a vision, prepared the ground thoroughly, and designated people or systems to carry on the work. Such an approach keeps their ideals and achievements alive, guiding others for decades.

When you reflect on these real-world stories, it becomes evident that the essence of legacy is in forging something that extends beyond personal recognition. By focusing on solutions that address social or environmental needs and establishing frameworks to maintain them, you can follow in the footsteps of those who built legacies that do not simply fade away with the passing of time.

8. Daily Actions and Habits to Strengthen Your Legacy

Though grand gestures and visionary projects capture headlines, the bedrock of a strong legacy often lies in small daily acts. Your habits, routines, and moment-to-moment decisions cumulatively shape how people perceive you and how your ideals take root in the world. By tending to these everyday patterns with intention, you set the stage for a legacy that is consistent, reliable, and deeply personal.

First and foremost, consistency of character is vital. Behaving differently in private from how you do in public can damage the trust and admiration you have cultivated. Reflect on the values you want to be known for, honesty, diligence, and compassion, and then integrate them into your daily life. This might mean double-checking any work for accuracy before finalising, offering encouragement to those around you rather than casual critique, or remaining steadfast when challenges arise. These actions may feel routine or unremarkable, but over time, they build credibility and strengthen the example you set.

Next, consider how you communicate with others. A simple message of support or a swift response to a query can leave a profound impression, particularly in an era where people often feel overlooked. Responding to emails or requests in a timely and considerate manner is more than professional courtesy; it shows that you value the people seeking your guidance. The same holds true for face-to-face interactions. Listening closely and showing genuine interest can shape someone's entire perception of you. Over years, these consistent acts of attentiveness form part of the legacy you leave in each personal relationship.

Setting micro-goals that align with your broader principles can also keep you oriented. For instance, if generosity is part of your ethos, commit to a small daily act of giving, be it a kind word, a helpful favour, or a short mentoring session. If you want to champion growth or innovation, spend a few minutes each evening reflecting on a new idea or reading about fresh developments in your field. These micro-tasks keep you invested in what truly matters so your bigger objectives never fall dormant.

Time management is another critical piece. Maintaining a schedule that balances professional obligations with the relationships and activities you hold dear safeguards your energy and presence. When you manage your day effectively, you keep burnout at bay, allowing you to consistently show up as the best version of yourself. This reliability becomes a key part of your legacy as others learn they can count on you to deliver, whether it is support, expertise, or just a friendly ear.

Ultimately, your daily habits form the backbone of your legacy. While dramatic achievements and influential projects are significant, the steadfast impression of your everyday behaviour carries equal weight. The small, private decisions you make, like how you treat a server at a café, how you handle criticism, or how readily you share knowledge, combine to create a mosaic that reveals your character. Align these tiny actions with your bigger vision, and you will find that your legacy is built steadily, day after day, in a manner no grand gesture alone can replicate.

9. Confronting Legacy Challenges and Roadblocks

Even with clear intentions, building a powerful legacy can be complicated by obstacles that threaten to dilute your impact. Personal doubts, practical limitations, and unexpected life changes can all disrupt your carefully laid plans. Identifying and acknowledging these potential challenges early will help you steer around them or address them head-on, safeguarding the longevity of your contribution.

One common hurdle is the fear that your efforts are insignificant. It is easy to feel overshadowed by large-scale projects or high-profile figures, leading you to question whether your endeavours hold any real weight. This self-doubt can stall your progress before it truly begins. To overcome it, remember that every major change often starts from modest roots. A single literacy programme can transform countless lives if nurtured with dedication. Your direct influence on even a handful of individuals might eventually spark an unimagined wave of progress.

Another obstacle is the clash of priorities. You might find yourself caught between immediate personal responsibilities, such as maintaining financial security or attending to family, and your larger vision for a legacy. In these moments, planning and compromise become essential. If limited resources or time hold you back, consider scaling your vision into manageable segments. You can develop your legacy step by step: introducing smaller initiatives, forming strategic partnerships, or saving funds steadily until you can make a bigger push. This flexibility allows you to remain aligned with your values while juggling life's daily demands.

Conflict within families or close associates can also threaten to derail your legacy. Differing opinions on how to allocate resources, conflicting visions for philanthropic projects, or even interpersonal rivalries may emerge. Address these challenges with open communication and a willingness to find common ground. By involving all key stakeholders in the decision-making process, you reduce misunderstandings and cultivate a sense of shared ownership in the legacy. Drawing up clear documents and guidelines about the scope and purpose of any resources can also prevent disputes from escalating.

Legal and bureaucratic barriers can pose further complications. Whether you want to set up a trust, found a charitable organisation, or draft a detailed will, you may encounter red tape that slows your progress. Seeking reliable, professional advice helps you navigate these complexities. Lawyers, financial advisors, and specialists in non-profit management can protect you from pitfalls and ensure your efforts meet regulatory standards. Although it may appear cumbersome, dealing with formalities promptly often prevents bigger headaches in the long term.

Finally, be aware that your own life circumstances can shift unexpectedly. You may relocate, face health challenges, or discover a new cause that reignites your passion. These changes need not undermine your legacy; they simply call for adaptation. Regularly review your goals and commitments, adjusting them when necessary to remain true to your overarching purpose.

Despite all these potential roadblocks, perseverance, thoughtful planning, and open communication can keep your legacy intact. Each hurdle you confront is an opportunity to refine your objectives and unify the people supporting you. Embracing these challenges with determination ensures that your lasting contribution remains resilient, purposeful, and ready to flourish, no matter what crosses your path.

10. Carrying Your Legacy Forward: A Lifelong Journey

As you approach the final step in crafting a lasting legacy, remember that this endeavour is not a project with a neat completion date but a lifelong journey that evolves with you. Each stage of your life adds fresh layers of experience, wisdom, and resources that can further fortify your impact. In essence, carrying your legacy forward is about continuous growth, adaptation, and genuine commitment to the principles you hold dear.

Begin with consistent self-reflection. At various points, whether you reach a personal milestone, endure a setback, or pass through a life transition, take stock of how your values may have shifted. Perhaps a cause you once championed fervently now feels less urgent, while another has taken on greater importance in light of new experiences. Do not hesitate to revise your legacy plan accordingly. This continuous shaping keeps your contributions relevant and ensures that your legacy remains an accurate reflection of your current self.

Sharing your evolving insights and goals with those who look up to you also keeps the momentum alive. If your family sees you regularly engage in honest self-assessment and adapt your course, they learn that legacy-building requires flexibility and renewal. If you work with a circle of peers who share similar ambitions, your ability to articulate these shifts can inspire them to pursue their own legacy work more actively. In both cases, you become a role model for growth, signalling that your dedication to leaving a mark is not static but ever-evolving.

Moreover, carrying your legacy forward demands a certain humility. You must be willing to accept that you do not control how everything unfolds. You can lay a robust foundation, but unforeseen societal changes, technological shifts, or personal tragedies may alter the course of your plans. Embracing humility means staying open to advice, sharing decision-making power where appropriate, and recognising when outside expertise is needed. Such openness allows your legacy to absorb shocks and thrive in new environments.

Patience is another virtue that fuels the longevity of your mission. Some initiatives will not reach their peak for many years, possibly long after you have stepped away. Seeds of transformation in education, healthcare, or social reforms can take a generation or more to mature. In that sense, you are planting trees whose shade you may never personally enjoy. However, that is the essence of legacy: a gift to those who follow, trusting that they will cherish and build upon what you started.

By viewing legacy as a journey, you remove the pressure to have everything perfectly arranged right away. Instead, you focus on steady progress, welcoming each chapter of your life as an opportunity to refine, expand, or shift your contributions. You hold fast to your overarching vision, anchored by your values, but allow it room to breathe and adapt to an ever-changing world. Ultimately, this approach grants your legacy the vitality it needs to flourish, carried along by your unwavering commitment and the cooperative energy of those who stand to benefit.

Final Word

Embrace the Journey to Abundance

You stand at the threshold of a life marked by genuine fulfilment and unshakeable purpose, ready to move forward from these pages and into your everyday reality. While you might feel a burst of excitement, you may also sense uncertainty about how to implement every insight you have gathered here. Know that this blend of exhilaration and hesitation is the greatest sign that you are indeed growing. You have taken ownership of your future by absorbing new perspectives on discipline, personal development, leadership, and legacy. Now, you hold the keys to a transformed path ahead.

From this day on, the core truths within this work can guide every decision and action you take. Picture your goals not as far-off ideals but as horizons you edge closer to each time you embrace a challenge. Whether you are aiming to refine your relationships, deepen your spiritual life, fortify your finances, or elevate your fitness, your renewed sense of purpose will serve as your compass. You have learned that victory does not favour those who wait in fear; it awaits those who step forward with confidence. As you proceed, remember that your setbacks do not define you. Rather, they are signposts encouraging you to adjust, learn, and push forward.

Your commitment to daily habits stands at the centre of any lasting change. Each morning offers a fresh opportunity to

Embrace the Journey to Abundance

practise the principles you value: kindness, perseverance, financial prudence, and thoughtful communication. By immersing yourself in these everyday disciplines, you will find that self-improvement eventually shifts from an uphill battle into a more natural part of who you are. If, on occasion, you slip or feel uncertain, look back on the insights you have collected within these pages. They serve not as rigid rules but as supportive allies, reminders of how capable you truly are.

Moreover, never lose sight of the larger perspective: you are not travelling through life alone. Seek camaraderie among friends, family, mentors, and those who share your hunger for growth. When you open yourself to community and collaboration, you amplify your own drive. Your relationships deepen, your successes carry more meaning, and your influence expands in ways you might never have anticipated. Your best life does not happen in isolation; it flourishes in the rich setting of shared victories, mutual learning, and collective hope.

Above all, keep your eyes firmly fixed on building a legacy that ignites positive transformation. Each thoughtful word, each compassionate act, and each decision grounded in your values plants seeds for future generations. As you go forth, speak from your heart, hold firmly to your guiding principles, and nurture the relationships and causes you truly value.

Embrace the journey to abundance, not as a far-off dream but as a lived reality that unfolds one purposeful step at a time. Your future self and all the people whose lives you will touch will thank you for summoning your courage, refining your vision, and stepping boldly into the life you have always been capable of creating.

Printed in Great Britain
by Amazon

67fecca8-4034-442f-9976-4b9bde7f92afR01